Towards a Praxis-based Media and Journalism Research

Towards a Praxis-based Media and Journalism Research

Edited by Leon Barkho

intellect Bristol, UK / Chicago, USA

First published in the UK in 2017 by
Intellect, The Mill, Parnall Road, Fishponds, Bristol, BS16 3JG, UK

First published in the USA in 2017 by
Intellect, The University of Chicago Press, 1427 E. 60th Street,
Chicago, IL 60637, USA

A catalogue record for this book is available from the
British Library.

Copy-editor: MPS Limited
Cover designers: Emily Dann and Lucy MacArthur
Production manager: Richard Kerr
Typesetting: Contentra Technologies

Print ISBN: 978-1-78320-745-9
ePDF ISBN: 978-1-78320-746-6
ePUB ISBN: 978-1-78320-747-3

Printed and bound by TJ International, UK.

This is a peer-reviewed publication.

MIX
Paper from
responsible sources
FSC® C013056

Contents

Introduction

Theory Is Not Enough: How to Convert Media and Journalism Studies into Relevant, Useful and Practical Research

Leon Barkho

Media academics rarely influence working professionals. The disconnect between theory and practice in media and journalism studies is obvious. Academic research seldom impresses practitioners and their organizations, while the academy has little faith in what practitioners do. Academic professors generally do not appreciate work by practitioner-turned-scholars. *The Guardian* (2015) ran an article by an anonymous academic under the headline: 'Journalism academics: Mocked by the media and stifled by universities'. The writer argued that the journalism practitioners universities hire to focus on practical vocational skills find themselves 'in the precarious position of bridge-builder between' two competing non-conciliatory camps of researchers and working professionals. Media and journalism scholars recognize the mutual antipathy and the dissonance that seems to prevent any agreement on how to move forward and bring rigour and relevance together. The relevant literature in journalism and mass communication, as far as the editor of this volume can see, lacks studies on how to bridge this divide.

Do we need to relate our theories to practice? Should our curricula include day-to-day training aspects of journalism? I think, if we in the academia want to be relevant, we should respond to the needs of the society we want to serve and the organizations we research. Academics at medical and nursing schools offer their students the type of education that combines theory with practice and prepares them to offer good service to patients in hospitals and clinics. One might wonder whether media and journalism schools take such a connection between practice and theory seriously. Alternatively, one might also wonder if it is possible for research to hypothesize whether our 'findings hold implications for our teaching practices' (Cohen 2005: 338). Academics need to balance student needs and demands when designing their curricula and doing their research. A medical doctor, an engineer or a veterinarian is equipped with the skills to practice the profession once leaving the university.

Media and journalism studies might be the closest to practice among other social science disciplines but the research – and the teaching – rarely has anything to do with the learning of professional skills the industry requires. A combination of theory and practice – the drive of this volume – would make media and journalism a wonderful subject to teach and practice at the same time.

Scholarship versus practice

The body of academic knowledge journalism schools offer is important. It provides students with the tools necessary to analyse and interpret the world around them and the media organizations they may encounter or work for. The practice-based approach or methodology this volume seeks to promote does not deny the role of journalism and media scholarship. It strives to build bridges and develop ways to help both academics and practitioners perform their teaching and research in a way that makes the convergence and merger of skills and theory possible. The nature of the media as a profession requires that universities pay attention to vocational skills. It demands media and journalism scholars produce knowledge that is useful and relevant to the profession's practitioners instead of always striving to meet the highest standard of scientific rigor and academic quality (de Burgh 2003).

No doubt, the academy has succeeded in unravelling the world of the media and journalism through rigorous studies based on critical and cultural concepts. The academy's emphasis on the role of power has uncovered a variety of news systems and patterns of production and reproduction of content. However, these studies have failed to bridge the theory-practice gap because, as Reese and Cohen (2000: 200) note, they 'do not typically engage much with the professions and are easily marginalized'. This state of affairs has led to the emergence of a few voices in the academy and the practitioner community urging a more praxis-based approach to research and teaching curriculum (Harcup 2012; Harrington 2008).

Journalism studies departments or their counterparts, in the wider defining category of communication, journalism and media studies, have done their best to produce 'conventional research' based on conceptual, theoretical and methodological frameworks prevalent in other social science disciplines. For many, this is the only way to get credits, promotion and higher ranking. This volume calls for a shift in research focus and approach, highlighting methodologies targeting the special workplace needs of media and journalism practitioners.

Student needs

Students at journalism and mass media colleges and departments seek the skills they need to work in the media. Media, communication and journalism academics should furnish them with the right skills and knowledge and have them prepared for real-life situations. Teaching theory is still vital but it should be 'infused into a practice-based curriculum' (Cohen 2005: 336).

The organizations our graduates aspire to join are witnessing drastic transformations. And when practitioners themselves strongly criticize academic language, writing and teaching modules (see Chapters 1–4), it should ring alarm bells about our curriculum and teaching practices. Many media (newspapers, radio and television outlets) have transformed their situations to meet the digital onslaught. When academics refuse demands by practitioners for theory not to lose its practical base, there are consequences: our 'ivory tower' or 'fortress' becomes target of practitioner attacks and our research findings rarely make it to the newsroom (Chapter 2).

Journalism in crisis

Today, there is much talk in the media and a plethora of research about the 'crisis in journalism'. The crisis has emanated from the way the media have struggled to adapt and respond to transformations brought about by the digital revolution. The crisis is reflected in the closure of newspapers, vanishing jobs and revenues, and plummeting circulations (see Barnett 2002; Blumler 2010; Fuller 2010; Franklin 2012).

These problems are not merely structural. In the United Kingdom, for instance, public trust in journalists and their output is declining. 'That goes right across the board – TV and newspapers', according to a survey by YouGov for *Prospect Magazine* (Kellner 2010). For instance, the survey found that the public trust rating of ITV's journalists nosedived to 33 per cent in 2010 from 80 per cent in 2003. The BBC fared no better, with the public trust rating of its journalists dipping to 21 per cent from 81 per cent over the same period.

A 2011 Pew survey found that 75 per cent of Americans thought that journalists could not get their facts straight (Moos 2011). A 2013 Ipsos MORI poll found that Britons' trust in journalists is even less than Americans, with only 21 per cent of British adults having faith in what reporters do (Beaujon 2013).

Journalism theory and scholarship define and measure issues and variables of impartiality and objectivity. We have theories that can help journalism students to produce news that is more fact than opinion and more objective than subjective. One wonders then why the public have the lowest trust in journalism out of all other professions universities teach as part of their curricula. We should not take lack of public trust in a profession we theorize and operationalize at tertiary education as an affront. It is a critique of academia whose teaching modules have not been effective enough to produce graduates capable in practical life to place fact over opinion and distance objective reporting from political agenda.

Working journalists do need conceptual and theoretical frameworks that help them analyse and explain the social reality of their output, their organizations and the world around them. At the same time, they need skills that help them to objectively and fairly reproduce and represent this world through signs – using the tools at their disposal like language, video and pictures. Media and journalism academics appear happy to interpret, investigate and understand the world of media journalism. But they normally shun 'intervention research' designed to not only interpret but also provide instructions and alternatives on how to improve conditions, news skills and the output of working journalists.

The 'hackademy'

Journalism and media studies is growing across the world. Most universities have their own departments, and some even separate colleges, offering both undergraduate and postgraduate degrees. Until very recently, some media organizations did their own training to improve the vocational skills of their employees. But plunging circulation and profits have forced media outlets to slash spending on training their journalists and instead restructure their newsrooms. Previously, many journalism departments would have scoffed at counterparts engaged in vocational training – they believed their core duty was a scientific study of the field rather than furnishing students with the type of training they needed to work as journalists (Franklin 2009; Wahl-Jorgensen and Franklin 2008).

In the United Kingdom, for instance, universities moved to fill in the gap and started employing practitioners to provide the kind of skills students need after graduation and conduct scholarly research (Harcup 2011). The presence of former reporters in the midst of journalism faculty is slowly transforming journalism academic landscape. There are calls for more emphasis on applied research partly geared towards meeting demands of the industry. In the past two decades, we have seen the promulgation of the type of language, particularly at the level terminology, to reflect a new 'hyprid' approach and methodology in academic research. The term 'hackademic' was first coined by Engel (2003) merging the word 'hack', British slang for journalist, with 'academic'. Errigo and Franklin (2004) used the term 'hackademy', a collective noun that groups the new breed of 'practitioner academics' and the emerging brand of applied research that binds theory with praxis.

But the arrival of former journalists as scholars in the journalism and mass communication faculty has not bridged the gap or alleviated tension between research and practice. Harcup (2011: 47) carried out a study based on 65 interviews with 'hackademics' – journalists who joined the academy to provide vocational training and share their newsroom and reporting experiences with faculty and students. He found the sides coexisting begrudgingly with conflicting and differing ideas and attitudes towards theory and practice. He says, '[T]here continues to exist a real tension for many hackademics, not simply between theory and practice, but between a world with which they are familiar (journalism) and a world in which they may feel like outsiders even after many years of service.'

Ongoing debate

There has been considerable debate in social science over the proper place of practice within the academy. In some disciplines, the debate has had serious implications and transformed scholars' perceptions of the nature of science and scientific research. These disciplines have seen a surge in praxis research, where academics take into account ways of helping the subjects of research improve the way they work and not merely interpret their world.

However, the academic-practitioner divide is still discernible in media and journalism studies 'where programs which compromise between vocational training and broader program of study [...] remain unsatisfactory because they put too much onus on students themselves to bridge the gap between theory and practice' (Skinner, Gasher and Compton 2001: 341). Practitioners, as many chapters in this volume testify, hold journalism and media research with suspicion. Academic research has documented the antipathy between the sides. Frith and Meech (2007) point out that journalism is a field in which subjects of research (practitioners) believe those investigating them (academics) to be doing something that is of no practical use, even irrelevant, to their profession and practice.

For academics, media and journalism studies is a discipline. For their students and the objects of their research (practitioners and their institutions), media and journalism is about the mastery of the vocational skills necessary for practice. The issue, as Bovée (1999) points out, is related to the reality of the situation in the academy, where scholars conducting research and teaching have not practiced the vocational skills that are vital for the discipline before or after obtaining their Ph.D. degrees.

When compared with other social science disciplines, where applied research and methodologies were established nearly half a century ago (Lather 1986; see also Freire 2000), praxis is a newcomer to journalism and media studies. Practice-based research is prevalent in many disciplines across the sciences, whether social, pure or natural. Some disciplines like engineering, medicine and finance have developed their applied research methodologies besides their rigorous and solid theoretical base (Barrows 1994; Addison 2002).

In the realm of media and journalism studies, practice research only gained some ground, albeit reluctantly, in the early twenty-first century and mostly at the hands of reporters-turned-academics. Works by Niblock (2007 and 2012; see also Chapter 8 of this book) as well as Bacon (2011, 2012), Lindgren and Phillips (2011) and Nash (2013, 2014) have sought to provide a theoretical framework for why such research is important and how to do it.

This book and its chapters

This book attempts to bridge the perceived gap in practice-based literature in media and journalism studies. In particular, it addresses questions raised about the relevance and practicality of research and education and the possibility of building bridges between theory and practice in the sphere of media and journalism studies. In the course of answering these questions, the volume discusses the reasoning behind the assertion that practice-based research is of vital importance to media and journalism as both practice and science.

The book was born from a symposium organized in Sweden by Jönköping University's College of Education and Communication in 2013 on praxis-based media and journalism research. In the years since then, many of the participants reworked their papers and had them published in the peer-reviewed *Journal of Applied Journalism and Media Studies*.

Nearly half of the volume's authors have had their papers already published in peer-reviewed academic journals.

Both practitioners and academics have contributed to the volume. The editor has strived to strike a balance in contributions in terms of size and number of chapters. The book is divided into three sections. The first, 'What Practitioners Say', includes articles by some renowned practitioners in which they voice their opinion of media and journalism academic research. The second, 'What Academics Say', is not a response to 'What Practitioners Say' but rather contributions from scholars with an interest in seeing how theory can be used to read media and journalism. The third, 'Who Gets It Right', comprises contributions that try to answer some of the queries and gripes practitioners make in the first section and attempts to carve out a path for future practitioner-academic collaboration. The first section comprises six chapters all of them written by practitioners:

- Chapter 1 outlines how practitioners view academic research and what they think academics need to do to make their work relevant, useful and practical. The chapter highlights the hurdles that prevent the two sides from bridging the existing gaps and then proposes three important ideas as to how the two camps can work together.

- Chapter 2 charts a path on how to bridge the scholar-practitioner divide. It calls for a 'genuine partnership' through which both sides can work together to help practitioners address the problems disrupting the industry. It cites examples of how a few academics have preserved the rigor of scientific research and at the same time made their work 'practical, relevant and useful' to the industry.

- Chapter 3 sheds light on the direct impact, for good or ill, media and journalism have on the health of the public discourse. It argues that despite their massive influence on society, media practitioners and the academy are as divided as ever, with practitioners seeing scholarly work as irrelevant to them and academics still unprepared to make their work timely and relevant to current issues or to abandon formats and language that alienates practitioners.

- Chapter 4 focuses on why practitioners complain about academic writing. It starts with how important it is for media and journalism academics to write in a lucid way to be clearly understood by their peers and the people they research. It provides a few samples of what the author sees as poor academic writing. It ends with a few suggestions.

- Chapter 5 starts with an examination of a popular Swedish radio programme and then moves on to the reaction it has received from both public and private media outlets in Sweden. The chapter dwells on both positive and negative aspects of the programme, shedding light on how its producer and presenter tried to establish a bridge with the academy in Sweden. It touches upon the producer's collaboration with media and journalism scholars.

- Chapter 6 explores the academic-practitioner divide on the relevance of journalism and media research to the problems the industry faces. Practitioners, it says, emphasize that much of media and journalism research is pointless and irrelevant to how they go about their work. Academics, it adds, point out that practitioners gloss over their research, its findings and implications.

The second section comprises seven chapters written by scholars or practitioners who joined the academy at some point of their career as faculty members:

- The section starts (Chapter 7) with a study that lays down the conceptual and methodological underpinnings of a praxis-based media and journalism research. It positions the keyword 'praxis' within the main schools of thought and philosophical deliberations that have characterized research in mainstream social science.

- Chapter 8 attempts to present methodologies that can help in understanding change in the dynamic field of media and journalism studies. It examines reflexive, praxis-based methodologies for conducting journalism research from a practitioner-academic perspective. Drawing on reflexive methodologies in the human sciences, such as hermeneutics, cybernetics and constructivism, this chapter envisions an immersive approach embracing phenomenology as a fully reflexive method of data collection.

- Chapter 9 justifies the need for minority-sensitive media, setting them out as a key plank of intercultural dialogue. To advance this argument, the chapter analyses minority-sensitive media in terms of the increasing recognition of minorities in international human rights discourse. It then attempts to appropriate minority discourse as communicative praxis, sketching three key normative communicative roles for minority media actors, namely, facilitating cultural interactions, unmasking cultural stereotypes and intolerance, and forging a common cultural-pluralistic narrative.

- Chapter 10 considers the position of newspaper sub-editors *within the larger organizational* model of the newsroom. It demonstrates how a newsroom's spatial setting, division of workload and the sub-editor's profile impact on sub-editors' ability to intervene in the news production process. It draws on participant observation in the newsrooms of a Belgian and a Dutch broadsheet, analysing the advantages, challenges and possible pitfalls media researchers are faced with when conducting research from within the newsroom.

- Chapter 11 looks at photojournalism from the perspective of the professional photojournalist and page editor and with regard to the way that images are actually used, commercially by news outlets. It shows that photojournalists appear to be aware of many of the limitations identified by academic work, yet formulate them in different terms. It argues that the limitations of the photograph appear to be well understood by professional photojournalists but are incorporated into how a photograph can best resonate with the requirements of different genres.

- Chapter 12 shows how readings of seminal works by influential cultural critics have helped us delve into issues of power and politics embedded in language representations. The chapter provides a 'tool box of political and cultural theories' and shows how to apply them through accessible language to bring about dialogue and change in a world ridden with conflicts.

The last section includes three chapters in which the authors provide some answers to the queries practitioners raise in the first section, respond to their critique of academic writing and chart a path for how to bridge the practitioner-scholar divide:

- Chapter 13 comes to academia's defence. While not absolving academics of the blame for a lack of praxis-based research, the chapter asserts that journalists also bear responsibility for the failure to find scholarly material useful and relevant to their profession.

- Chapter 14 emphasizes the need to develop a praxis-oriented approach to deal with the questions media and journalism academics face during their ethnographic encounters with those we research. It discusses the issue of how to relate theory to practice and examines why the gap between those who practice and those who theorize is still so wide. The chapter touches on the type of learning most appropriate for media and journalism research and ends with a conclusion about the type of research the volume wants to promote in order to accomplish its praxis-oriented mission.

- Chapter 15 considers the major concerns voiced by nearly a dozen practitioners about much of the research media academics carry out. It then presents a synopsis of their responses to two major questions: (1) Why do media practitioners generally discard or not trust findings by media scholars? (2) Are media scholars under any obligation to relate their theories to practice? It ends with the lessons that academics can draw from the way practitioners view their world and assess their research.

References

Addison, P. S. (2002), *The Illustrated Wavelet Transform Handbook: Introductory Theory and Applications in Science, Engineering, Medicine and Finance*, Boca Raton: CRC Press.

Anonymous Academic (2015), 'Journalism academics: Mocked by the media and stifled by universities', *The Guardian*, http://www.theguardian.com/higher-education-network/2015/may/07/journalism-academics-mocked-by-the-media-and-stifled-by-universities. Accessed 27 January 2016.

Bacon, W. (2011), 'Investigative journalism in the academy: Possibilities for storytelling across time and space', *Pacific Journalism Review*, 17: 1, pp. 45–66.

Bacon, W. (2012), 'Frontline: An innovative direction in academic journalism', *Pacific Journalism Review*, 18: 2, pp. 153–165.

Barnett, S. (2002), 'Will a crisis in journalism provoke a crisis in democracy?', *The Political Quarterly*, 73: 4, pp. 400–408.

Barrows, H. S. (1994), *Practice-based Learning: Problem-based Learning Applied to Medical Education*. Springfield, IL: Southern Illinois University.

Beaujon, A. (2013), 'As BBC strikes, Brits trust journalists less than Americans do', *Poynter: A Global Leader in Journalism*, http://www.poynter.org/news/mediawire/204599/as-bbc-strikes-brits-trust-journalists-less-than-americans-do/. Accessed 25 January 2016.

Blumler, J. G. (2010), 'Foreword: The two-legged crisis of journalism', *Journalism Practice*, 4: 3, pp. 243–245.

Bourdieu, P. (1990), *The Logic of Practice*, Cambridge: Polity Press.

—— (2003), 'Participant objectivation', *Journal of the Royal Anthropological Institute*, 9, pp. 281–294.

Bovée, W. G. (1999), *Discovering Journalism*, Westport, CT: Greenwood Publishing Group.

de Burgh, H. (2003), 'Skills are not enough: The case for journalism as an academic discipline', *Journalism*, 4: 1, pp. 95–112.

Cohen, J. (2005), 'Connecting the dots between journalism practice and communication scholarship', *Journalism & Mass Communication Educator*, 59: 4, pp. 335–36.

Engel, M. (2003), 'Book review: Hackademic heavyweight', *British Journalism Review*, 14: 4, pp. 61–62.

Errigo, J. and Franklin, B. (2004), 'Surviving in the Hackademy', *British Journalism Review*, 15: 2, pp. 43–48.

Franklin, B. (2009), '"Editorial: On Journalism Studies" tenth anniversary', *Journalism Studies*, 10: 6, pp. 729–733.

—— (2012), 'The future of journalism', *Journalism Studies*, 13, pp. 5–6.

Freire, P. (2000), *Pedagogy of the Oppressed*, London: Bloomsbury Publishing.

Frith, S. and Meech, P. (2007), 'Becoming a journalist: Journalism education and journalism culture', *Journalism*, 8, pp. 137–164.

Fuller, J. (2010), *What Is Happening to News: The Information Explosion and the Crisis in Journalism*, Chicago: University of Chicago Press.

Harcup, T. (2011), 'Hackademics at the chalkface: To what extent have journalism teachers become journalism researchers?', *Journalism Practice*, 5: 1, pp. 34–50.

—— (2012), 'Questioning the "bleeding obvious": What's the point of researching journalism?', *Journalism*, 13: 1, pp. 21–37.

Harrington, S. (2008), 'Popular news in the 21st century: Time for a new critical approach?' *Journalism*, 9: 3, pp. 266–84.

Kellner, P. (2010), 'Number cruncher: A matter of trust', *Prospect Magazine*, October, http://www.prospectmagazine.co.uk/columns/peter-kellner-yougov-trust-journalists. Accessed 12 January 2016.

Lather, P. (1986), 'Research as Praxis', *Harvard Educational Review*, September, 56: 3, pp. 257–78.

Lindgren, M. and Phillips, G. (2011), 'Conceptualising journalism as research: Two paradigms', *Australian Journalism Review*, 33: 2, pp. 73–83.

Moos, J. (2011), 'Pew: 75% of Americans say journalists can't get their facts straight', Poynter, 23 September, http://www.poynter.org/2011/pew-75-of-americans-say-press-cant-get-their-facts-straight/147038/. Accessed 14 January 2016.

Nash, C. (2013), 'Journalism as a research discipline', *Pacific Journalism Review*, 19: 2, pp. 123–35.

———— (2014), 'Research degrees in journalism: What is an exegesis?', *Pacific Journalism Review*, 20: 1, pp. 76–98.

Niblock, S. (2007), '"From knowing how" to "being able": Negotiating the meanings of reflective practice and reflexive research in journalism studies', *Journalism Practice*, 1: 1, pp. 30–32.

Niblock, S. (2012), 'Envisioning journalism practice as research', *Journalism Practice*, 6: 4, pp. 497–512.

Reese, S. D. and Cohen, J. (2000), 'Educating for journalism: The professionalism of scholarship', *Journalism Studies*, 1: 2, pp. 213–27.

Skinner, D., Gasher, M. J. and Compton, J. (2001), 'Putting theory to practice: A critical approach to journalism studies', *Journalism*, 2: 3, pp. 341–60.

Wahl-Jorgensen, K. and Franklin, B. (2008), 'Journalism research in the UK: From isolated efforts to an established discipline', in M. Loffelholz and D. Weaver (eds), *Global Journalism Research: Theories, Methods, Findings, Future*, Oxford: Blackwell, pp. 172–184.

Part I

What Media Practitioners Say

Chapter 1

Journalists and Scholars: A Short Manifesto

Vin Ray

If it is true that 'opposites attract' then journalists and academics should be working in blissful unison. Where one works at breakneck speed, the other takes time. Where one works in the practical world, the other works in a theoretical space. Where one deals in stories, the other deals in research.

So what's the problem? Well, the default narratives each side has about the other, for a start. The role of stereotypes looms large in any discussion about the relationship between journalism and the academy. So let us put them out there and get them out of the way. Our scholar can picture a downtrodden journalist dragged from the wine bar back to the hype-factory to transform a snippet of celebrity gossip into a front-page lead. The healthy scepticism with which he left journalism school has long since degenerated into cynicism. Meanwhile, the same journalist can envisage our scholar toiling away at home, the leather patches on his elbows wearing away the varnish on his wooden study chair. The crumbs stuck in his beard keep dropping onto the keyboard he is using to write an obscure paper that, if it is ever finished, no one will ever read, let alone understand.

Praxis-based media and journalism researchers should work to break down and overturn these stereotypes, and seek to find ways in which practitioners and scholars can help each other. It is worth highlighting the fact that *Journal of Applied Journalism and Media Studies* is the first scholarly journal to actively encourage practitioners to write for each and every edition. It is possible that no other journal would have allowed me – a journalist – to write this piece. While I have tried to be fair to both sides in this debate, I am writing from the perspective of a journalist, albeit one with strong links to the academic world.

It has often been said that journalists are at best dismissive towards academics and, at worst, antagonistic. The truth is more prosaic and, perhaps, more depressing. To the vast majority of working journalists the work of academics is invisible: they don't think about academia at all. The phrase 'it's academic' has never been more apt.

To the extent that they do think about it, journalists are less than charitable. For journalists, academic work is too often irrelevant, out of date and written in impenetrable language. The wall that exists between them and scholars is more of a time warp, so fast is the world of journalism changing and so slow is the adaptation of the academy.

A growing number of scholars agree. Professor Patrick Dunleavy and Chris Gilson (2012) from the London School of Economics – both academics – recently put it like this:

> … social scientists have an obligation to society to contribute their observations to the wider world – and at the moment that's often being done in ramshackle and impoverished

ways, in pointlessly obscure or charged-for forums, in language where you need to look up every second word in Wikipedia, with acres of 'dead-on-arrival' data in unreadable tables, and all delivered over bizarrely long-winded timescales. So the public pay for all our research, and then we shunt back to them a few press releases and a lot of out-of-date academic junk.

Even journalists might not have put it that bluntly. But it perfectly articulates what they too often feel. That 'obligation to society' that Dunleavy and Gilson cite is felt deeply by journalists. They are driven by a belief that they can make the world a better place; that their work can help people make better choices in their lives. In short, they believe they can make a difference. At least, that's why most of them became journalists. Their work is publicly and immediately available, often to millions of people.

If we can put the stereotypes to one side, there would be huge and mutual benefits to working together. We just need to establish the best mechanisms to make it work. Journalists and academics need to engage in more collaborative research. For that to happen, academics need to ask themselves three questions about any piece of research they undertake. First, is this a subject that has some relevance or some application? Second, can it be published in a timely manner – when it still matters or while it can still make a difference? Finally, is it written in a way that can be understood by an averagely intelligent person? Positively answering these questions would go a long way to helping journalists trust and respect the work of academics.

Not all theory is bad

So far so good. But journalists too must play their part. They need to accept that some theoretical research might have a value and might make a beneficial difference to the way they work – and think. They need to set aside an almost visceral distrust of media studies. News executives need to be more open and less defensive about giving academics the access they need to carry out their research.

News organizations need to think carefully – and honestly – about areas of research that might genuinely help them. There are plenty of areas of meaningful studies that could benefit journalists' organizational and editorial strategies. What does audience research tell us about the extent to which the news media help audiences understand certain subjects like the economy? What drives the way the media extensively cover certain missing children and not others? To what extent could the use of data overturn default narratives around issues like knife crime or road deaths? What can we learn from gathering quantitative and qualitative analysis of the way journalists are educated, recruited and trained? How much graphic and distressing imagery should broadcasters use; can international comparisons help us understand how best to handle these pictures? Of all the techniques and formats now available to the media, which are best suited to explaining complex issues to audiences and readers? The list could go on. Perhaps some of this has been done by academics, but it is rarely, if ever, in a form that can be easily found (or understood).

Relevance, timeliness and language

Even when it can be found, it needs to be done within an appropriate time frame if it has any chance of making a difference. Speed is crucial if academic research is to be useful. Practitioners have little time for reflection and this is where academic research can really help. If the media are giving too much time to a particular crime, can academics reflect on what the data tells us and suggest the ways in which we can put these stories in better context? Can some content analysis tell whether our coverage of China is too focused on human rights issues at the expense of economic growth? Can some linguistic analysis tell us whether we are unwittingly adopting the language of one side or another in a long-running debate? These would be very helpful kinds of analyses – but only if they can be done in a time frame that makes them useful. Waiting for journals to publish articles will often not be quick enough.

Assuming the subjects are timely and relevant, there is one final hurdle to overcome: language. The way scholars write is a direct offence to the craft skills of journalists. It goes against everything they believe and everything they teach their staff. They see their own job as achieving clarity and regard academics as delivering obfuscation – overlong papers, windy jargon, cloudy meaning, invented language.

Academics rarely have a solution or an answer to the questions they pose. This is immensely frustrating to journalists who are, on the whole, doers – practical people. In fact, if their research is presented properly, social scientists can help journalists consider whether they are asking the right questions in the first place – whether there is a different way of approaching an issue. But without a commonality of language, the discussion remains mired in stereotypes and misunderstanding.

Three steps

So, what can be done? The *Journal of Applied Journalism and Media Studies* is seeking to bridge the chasm between the two camps and this chapter proposes three developments to that end:

1. The journalism research forum

There is an urgent need for a journalism research forum that connects media organizations with research scholars. Its role would be first to agree research topics that had some useful application in the world of journalism, then, second, to 'pair' journalists and scholars to work together on the agreed subjects. The scholars would ensure the rigour of the research and a suitable distance, while the journalist could interpret its real-world application. In many cases, journalists and scholars would be trading access for relevant and useful research. This does not preclude the role of academic journals, but it would ensure a wider audience and impact for the research and its findings.

2. The journalism research database

Journalists should be much better at using academic research as source material. Yet, the work of academics so often appears to be hidden or fractured across a diverse and obscure range of locations. There is simply no easy way for anyone to access it. If, for example, a news executive wants to look at all the research done on, say, the reporting of gun crime, where can he or she go to find it in one place? If they are lucky enough to find something that *might* be of interest, the chances are that they will need to pay for it. (This is a curious state of affairs. It is analogous to a publicly funded broadcaster like the BBC charging all of the British public a licence fee to fund it – and then asking people to pay additional amounts to watch its programmes.)

There is an acute need for a Web-based database that curates and links to all the research related to the media and journalism. Allowing journalists to browse abstracts (at the very least) would be a huge leap in helping them find and access material germane to their editorial processes and even, depending on the research, their strategic approach to any number of areas. In many cases, it would greatly increase the readership of scholars' work. Any interested party could subscribe to the database and receive updates every time some relevant research was being made available. There may even be circumstances where preliminary findings or research could be made available before the (often interminable) wait for publication in journals.

3. Blogging and social media

If scholars do want to achieve more impact from their research, they need to develop a wider range of tools to disseminate it. Yet, many scholars appear to distrust the value of blogging and social media as much as journalists distrust media studies. In their book, *The Impact of the Social Sciences – How Academics and their Research make a Difference*, Bastow et al. (2014) identify five challenges to creating impact from research:

- Making connections with potential partners and users
- Identifying a 'quid pro quo' in applying research
- Finding traction for applying research within the organization
- Building and extending the relationship
- Demonstrating specific impacts or benefits to the organization

These criteria could easily be applied to research in the field of journalism. But the authors' main conclusion is that social media and blogging increase exponentially the academic and external impact of social science research. Similarly, two senior economists at the World Bank, David McKenzie and Berk Özler (2011) measured the impact of economics blogs in pointing interested parties to academic research papers. Their conclusion:

> First, links from blogs cause a striking increase in the number of abstract views and downloads of economics papers. Second, blogging raises the profile of the blogger (and his or her institution) and boosts their reputation above economists with similar publication records. Finally, a blog can transform attitudes about some of the topics it covers.

Dunleavy and Gilson (2012) argue that,

> [...] a new paradigm of research communications has grown up – one that de-emphasizes the traditional journals route, and re-prioritizes faster, real-time academic communication in which blogs play a critical intermediate role. They link to research reports and articles on the one hand, and they are linked to from Twitter, Facebook and Google+ news-streams and communities. So in research terms blogging is quite simply, one of the most important things that an academic should be doing right now.

For scholars to blog about their work is not just about impact – it's about accountability. Too much research is hidden behind the paywalls of scholarly journals where, aside from the peer review process, it is subject to very little scrutiny. Why shouldn't scholars present their work to a wider interested public?

The notion that every piece of academic research related to journalism and journalists should have a blog and a social media strategy would no doubt horrify some scholars. Blogging and social media horrifies plenty of journalists too. But it is the space where the two can meet. There will be refuseniks, of course. But they must ask themselves – truthfully – if their reluctance is for genuine reasons or a fear of the kind of scrutiny and accountability that comes with exposure.

Some academics *are* starting to blog. The gap between journalists and scholars is closing – slowly. But there is a very long way to go before the two groups are working in a way that is mutually beneficial.

Conclusion

Academics might be surprised to see how much impact their work had if it was timely, well written and easier to access; journalists would be surprised how much good work scholars are doing.

We do not want journalists and scholars to do the same thing. They both have distinct and important functions. Praxis-based media and journalism research is to encourage both sides to work together – and do their jobs *better*. A journalism research forum pairing individual scholars and journalists on research projects, a journalism research database that curates and links to all journalism and media-related research papers and an increased engagement through blogging and social media are all developments that would at least help journalists and scholars to begin to speak the same language.

References

Bastow, S., Tinkler, J. and Dunleavy, P. (2014), *The Impact of the Social Sciences – How Academics and Their Research Make a Difference*, London: SAGE.

Dunleavy, P. and Gilson, C. (2012), 'Five minutes with Patrick Dunleavy and Chris Gilson: "Blogging is quite simply, one of the most important things that an academic should be doing right now"', http://blogs.lse.ac.uk/impactofsocialsciences/2012/02/24/five-minutes-patrick-dunleavy-chris-gilson/. Accessed 12 June 2014.

McKenzie, D. and Özler, B. (2011), 'The impact of economics blogs', http://elibrary.worldbank.org/doi/pdf/10.1596/1813-9450-5783. Accessed 25 June 2014.

Chapter 2

Towards a New Relevance: Why the New Media Landscape Requires Journalists and Media Scholars to Forge a Genuine Partnership for the First Time

Matthew Eltringham

Having spent more than 20 years of my life in newsrooms across the United Kingdom I intend to take a journalistic approach – personal, opinionated and full of sweeping generalizations – to the issue of how to bridge the gap between media theory and practice. However, I hope that I'll get some of my facts right and there is a kernel of truth and a little insight in what I have to say, and that you will find some of it at least useful.

I've been at the BBC for more than 18 years – most, but not all, of my journalism career. I've worked in TV, radio and online. I've edited the late, great Sir David Frost and as a result interviewed many presidents and prime ministers. I've interviewed global celebs like George Michael and Julie Andrews, drugs barons in Colombia and child soldiers in Liberia.

And I've even worked with a fair few academics.

My biggest regret? Having to turn down an interview with the footballer George Best, because we didn't have a programme that week!

My current incarnation is as executive editor at the BBC's College of Journalism – the part of the BBC that is primarily responsible for training the 8000 or so journalists we have at the Corporation. In particular I run our website, which tells you all you need to know about how the BBC does its journalism.

At the College of Journalism, I spend even more time talking to media academics and journalism schools.

So my first observation is that journalists and academics have an awful lot in common. We all have egos; we speak our own unique language; we all think we're right and the other guy is wrong; and we all want to make a difference. Perhaps that's why the current relationship between academia and journalism is like two hedgehogs mating – prickly and standoffish. Please play this short clip: http://www.ted.com/talks/brene_brown_on_vulnerability.html

That was a clip from a TEDex talk that many of you may have seen. Professor Brene Brown is a research professor at the University of Houston – her field is social work rather than journalism but the clip, I thought, said a lot about the relationship between journalists and academics.

Fortress Journalism versus Fortress Academia

However, despite their differences, the cultural institutions – journalism and academia – are facing similar challenges to the way they operate as they lurch through the early part of the twenty-first century.

Old style Fortress Journalism has been under relentless attack for some years from the changing digital and social frontlines. No longer can the white, male journalist sit in his ivory towered newsroom holding onto 'The News' until six o'clock, when a grateful public will listen quietly and respectfully to his words of wisdom.

That 'The News' now appears first on Twitter has already become a truism ... the Arab Spring and many, many other stories are testament to the power and importance of social media. That is why the BBC has focused substantial resources in engaging with social media to both source and share our journalism. We embrace it or risk becoming irrelevant at best, redundant at worst.

Meanwhile, Fortress Academia similarly struggles to maintain its traditional ways of working. The cycle of research, funding, writing, peer review, publication, citation are being challenged by all of the same digital and social forces that are assailing journalism.

Why wait eighteen months to publish your research in a fusty old journal when you can blog about it instantly? That clip from Brene Brown has been viewed about 12 million times. I'm not surprised – she's an incredibly charismatic speaker and has a powerful message. Professor Brown hasn't just appeared on YouTube, Oprah Winfrey and CNN. She's topped the *New York Times* bestseller list and published in a wide range of conventionally respected academic journals.

I'm as envious and impressed by Professor Brown and her career as the next person. It's easy to make cheap jibes about dumbing down and hide behind the walls of Fortress Academia, in the same way that I used to hide behind the walls of Fortress Journalism – I am telling you the news and you need to listen to me because I am a BBC journalist.

Relevance

But if we succumb to that temptation we risk throwing away one of the key values that has to define our new relationship – one of relevance. These digital and social forces are the ones that are shaping our world now. We need to understand them and use them in order to continue to connect to both an academic audience and a journalistic one.

Professor Brown's ability to communicate to both academic and lay alike, and her willingness to use the new digital tools to do so (she blogs and she tweets as well, for example) has meant that her work and her research is having a much bigger impact and public good than if she had stayed within the safety of her fortress walls.

So far so familiar really – but this challenge was really brought home to me when I spoke to an academic colleague who, unlike Professor Brown, is at the start of his academic career. He has just published his doctoral thesis after three years of hard grind – researching digital media and reporting conflict – seen particularly through the eyes of the BBC's coverage of war and terrorism.

Routledge published his work a few months ago and he has yet to harvest any citations – but throughout his research he blogged, and one of the most rewarding responses he has had throughout this period is not to the many thousands of words of his thesis, but to something that came out of his research that he posted to the Frontline Club's blog unpicking the myth of the Moldovan 'Twitter Revolution'. The Frontline Club is a home in the heart of London for foreign correspondents.[1]

His profound satisfaction came in the knowledge that his work had made a practical difference to the journalism he was studying, not that he had been cited in some learned journal.

The impact of his blogging meant he thought seriously about publishing the entire thesis online in a blogging format rather than in a conventional format. But because he's looking to pursue an academic career, he felt had little real option and Routledge published his work a few months ago.

He is convinced that his blogging hasn't helped his academic job prospects – and has possibly hindered them.

Meanwhile Andy Miah, Professor of Ethics & Emerging Technologies at the University of the West of Scotland tweeted from a workshop run in November 2013 by the academic publishers Taylor and Francis: "'the average journal article is cited once" says David Green #TandFeditors #yikes'.

David Green is the Global Journals Publishing Director for Taylor and Francis; Peter Neumann – who tweets here, even more skeptically – is Professor of Security Studies at Kings College London.

'What's in it for me?'

So if impact is measured simply in the traditional academic sense of citations, it looks like a pretty tough game to play. I'm not going to argue that we should never engage in, fund or support purely academic work in journalism – of course we should. But don't expect me or my journalist colleagues to be tremendously interested in it. And to be brutally honest – looking at these tweets – it's not entirely clear how much other academics are either.

Translate that response to a journalistic environment and it's difficult to imagine working journalists promoted or even surviving for very long writing stories no one ever mentioned.

Newsrooms are stressful, pressured environments – even well-resourced ones like the BBC, who also have a public service remit. We have a lot of requests from academics across the United Kingdom to partner or help them in their research. We are nice helpful people, but the first question we ask when assessing whether or not to agree to work with an academic is 'what's in it for me?'

We reject the overwhelming majority.

There's a very provocative blog written this time last year for the Knight Foundation by the journalist Eric Newton questioning the value of academic research in journalism that I would point you to, if you're not already familiar with it: http://www.knightfoundation.org/blogs/knightblog/2012/9/5/exploring-the-value-of-academic-research-in-journalism/

If I can quote a pithy par from his blog post!

Perhaps the good research is *really* good. At the 2012 convention, the Association of Educators in Journalism and Mass Communication gave out a thumb drive with the 'best' scholarly articles from decades of the journals. We reviewed them. Alas, for the most part, they seemed derivative, obvious or obtuse. To quote a senior journalism educator: 'There are three categories of research these days: 1. Who cares? 2. No shit! 3. I don't have any idea what you are talking about'. To be generous, perhaps we should add a category: '4. Needs more work, but there might be something there. (Or, Close But No Cigar.)'

Needless to say there were dissenters.

Genuine partnership

So what should be the foundation of a fruitful – and genuine – partnership between academics and journalists? From where I stand it has to be relevant, practical and useful. Mutually relevant, practical and useful – for both journalists and for academics.

What does that actually mean? What does that work or research look like? And why does it matter? Perhaps if I offer two examples of the kind of work I am talking about I can illustrate what I mean and why this kind of research in partnership with the industry is essential.

The first was produced by Dr Claire Wardle and Dr. Andrew Williams (2008). Claire was an academic at Cardiff University's Journalism School. Claire left the academic world for journalism, where she now works closely as a consultant and trainer with a number of media organizations around the world.

The second was produced by Emily Bell, who was a very senior journalist at *The Guardian* newspaper in the United Kingdom, where she was director of digital content. She's now an academic – Professor of Professional Practice and Director of the Tow Center for Digital Journalism at Columbia University.

They both have what I would call 'Crossover Appeal' – because they understand the interests, demands and pressures of both academia and journalism.

User-Generated Content (UGC)

Claire and Williams' work (2008), 'UGC: Understanding its impact upon contributors, non-contributors and the BBC', was co-funded by the Arts and Humanities Research Council and the BBC, in conjunction with her colleague Andy Williams – way back in 2007/2008 – was the first proper look at the way user-generated content was affecting journalism and journalists.[2]

I met her first when she was working on her paper. It involved six different methodologies: ten weeks of newsroom observations at different newsrooms across the BBC; a nationally representative Ipsos MORI survey of 944 people; an online survey of 695 BBC website contributors; 12 focus groups with 100 people; 115 interviews with BBC journalists; ten interviews with senior managers and BBC executives; and analysis of 105 hours of news output from 13 national and regional TV and radio programmes (and associated websites).

It remains a seminal piece of work on the subject, providing insight into what people thought about participation in the news process, what kinds of people did it and why. It is insight that is still relevant today – even though it was written and researched in the days before Twitter and Facebook, the principles still apply.

It provided significant signposts for the BBC in its foray into the use of UGC, or user-generated content. I was at the time running a small experimental team in the BBC's network newsroom called the UGC Hub – it still exists and is now integral to our news operation.

It is a significant operation now of 20 journalists, whose job it is to find, verify and then share across the news operation key bits of user-generated content that we incorporate into our daily output.

When Claire produced her research we were still finding our way towards an effective and sustainable modus operandi and although we were stumbling towards some of the conclusions she reached, she and her team were able to clarify and codify those thoughts in a way that helped drive the project on.

In 2008 she wrote:

For all the excitement about 'UGC' democratising news, the vast majority of the population have never contributed material. There are significant barriers to participation and news organisations should be thinking about ways of minimising those barriers to broaden the range of views and opinions included in their news output.

Emily Bell's work

Published earlier this year, Emily Bell's report drawn up with others, notably C. W. Anderson and Clay Shirky (2014), is entitled 'Post-industrial journalism: Adapting to the present'.[3]

In it she and her co-authors examine the present state of American journalism and what can be learnt from it in a way that might offer clues and insight into the new possibilities for journalism. They look at the news ecosystem, news organization and business models.

Merely bolting on a few new techniques will not be enough to adapt to the ever-changing ecosystem; taking advantage of access to individuals, crowds and machines will mean changing organizational structure. We recognize – she adds – that many existing organizations will regard these recommendations as anathema.

Emily admits that her report is 'more an essay than a piece of testable scholarship' describing it as a call to arms for further 'more traditional' academic research.

'Nonetheless' she says, she and her co-authors draw on a 'variety' of methods including qualitative interviews and industry experience.

Pioneers of praxis

The pieces by Claire and Bell have a lot in common – both tackle the key issues that are right now challenging journalism, journalists and the industry built on them.

They help journalists understand the fundamental changes that are being driven by the inexorable and inexhaustible rise of the digital world and the social Web.

They therefore help us find a route through to the 'next world'.

They are – frankly – written in a language and style that we understand or, perhaps more accurately, one that we are prepared to put up with.

They retain academic worth and credibility.

They explain why a genuine partnership between journalists and academics is important – because they help us understand the issues that are disrupting our industry and threaten to unseat us all.

They have real impact in the real world

They are practical, relevant and useful.

Let's be clear that 'practical' doesn't have to mean rooted in the sordid world of the newsroom, who does what, where, when and how. Practical can also mean theoretical, as long as those ideas have a practical application.

Look at the work of Jeff Jarvis (2016), for example, at buzzmachine.com. We all know him. He's a bit of a Marmite character. You either love him or loathe him. A former journalist turned academic – now Associate Professor at City University of New York and he certainly makes a lot of noise.

A lot of his work is as theoretically-based as it is practical – but his books *What Would Google Do?* and *Public Parts,* along with his blog BuzzMachine and his 130,000 followers on Twitter have certainly got many in the media and academia arguing. And they have also – I would suggest – had substantial impact, got many people thinking and driven significant change in minds at least, if not in practice.

Or what about Paul Bradshaw of onlinejournalismblog.org and helpmeinvestigate.com – a visiting professor at City University London who also teaches at Birmingham City University?

He has done a lot of thinking on the organization of twenty-first-century news-rooms – his 2007 theory of the news diamond, for example, engaged the interest of many at the BBC. His background is more academic than practitioner, and he approaches his research from that perspective.

His work on data journalism and social media and investigative journalism – all brought together in two websites: HelpMeInvestigate and OnlineJournalismBlog – put some of his theories to the practical test and, again, has driven change.

Paul and Jeff have two further things in common that are central to realizing a new partnership between journalists and academics – and indeed explain why it is necessary.

First, they teach as well as write and research, and second they both operate in and fully understand the digital world we all now live in.

Three years ago, the Head of the BBC Newsroom made it pretty clear what he thought were the essential skills for twenty-first-century journalists.

Prominence of social and digital

If it was true then, it is even more true now: most programme editors at the BBC have said explicitly that if you don't understand the social and digital world don't bother applying to them for a job, because you won't get one.

For a lot of journalists who have found a comfortable niche behind the castle walls and bedded down for what they thought was the duration, that's pretty scary – and I'm sure that's the same for many academics too.

But once you've been given the new tools and been taught how to use them, you realize pretty quickly that in fact it makes our jobs far more interesting and creative.

You also realize that it doesn't fundamentally change what we do – although it may change what it looks like and where it appears.

Journalism remains about narrative, context and analysis; it demands independence, accuracy and impartiality. Sound familiar?

The BBC – and my colleagues at the College of Journalism in particular – have invested substantial resources in training our editorial staff in these core skills of understanding how to use the social media and the Web.

Encouraged by senior editorial figures like Peter Horrocks, rather than support an identified need from the business, we led from the front and enabled a huge cultural change across BBC News in the understanding and use of social media in particular.

We're now looking at enhanced digital skills and data journalism – even, possibly, basic coding.

That's what we as an industry need from our journalism schools – to teach those skills and more to those coming into journalism; not just to provide willing troops but those ready to meet the future head on, and even help shape it too.

And we need to talk to them more about that, because even as the need for practical, relevant and useful courses becomes sharper, so do the financial pressures.

Journalism students and jobs

In the United Kingdom most mainstream media organizations – including the BBC – are shedding jobs, not hiring. And most courses that offer a realistic chance of gainful employment in your chosen career are postgraduate M.A.s.

That means most UK students will be carrying debts of £50,000 or more (more than $80,000) – into a profession, that I can personally vouch, is not the most lucrative in the world. Students will be faced with a very clear choice – is this course going to get me the job I want or am I wasting my money?

The industry needs J-Schools to turn out the right graduates and the J-Schools need media organizations to recruit their graduates and justify their fees.

The industry also badly needs them to innovate and explore the new worlds of digital, data, coding and social.

So between them they need to work out a way forward.

It wouldn't be entirely untrue either to say that parts of the media industry don't always know exactly what they want or even what they really need. Which ought to be a huge opportunity for journalism educators.

Even if they saw it as their responsibility, most media organizations – in the United Kingdom at least – have limited resources or time to invest in significant training for their own staff, let alone graduates. What postgraduate training they do is highly focused on the specific needs of their own organization rather than anything with a broader ambition.

The BBC offers about a dozen places a year on their Journalism Trainee Scheme. *The Guardian* newspaper, after months of discussion and even advertising for staff, after arguing that '[e]verything about the media is there to be re-imagined and reshaped', scrapped a partnership in September with Cardiff University to set up a Master's degree.

However, at the last count there were more than 30 centres in the United Kingdom offering more than 50 different postgraduate courses in journalism. There are many more B.A. courses in journalism studies.

Digital challenges

And then there are the digital challenges to those courses – e-learning, online courses, part-time, short-term modules, all abbreviated as MOOCS.

If the digital world now allows you to be a journalist without working for a media organization, you can certainly acquire the skills to be a journalist without ever going to university. Will training overtake education? If it does, what impact will that have on the quality of our journalism?

I might be prepared to spend a few hundred pounds on a course that teaches me to use my iPhone as a camera or audio recorder – but would I spend the same amount of time and money on a short course on journalism ethics, or even the law? I doubt it.

That – needless to say – is a huge threat to journalism standards everywhere.

A survey this year of United States J-Schools by the Poynter Institute[4] suggests that, where there should be collaboration, there is dysfunction. First among a number of worrying findings was that barely half – 53 per cent – of educators think a journalism degree is very to extremely important to getting a job. About 41 per cent of professionals share that belief.

If journalism academics don't think their courses are important, what is anyone else going to think – be they students or employers?

But, particularly in the United Kingdom in a post-Leveson world, where standards of journalism and journalistic activity are being challenged more than ever before, journalism educators should be leading journalism into the digital age.

The Poynter Institute's Howard Finberg has written that he worries more about the future of journalism degrees than he worries about the future of journalism.

He says 'those who don't innovate in the classroom will be left behind – just like those who chose not to innovate in the newsroom'.

I share a lot of his worries, but there is also a huge opportunity to work together at a time of huge disruption, and find a way to forge a new and genuine partnership that will benefit us all.

Tell us something we don't know, tell us something that matters to us and tell us something that will make a difference to what we do.

References

Anderson, Chris, Bell, Emily and Shirky, Clay (2014), 'Post industrial journalism: Adapting to the Present', Tow Center for Digital Journalism, http://towcenter.org/research/post-industrial-journalism-adapting-to-the-present-2/. Accessed 9 September 2016.

Jarvis, Jeff (2016), BuzzMachine, http://buzzmachine.com/. Accessed 12 September 2016.

——— (2010), *What Would Google Do?*, New York: Harper Collins, https://aszapla.files.wordpress.com/2011/12/what-would-google-do.pdf. Accessed 14 September 2016.

——— (2011), *Public Parts: How Sharing In The Digital Age Is Revolutionizing Life Business And Society Jeff Jarvis*, New York: Simon & Schuster.

Wardle, Claire and Williams, Andrew (2008), 'UGC: Understanding its impact upon contributors, non-contributors and the BBC', ugc @thebbc, http://www.bbc.co.uk/blogs/knowledgeexchange/cardiffone.pdf. Accessed 28 August 2016.

Notes

1 More information on this can be found through the following address: http://www.frontlineclub.com/the_myth_of_the_moldova_twitter_revolution-2/.

2 Her work can be accessed at: http://cardiff.ac.uk/jomec/ research/researchgroups/journalismstudies/fundedprojects/usergeneratedcontent. html.

3 This can be retrieved from: http://towcenter.org/research/post-industrial-journalism/.

4 This can be retrieved from the following address: http://www.poynter.org/how-tos/journalism-education/220410/scary-future-journalism-education/.

Chapter 3

Journalism's Practitioners and the Academy: Must They Eternally Live in Different Universes?

Kevin Marsh

If you're still alive thanks to modern surgery, whisper a quiet word of gratitude to Ambroise Paré. He was a sixteenth-century barber-surgeon who served the Valois kings of France. A hero to those patients whose lives he saved, a heretic to most of his fellows. That heroism/heresy lay in two revolutionary ideas.

One, the point of surgery was to improve the health of patients, not to provide a stage for the surgeon to show the speed, sophistication and skill of his sanguineous sawing.

Two, patients' health and life chances were dramatically enhanced if surgeons studied the effects of their interventions and did more of those things that didn't kill the patient, fewer of those that did.

Paré's fellow surgeons saw the orthodoxies of their trade as something close to the revealed truths of religion. Beliefs, techniques and practices reverently handed down from generation to generation. They weren't to be questioned – not even with hard evidence that showed beyond doubt they did more harm than good.

Self-regard, self-validation and indifference to the effects of their work were defining features of these pre-enlightenment sawbones. So was their disregard for evidence-based critique and disdain for those who suggested putting their practices to the test. Attitudes that have some parallels with Anglo-Saxon and European journalists today.

Even now, after major scandals in the United States and Europe and with the public's confidence in journalism barely measurable, many practitioners still reject the notion that they have anything to learn from the academy, the men and women who, in theory at least, study journalism and its effects on the public sphere.

The parallel isn't exact, though. Paré's 'academic' study of surgery was calculated to be relevant to practice, to improve it for the sake of the public health. The same has not been true of far too many academics who have 'studied' journalism and the media.

Before defecting to the academy, I spent thirty years as a senior BBC editor, a practitioner in journalism's front line. Unlike almost all my colleagues, I had an interest in what the academy had to say about media – yet I cannot recall a single academic paper issuing from 'pure' media scholars that I found relevant or useful to the work I did or that resulted in me changing my practice in any way. Nor can I recall any of the hundreds of journalists I knew in other branches of the British media even discussing academic work.

Different universes

Until the last few years, journalism's practitioners and academics inhabited different universes. Most still do.

The mission of praxis-based media and journalism research is to play some part in linking those universes. In that mission, it's not alone. But it's no easy task. There are many reasons for journalism's and the academy's mutual estrangement. Some valid, some less so.

In the 'valid' column is the most familiar argument of all: journalism is essentially institutionalized free speech. Constraint is anathema and that includes intellectual constraint emerging from the academy.

It is valid, too, to argue that journalism is not a profession. It does not require the academy to devise for it and teach entry requirements, professional development or regulation as do medicine, the law, architecture, accountancy and any number of other true professions.

The former *LA Times* editor John S. Carroll put it succinctly when he spoke to students at the University of Oregon a decade ago:

> it is the constitutional right of every citizen, no matter how ignorant or how depraved, to be a journalist [...].

He went on:

> This wild liberty, this official laxity, is one of journalism's appeals.
>
> (2004)

Carroll couldn't know it – he was speaking before the social media explosion of the mid-2000s – but that 'wild liberty' was soon to be a more apt description of the lawless frontier where paid and unpaid journalism collide. A frontier where those who earn their living from journalism might want to distinguish themselves from those who do not – and might want to do so by thinking more deeply about the effects of their trade on the health of the public sphere.

There is, or should be, a clear distinction between journalists' stubborn independence that pushes back against power or onerous regulation – the 'valid' column – and the cussed refusal even to acknowledge any and every critique. Yet it's not a difference many practitioners in Western European and Anglo-Saxon journalism make.

Resistance to the academy

Here in the United Kingdom, there is ample evidence in the notorious refusal of some newspapers to correct errors of fact, their acquiescence in criminal activity – phone hacking, personation, theft – and their refusal to implement the recommendations of the Leveson

Inquiry into the 'culture, practices and ethics' of the press, recommendations that have overwhelming public support (YouGov Poll 2013).

But even those practitioners who are more receptive to critique, more prepared to listen and take account of study and analysis, are still resistant to the influence of scholars and academics.

Journalism, these practitioners argue, is an instinctive trade. While news *production* is increasingly process-driven, the *practice* of news journalism itself is not. What's 'on agenda' at any time; priorities between stories, the lead, the tailpiece; when a story becomes live, when it 'loses legs', when it's revived; narratives, framings and language – all of these and other practical journalistic decisions are context-, time- and place-specific. Practitioners argue that they depend on the journalists' 'nose' and cannot – like cardiac surgery, the preparation of a contract or annual audit – be reduced to procedures susceptible to continual improvement through both academic and practical observation, study and analysis.

Practitioners who do think more seriously about their trade still see little relevance in the academy. My own failure to find relevance in the academic papers I read as a senior BBC editor derived largely from their relentlessly negative, 'holier-than-thou' mindset. An alienating mindset that seemed designed only to lecture me on how blind I was to whichever social, economic or political interpretation was fashionable in the academy at the time.

At various moments, the academy charged me with failing to recognize the controlling hand of capitalism's self-interest; naïve exercises in self-delusion as I tried to report impartially on Northern Ireland, the Middle East, the Balkan Wars, consolidating power's grip on the lives of the downtrodden. All of which I was too feeble-minded to see.

Timely relevance to practice never seemed to be of any interest to the academy – and for that reason if no other, the academy was never relevant to me nor to any other practitioner I knew.

The limits of the academic method

Others have written here (Chapters 1 and 4) about the obscure, impenetrable language that is characteristic of the academy – a characteristic that too many academics wear as badges of pride. Others have written about the lack of timeliness, too. A lengthy, comprehensive study of an issue that has long passed from human memory might win the acclaim of other social scientists. It is of no conceivable relevance to practitioners.

But there's a third barrier, linked to these first two. And that is the standard format of the academic offer. The 'paper'.

The defining feature of the 'paper' or dissertation is its theoretical and conceptual anchoring in previous academic study, embodied in the customary critical literature review and referencing – features that seem to non-academics fetishistic.

To a social scientist, a media studies academic, a paper without a review and pages of references is unthinkable – 'not scholarly'. To a practitioner, a paper packed with precedent is unreadable. More importantly, however, the academic paper's format locks all thinking inside current academic orthodoxy, as if its author hadn't dared leave the intellectual harbour without a surrounding scholarly flotilla.

Practitioners have no need for literature reviews and references that are designed to show how this latest offering from the academy nudges some slice of thinking within this or that conceptual framework a millimetre further forward, especially when those practitioners find the conceptual framework alien in the first place.

If practitioners are to accept more readily the interventions of the academy, and if the academy is to have any real relevance to practice, both have to shift positions. Bringing together practice and scholarly thought is an important component in that.

There are other models, too, whose influence on journalistic practice is worth considering.

One of the academy's more effective and insistent interventions in the practice of journalism was the American Public Journalism movement that flourished in the 1990s (Glasser 1999).

That movement grew out of something close to despair at the state of American political journalism – in particular, the threadbare coverage of the 1988 presidential election. By then, journalism had, according to Larry Sabato, Politics Professor at Virginia University, completed its transformation from 'lapdog' via 'watchdog' to 'junkyard dog' (1991).

Public Journalism's declared purpose was to shift journalism's understanding of itself: to see itself as part of the public not separate from it; to acknowledge its responsibility for making the public go well or go badly. And it was a movement whose most energetic agents were academics – most prominently, New York University's Jay Rosen.

It gained traction, however, from the adherence of senior editors and influential journalists in what was at the time America's second biggest newspaper group, Knight Ridder. And even those journalists who rejected the movement's ideas – among them some of America's senior TV anchors – were forced to confront them.

What was different about the academic component of Public Journalism was its calculated intent to change journalistic practice. To cause practitioners to think in a different way about the kind of stories that newspapers covered, the way they framed them, the balance between the negatives and positives, the way TV interviews were conducted and political positions were analysed.

Rosen and the other academics involved produced short, intense, sharply critical interventions, delivered in non-scholarly formats via non-traditional academic channels (2003): short blog posts, TV interviews, newspaper op-eds, workshops held in newsrooms – though for those in the academy who couldn't break the habit, there were also more traditional academic offers.

That preparedness to embrace the 'non-academic' was key to penetrating the protective shield many practitioners had erected between themselves and informed critique. As was the generally 'positive' nature of the interventions, practitioners weren't lectured on their failures alone; a vital part of Public Journalism was to present a vision of journalistic practice that was, according to its proponents, calculated to improve the health of public discourse.

Public Journalism's direct influence was relatively short-lived, in part, because it reached maximum influence just as 'Big Journalism's' monopoly was being unpicked by the Web and the free read–write blogging software that made publishers of us all and led eventually to social media. But its influence was critical in creating the atmosphere for the genuinely practical research and critique of American journalism's rites and rituals that we now find in the Pew Centre, the Nieman Journalism Lab and the Columbia Journalism Review to name but three.

Here in the United Kingdom, the Reuters Institute for the Study of Journalism provides a second model. The beating heart of the institute is its programme of fellowships, aimed at international mid-career practitioners offering time-out at the University of Oxford to study an aspect of journalistic practice directly relevant to their place of work.

Recent work includes 'How to reinvent a regional newspaper in the digital age' (Hakaniemi 2014); 'New media and the Syrian conflict' (Harkin 2014); and 'New pressures on old ethics' (Mayo 2013) – all researched and written to meet the highest academic standards but in a language, format and timeliness that renders them instantly readable and relevant to practice.

A third model is offered by my former employer, the BBC.

The BBC is publicly funded. Not, as some mistakenly believe, by the government of the day but by a continuing levy on households who own and use a TV set. That method of funding has driven the evolution of a range of practices designed to demonstrate the corporation's accountability to its public.

One of those is a process of regular editorial review. These reviews are led by a prominent subject expert who may or may not be drawn from the academy, often assisted by a panel of other specialists. And in recent years they've considered many aspects of news coverage: business, religion, the EU, rural life and, most recently, the Arab World and the Middle East (Mortimer 2012) and science (Jones 2011).

The purpose of the reviews is threefold: to analyse output; to determine what has actually been broadcast or published, the narratives, language and framings routinely selected; to examine attitudes amongst both senior and junior editorial staff; and to conclude with recommendations for practical improvements while such improvement is still relevant to coverage.

As a senior BBC editor, I often found these reviews uncomfortable. But I could not ignore them – and not just because it was in my contract to follow their recommendations. They were and are thorough, researched to high academic standards, in particular their analysis of data. But they also always have three characteristics lacking in the majority of pure academic work: timeliness; relevance to practice; accessibility.

They had and have the status of pieces of research and analysis carried out on behalf of BBC journalism's paymasters and, for that reason they also had and have genuine traction with practitioners. It's possible to point to dozens of tangible changes deriving from these reviews – the appointment of new specialists in new specialisms and distribution of bureaux and teaching programmes around journalistic ethics and knowledge areas.

Conclusions

Journalism's practitioners and academics have never been the closest allies – for both valid and invalid reasons. Perhaps unsurprisingly, journalists and academics do different jobs and have different criteria by which they judge what 'good' looks like.

Journalists feel keenly the need to protect the freedom of their trade, to resist power and pressure and they tend to trust instinct rather than process. The academy, on the other hand, sees intellectual progress as an end in itself for which relevance to practice has little if any significance and for which the continuity of scholarship expressed in scholarly language and formats is essential.

These mindsets might be understandable. Others less so.

Journalism's arrogant resistance to critique from any source, for example, including its own audiences; its belief that listening to critique and changing practice for the better is 'caving in to pressure'; its habit of excusing the worst in journalism with the arguments needed to protect the best; its certainty that the health of the public discourse is not its concern.

Or, on the academy's side, the relentless negativity that insists on lecturing practitioners on how wrong they are, not how right they could be; its insistence on 'revealing' the hidden hands that we mere practitioners are too foolish to see; its methodologies that lock-in orthodoxy and bar the door to the heterodox; its other-worldly sense of time and relevance and what effective communication truly is.

The keys to unlocking this are already known – what is needed is the will, both among practitioners and in the academy, to turn them.

Practitioners and academics need as many places as possible where they share in a dialogue of equals, and that means both sides stepping outside their norms.

Practitioners need to understand they do have a responsibility for the public sphere, certainly for the effects of their role in it – they can be a force for good or for ill. Listening to critique and analysis and perhaps changing practice isn't 'caving in'; as public service broadcasters such as the BBC demonstrate, listening to the public and changing practice to serve them is a sign of strength, not weakness.

Academics need to understand that they too have a responsibility to the public. That sterile, self-regarding scholarly research designed only to score intellectual points or win real points within an academic hierarchy will never influence practice – worse, it's an approach that will widen, not close, the gulf between practitioners and the academy.

Journalism will never – should never, perhaps – achieve the kind of synergy between practice and the academy that Ambroise Paré forged between observation, analysis and practical surgery. But there can be no argument now – as any number of models demonstrate – against a closer, more respectful, continual dialogue in terms and formats both sides accept and find relevant.

References

Carroll, J. S. (2004), 'Ruhl lecture – the wolf in reporter's clothing: The rise of pseudo- journalism in America', University of Oregon, http://journalism.uoregon.edu/ events/2004-ruhl-lecture-john-carroll/. Accessed 20 January 2015.

Glasser, T. L. (ed.) (1999), *The Idea of Public Journalism*, New York: The Guildford Press.

Hakaniemi, K. (2014), 'From a print house to a technology company: How to reinvent a regional newspaper in the digital age?', RISJ, http://reutersinstitute.politics.ox.ac.uk/publication/ print-house-technology-company-how-reinvent-regional-newspaper-digital-age. Accessed 20 January 2015.

Harkin, J. (2014), 'Good media, bad politics? New media and the Syrian conflict', RISJ, http:// reutersinstitute.politics.ox.ac.uk/publication/good-media-bad-politics-new-media-and-syrian-conflict. Accessed 20 January 2015.

Jones, S. (2011), 'BBC Trust review of impartiality and accuracy of the BBC's coverage of science', BBC Trust, http://downloads.bbc.co.uk/bbctrust/assets/files/pdf/our_work/science_ impartiality/science_impartiality.pdf. Accessed 20 January 2015.

Mayo, K. (2013), 'New pressures on old ethics', RISJ, http://reutersinstitute.politics.ox.ac.uk/ publication/new-pressures-old-ethics. Accessed 20 January 2015.

Mortimer, E. (2012), 'A BBC Trust report on the impartiality and accuracy of the BBC's coverage of the events known as the "Arab Spring"', BBC Trust, http://downloads.bbc.co.uk/bbctrust/ assets/files/pdf/our_work/arabspring_impartiality/arab_spring.pdf. Accessed 20 January 2015.

Rosen, J. (2003), 'Pressthink: The ghost of democracy in the media machine', http://pressthink. org/. Accessed 20 January 2015.

Sabato, L. J. (1991), *Feeding Frenzy: How Attack Journalism Has Transformed American Politics*, New York: Free Press.

YouGov Poll (2013), 'Poll for the media standards trust', YouGov, http://cdn.yougov.com/ cumulus_uploads/document/mry6s51f2n/YouGov-Media-Standards-Trust-Archive-results-010213-Leveson-Inquiry-press-regulation.pdf. Accessed 20 January 2015.

Chapter 4

Why Practitioners Resent Academic Writing

Leon Barkho

Ask a practitioner or journalist what annoys them about academic writing, and language will come near the top of the list of their grievances. But it is not only practitioners who are complaining. Today many academics moan about the way journal papers are written. As criticism about academic writing mounts, the gripes can no longer be ignored. The volume of free and readily available academic content on the Internet is steadily growing. Therefore, more than at any time before, media and journalism scholars must improve their writing and make it as 'digestible' to the people they research as possible. Nearly half of this book includes submissions by practitioners. In most of them, poor language tops complaints about journal articles. Vin Ray (Chapter 1), who founded the BBC College of Journalism and was its director for four years, puts it like this:

> The way scholars write is a direct offence to the craft skills of journalists. It goes against everything they believe and everything they teach their staff. They see their own job as achieving clarity and regard academics as delivering obfuscation – over-long papers, windy jargon, cloudy meaning, invented language.

Why do we write?

We write to communicate to others our ideas, our opinions, and the result of our work and findings. Writing is the most important means through which media and journalism scholars communicate with each other and with the world outside their campuses. Of course, we must distinguish between good and bad writing. We must also write in a way that tells others – with clarity – what we want to say. George Orwell (1964) in his masterpiece *Politics and the English Language* links bad language to 'foolish' thought. Slovenliness of writing, he says, points to slovenliness of ideas, and bad language corrupts good thought.

If we lack the ability to lucidly write what we have in our mind, there is a problem with the way we are using language as a carrier of our thoughts. The 'greatest virtue' of speech and writing, says Aristotle (1965), 'is to be clear'. Clarity on the part of the writer is closely linked to honesty and sincerity and it is 'insincerity' that is 'the great enemy of clear language' because lack of clarity in writing and speech points to 'a gap between one's real and one's declared aims' (Orwell 1964).

Which language are media and journalism academics supposed to speak? Scholars, practitioners claim, talk in a language that could even be hard for other academics to follow.

If academics want media and journalism practitioners to take them and their work seriously, they should talk to them in their own language. Then, and only then, will practitioners begin to respect academics and their writings and listen to what they say. In one of his most oft-cited quotes, Lee Iacocca (Iacocca and Novak 2007: 58), the legendary US businessman and newsmaker, drives home the same message: 'Talk to people in their own language. If you do it well [...] they'll follow you to the death'.

What philosophers say

Linguists, anthropologists and philosophers have long grappled with the issue of the correlation between language and thought. They say that language is the area where our differences in terms of customs, habits, thoughts, experiences, conventions and rules are represented. They broadly agree that language shapes the way we think and that the way we think determines the way we speak and write (e.g. Sapir 1921; Wittgenstein 1969; Hoijer 1959; Whorf 1969; Cooper 1973). China's greatest teacher, philosopher and theorist Confucius (1980, Book 13, Verse 3) links language that is quickly and easily understood to morality and justice. If what we say and write is obscure, complex, incoherent and cloudy, then 'morals and art will deteriorate [...] justice goes astray [and] the people will stand about in helpless confusion'. What matters above everything in language is that there must be no confusion in what is said or written. Bad language breeds confusion.

Academics draw a lot on social science philosophers and try to pursue their style of writing. Some of the most cited philosophers in social sciences, such as Habermas, Wittgenstein, Kant, Ricoeur, Derrida, Bourdieu, Foucault or Hegel, generally write in a difficult way because they mainly deal with some of the most complex and difficult social and mental problems in life. But this is not the case with the majority of the issues covered by media and journalism academics. These are mostly of a practical nature, with the results arrived at mainly through interviewing and immersion in the social reality of the people and output they research.

New outlets require a new academic language

Media and journalism academics must bear in mind the issue of free and open access. Much of their writings are, for the first time, freely available for the public to read. We are seeing the emergence of university presses that are wholly dedicated to free and open access publishing. Cardiff University has set up its own open access publishing house with no fees or pay walls (Bowman 2014). Academic writing is in the throes of drastic transformations for two major reasons. First, digitization that has made it easy for scholars, their institutions and publishers to allow for free and open access. The second relates to rules and regulations in Europe and North America that make it incumbent on academics and their institutions to provide free access to all scientific output financed by charities or taxpayers' money. In the United Kingdom for instance it is now mandatory that the results of taxpayer-financed research are made available free online for others to read and redistribute. The European Union and charities are following suit (*The Economist* 2012a, 2013b). The point is whether academics are prepared to change the way they write in response to these transformations.

Another important issue is whether academic publishers are willing to invest in editing and proofreading as part of attempts to improve academic language. Journal publishers cash in on other academics' work submitted to them almost free of charge as it is written and then vetted for nearly nothing. The number of submissions to academic journals outpaces the capacity to review them. But despite the increasing demand for peer review and publishers' skyrocketing profit margins, academic journal editors, reviewers and authors are rarely paid for what they do. In fact, the Public Library of Science, a pioneer of open access publishing, charges its authors 'a fee (between $1350 and $2900)' for each article it issues (*The Economist* 2012b, 2013a).

Academic journal publishing is a lucrative business – but not for editors, reviewers or authors who work for little or nothing. Annual subscription rates for top scientific journals such as *Tetrahedron* or the *Journal of Mathematical Sciences* costs up to $20,000. In Britain, 65 per cent of the money spent on content by university libraries goes to academic journal subscription. Elsevier is the biggest academic journal publisher with more than 2000 titles, including such top ranking ones as *Cell* and *The Lancet*. It made a profit of £768 million ($1.2 billion) on revenues of £2.1 billion in 2011 (*The Economist* 2011, 2014). Improving the language in the articles is not a priority for the publishers. Any copy-editing is mainly restricted to ensuring that the format is in line with the publisher's style guide. Editors, peer reviewers and authors form an 'academic cheap labour force': employed but rarely paid. Hired for free, peer reviewers seldom pay attention to language. Their ultimate aim is to see whether content meets scientific criteria or not.

There is a big difference in the editing procedures of news organizations and academic journals. In many cases, sub-editors correct and polish articles with a view to making them as stylish and comprehensible as possible. Journalists attend specially designed courses, arranged by their own institutions, on how to write well. No such help is available in most universities and academic journals. Editing geared towards improving the language of journal articles and academic textbooks is generally poor or non-existent. Many of the poor writing habits I refer to below persist because scholars get little or no help in this field. Journal peer reviewers and editors rarely help writers improve the clarity of their prose (Takoma 2013; Walt 2013).

What is wrong with academic writing?

Samples of poor academic writing are not hard to find. In a bid to raise the consciousness of the 'low' state of the language of scholarly articles, the journal *Philosophy and Literature* sponsored a 'Bad Writing Contest' (*Philosophy and Literature* 1996–98). The gripes are voluminous and it is beyond the scope of this chapter to cover them. But before I cite some of the most common complaints, let me focus on a few examples that I picked up from an international media and journalism conference I attended in Brazil in June 2014. I will concentrate on the titles of some presentations and cite them as they were written, all in upper-case letters. The lower-case sentences are my own. I have tried – as far as possible – to 'demystify' the titles by writing them differently to make them acceptable to practitioners and academics alike:

1. JOURNALISM RECONFIGURATION OF INTERNATIONAL NEWS AGENCIES: THE NEW LANDSCAPE OF EFE WITH THE 'DIGITAL AGE'
    How EFE, the Spanish newswire, is going digital
2. NEWSPAPER OWNERSHIP AND PRIORITIZATION OF DIGITAL COMPETENCES
    How much emphasis should newspapers place on digital skills?
3. CONCEPTUALIZING MEDIA WORK: HUMAN-LED VS TECHNOLOGY-LED APPROACHES
    It is hard to know what exactly this title means but it might be: To what extent can technology replace humans?
4. THROUGH THE LOOKING CLASS: NEW TOOLS FOR JOURNALISTS USING SOCIAL MEDIA
    New tools for journalists using social media
5. WEBTV FOR PRINTED NEWS? A FIT-VIABILITY PERSPECTIVE ON ADOPTION OF WEBTV TECHNOLOGY IN REGIONAL NEWS PUBLISHING IN GERMANY
    Does Web TV work for regional newspapers? A case study from Germany
6. MOBILE NEWS UPTAKE AND ITS DISPLACING – AND COMPLIMENTARY – EFFECTS ON PRINT- AND ONLINE-NEWS
    How mobile is changing online news
7. PAYING FOR LOCAL ONLINE NEWSPAPERS: AN ANALYSIS ON PAYING INTENT, PRICE ELASTICITY OF DEMAND, AND PREDICTORS OF PAYING INTENT
    Is there a viable business model for local online news?

These titles may be good examples of the complaints Rachel Toor (2010) makes in her article 'Bad writing and bad thinking'. They are 'dense and boring' with many 'multisyllabic words [and] complex phrasing'.

A major complaint about academic writing relates to its failure to convey in lucid and lively language what their authors want to say. That is the problem with the language of the samples above. Denis Dutton (1999) goes as far as accusing academics, whose writing is obscure and difficult to comprehend, of 'committing language crimes'. Language is a means to facilitate communication and not the other way round, Dutton says. What gives credence to Dutton's outburst published in the *Wall Street Journal* is the fact that he himself was an outstanding academic and for 23 years the editor of the scholarly journal *Philosophy and*

Literature. He shows 'how the state of academic writing had sunk' with 'most egregious examples of awkward, jargon-clogged academic prose from all over the English-speaking world' (Dutton 1999).

Writing in *Foreign Policy*, Stephen Walt (2013) says 'academic writing is both aesthetically offensive and highly inefficient' and readers are usually scornful of its 'trendy neologisms'. He calls for an 'endless war against academic obscurantism'. Undoubtedly, many practitioners will view the language of the titles I have selected as samples as an 'affront' to the public and civic values the media strive to promote in a democracy.

Roger Alford (2013) believes it has become increasingly difficult for academics to break away from their own habitual writing practices and formulaic prose. They feel that such a style of writing is an important prerequisite to get printed in scholarly journals. 'We [academics] love the research, but not the writing', he argues. The authors of the sample titles above seem to be much more concerned with meeting research requirements than communicating in a lucid language.

It is not only practitioners who feel alienated by such writing. Media, journalism and communication students are rarely happy with the language of the academic texts they are forced to read as part of their curriculum. Asked about memories of his university life as a media and journalism student, Pal Aam of Norway's Volda University said: 'I vividly remember my own frustration over academic books as a student' (Chapter 16). Waller (1993) attributes students' displeasure with their textbooks to their 'big' words, 'awkward' phraseology and long, convoluted sentences. 'Students might behave intelligently if they could understand what their textbooks were trying to say' (Waller 1993).

Why do academics stick so tenaciously to their own writing habits? One of the reasons might be due to the idea prevalent in academic quarters that 'tangled [...] breathless [...] impenetrable [...] long, obscure, jargonized' language points to a 'sophisticated' mind (Limerick 1993). Writing in the *New York Times Book Review*, Limerick dismisses the correlation between 'unintelligible prose' and a 'sophisticated mind' as a myth.

Academic writing blamed for government 'gibberish'

Language we cannot understand has even become a case of concern for governments and public institutions who blame academics and their 'gibberish' that 'is spreading like a virus' outside the confines of their campuses (Lewis 2014). Jemima Lewis (2014) refers to the case of MIT researchers who churned out a nonsense paper using 'Sclgen software', put their names on it and got it published in an academic journal. The aim was to show that many academic conferences and journals would accept any 'old gobbledygook, so as long as it was stuff with fancy language and contained enough long words' (Lewis 2014).

Writing in *The Telegraph*, Amy Willis (2009) shows how government 'gobbledygook', characterized by jargonized and dense academic prose, has been causing Brits 'tangible harm'. Willis, drawing on a 28-page public inquiry into the abuse and use of official language, says excessive jargon was causing Britons to 'miss out on government services and benefits' and was causing the treasury hundreds of millions of dollars in unpaid taxes due to clients' inability to understand how to complete assessment forms. One wonders how many more losses we academics could be incurring if the consequences of others failing to understand what we write were ever estimated.

What to do about it?

Of course, not all academic prose is deficient. There are many lucid and lively writers in academia. However, the advent of the Internet and the success of free and open access peer-reviewed journals has put an end to the notion of academia as an exclusive and reserved arena where academics only write for and communicate with academics. If media and journalism scholars are keen to share their findings with the public, with practitioners and with the organizations they study, they should speak a language that can be understood.

It is time academics developed a new language beyond the limits of professional boundaries, a language that speaks directly to practitioners. It is time academics followed Orwell's (1964) advice: 'What is above all needed is to let meaning choose the word, and not the other way around'. Orwell thinks it is not that difficult to get rid of bad writing habits 'if one is willing to take the necessary trouble' of avoiding prose that is awkward and convoluted. Clear and lucid writing, he says, is a prerequisite of clear thinking. Limerick (1993) advises social science academics to get rid of cramming together many ideas in one long sentence, concealing the points they want to make 'under layers of clauses and phrases' which make it difficult for their readers to follow.

It is time the social science scholarly community revised the assumption that ordinary language is not appropriate for 'grand thinking' because it is 'full of chaos and error' (Elbow 2013). It is not clear how academics have come to hold such a belief, which for language philosophers and thinkers is nothing more than a fallacy. Ordinary language has the ability to explain the most difficult of subjects and with a high degree of precision (James 1980; Labov 2013; Halliday and Matthiessen 2013).

Most of our research deals with simple ideas. Simple language will convey them more effectively, to peers and practitioners alike. Precision in media and journalism research does not require awkward terminology, big words, complex phrases and convoluted sentences. As far as I know, there is no scientific evidence in support of such a correlation. In most cases the opposite will be true.

References

Alford, R. (2013), 'Why is academic writing so bad?', http://opiniojuris.org/2013/02/18/why-is-academic-writing-so-bad/. Accessed 10 September 2014.

Alyssavance (2012), 'Why academic papers are a terrible discussion forum', 20 June, http://lesswrong.com/lw/d5y/why_academic_papers_are_a_terrible_discussion/. Accessed 8 August 2014.

Aristotle (1965), 'On the art of poetry' (trans. T. S. Dorsch), in T. S. Dorsch (ed.), *Classical Literary Criticism*, Harmondsworth, UK: Penguin, pp. 29–76, http://www.rlwclarke.net/courses/lits2306/2012–2013/06AAristotle,Poetics.pdf. Accessed 6 September 2014.

Billig, M. (2013), 'Why academics can't write', *Prospector*, 8 August, http://www.prospectmagazine.co.uk/blogs/prospector-blog/bad-academic-writing. Accessed 29 September 2014.

Bowman, P. (2014), 'Cardiff University seeks new journals for Academic Press', http://cultstud.blogspot.se/2014/07/cardiff-university-press-invites.html. Accessed 27 August 2014.

Confucius (1980), *The Analects of Confucius* (trans. J. R. Ware), Book 13, Verse 3, http://www.princeton.edu/chinese-historiography/tools-1/8-classical-quotations-a/. Accessed 2 October 2014.

Cooper, D. E. (1973), *Philosophy and the Nature of Language*, London: Longman.

Dutton, D. (1999), 'Language crimes: A lesson in how not to write, courtesy of the professoriate', *The Wall Street Journal*, 5 February, http://denisdutton.Com/language_crimes.htm. Accessed 8 October 2014.

The Economist (2011), 'Academic publishing: Of goats and headaches', 26 May, http://www.economist.com/node/18744177. Accessed 29 August 2014.

The Economist (2012a), 'Academic publishing: Open sesame', 12 April, http://www.economist.com/node/21552574. Accessed 2 September 2014.

The Economist (2012b), 'Scientific publishing: Brought to book', 19 July, http://www.economist.com/node/21559317. Accessed 2 September 2104.

The Economist (2013a), 'Academic publishing: Science's Sokal moment', 19 July, http://www.economist.com/news/science-and-technology/21587197-it-seems-dangerously-easy-get-scientific-nonsense-published-science-sokal. Accessed 2 September 2014.

The Economist (2013b), 'Academic publishing: Free-for-all', 4 May, http://www.economist.com/news/science-and-technology/21577035-open-access-scienti-fic-publishing-gaining-ground-free-all. Accessed 2 September 2014.

The Economist (2014), 'A publishing giant goes after the authors of its journals' papers', 11 January, http://www.economist.com/news/science-and-technology/21593408-publishing-giant-goes-after-authors-its-journals-papers-no-peeking. Accessed 2 September 2014.

Elbow, P. (2013), 'Maybe academics aren't so stupid after all', http://blog.oup.com/2013/02/academic-speech-patterns-linguistics/. Accessed 25 August 2014.

Halliday, M. A. K. and Matthiessen, C. M. I. M. (2013), *Halliday's Introduction to Functional Grammar*, 4th ed, London: Routledge.

Hoijer, H. (1959), 'The Sapir-Whorf hypothesis', in H. Holier (ed.), *Language and Culture*, Chicago: University of Chicago Press.

Iacocca, L. and Novak, W. (2011), *Iacocca: An Autobiography*, New York: Bantam Books.

James, C. (1980), *Contrastive Analysis*, London: Longman.

Labov, W. (2013), *The Language of Life and Death: The Transformation of Experience in Oral Narrative*, Cambridge: Cambridge University Press.

Lewis, J. (2014), 'Gibberish is spreading like a virus from academia', *The Telegraph*, 28 February, http://www.telegraph.co.uk/technology/10665312/Gibberish-is-spreading-like-a-virus-from-academia.html. Accessed 12 August 2014.

Limerick, P. N. (1993), 'Dancing with professors: The trouble with academic prose', *The New York Times Book Review*, 31 October, http://www.cs.tufts.edu/~nr/cs257/archive/patricia-limerick/dancing.htm. Accessed 16 August 2014.

Lyons, J. (1968), *Introduction to Theoretical Linguistics*, Cambridge: Cambridge University Press.

Michael, A. P. (1993), 'Academics and their prose', *The New York Times*, 5 December, http://www.nytimes.com/1993/12/05/books/l-academics-and-their-prose-960193.html. Accessed 3 August 2014.

Orwell, G. (1964), 'Politics and the English language', https://www.mtholyoke.edu/acad/intrel/orwell46.htm. Accessed 3 August 2014.

Palmer, F. (1976), *Semantics*, Cambridge: Cambridge University Press.

Park, T. (2013), 'Why is academic writing so bad? A brief response to Stephen Walt', http://dartthrowingchimp.wordpress.com/2013/02/16/why-is-academic-writing-so-bad-a-brief-response-to-stephen-walt/. Accessed 28 July 2014.

Philosophy and Literature (1996–98), 'The bad writing contest: Press releases 1996–98', http://denisdutton.com/bad_writing.htm. Accessed 4 October 2014.

Ray, V. (2014), 'Journalists and scholars: A short manifesto', *Journal of Applied Journalism & Media Studies*, 3: 2, pp. 125–131.

Sapir, E. (1921), *Language*, New York: Harcourt and Brace.

Sullivan, A. (2013), 'How blogging makes you a better writer', http://dish.andrewsullivan.com/2013/09/18/blogging-makes-you-a-better-writer/. Accessed 9 August 2014.

Toor, R. (2010), 'Bad writing and bad thinking', http://chronicle.com/article/Bad-WritingBad-Thinking/65031/. Accessed 17 August 2014.

Waller, L. (1993), 'Academics and their prose', http://www.nytimes.com/1993/12/05/books/l-academics-and-their-prose-951293.html. Accessed 12 June 2014.

Walt, S. M. (2013), 'On writing well', http://www.foreignpolicy.com/posts/2013/02/15/on_writing_well. Accessed 20 July 2014.

Whorf, B. L. (1969), *Language, Thought, and Reality*, Cambridge: MIT Press.

Willis, A. (2009), 'Government "gobbledegook" is "harmful", says select committee', *The Telegraph*, 30 November, http://www.telegraph.co.uk/news/uknews/6684670/Government-gobbledegook-is-harmful-says-select-committee.html. Accessed 2 June 2014.

Wittgenstein, L. (1969), *Philosophical Investigations*, 3rd ed, New York: Macmillan.

Chapter 5

When the Media Criticize the Media

Åke Pettersson

Introduction

I have been working for Sveriges Radio, Sweden's non-commercial, independent public service radio broadcaster, since 1981. More specifically, I have been working for P1, one of four main public radio channels in Sweden. P1 is a talk radio channel, focusing on in-depth news analysis, current affairs, culture and debate. I have mostly been the editor, producer and presenter of a nationwide-media programme initially called *Vår grundade mening* and then *Publicerat*. My programme's major task has been to scrutinize and discuss the media. One could say that my job has been to *produce journalism about journalism*.

I am based in Malmö, in southern Sweden, although Sveriges Radio was headquartered in Stockholm. Traditionally, Sweden's public service corporation, both radio and television, shifted the production of many of their national programmes to provinces outside the capital, but the number of such programmes has been slashed recently due to restructuring and cost cutting. Even my own programme, *Publicerat,* was shelved when I was put on part-time pension almost a year ago. For a radio programme to continue without interruption for more than 30 years is in itself an achievement.

Vår grundade mening/Publicerat is not the only media affairs programme broadcast by Swedish public service radio or television. There have been other media programmes but unfortunately, they would only last for a few years because of either lack of resources or lack of interest. My programme broke the record in terms of longevity as it has been going on without interruption since 1981.

In this chapter, I shall first say a few words about the programme and its history and then focus on the reaction, impact and effect that it has had on the Swedish media scene and the responses and criticism it has received. The chapter dwells on events, both positive and negative, with a bearing on the programme and its broadcasts. Finally, I will touch on how the programme, representing the media's practitioner side, collaborated with academia, namely media and journalism scholars.

Critique of the media by the media

It might not be surprising to see a public service broadcasting company paying such attention to scrutinizing the media and monitoring its behaviour and coverage. It is a bit easy for us, the people in public media, to criticize what is happening in areas inside our realm. Doing so, we cannot be accused of using criticism the way commercial media do. Our job as public broadcasters is not to make a lot of money. We are owned and financed by our audiences, our listeners and viewers, through a government-imposed 'tax' euphemistically called *license fee*. We owe our independence and existence to our license fee payers.

Public radio versus public television

I should point out that in Sweden, unlike in other countries, public radio and television are two different companies. This is probably the reason why public radio in Sweden is so influential. In a public service corporation dominated by television, radio usually trails behind. There were precursors to *Vår grundade mening*, particularly in the 1970s, but it was only in 1981 that the programme was aired continuously 52 weeks a year.

The philosophical foundation of the programme emanated from the fact that, since the media have power, the media should be examined like any other power centre. I was the programme's sole employee, but leaned on a fairly generous budget. This meant that I could order and purchase reports from freelancers, especially if they had interesting experiences from or about other countries. Sometimes I travelled abroad as well, and I could request a freelancer to do the programme while I was away. But I must say that topics, debates and discussions concerning the media situation and journalism in Sweden have always been the most interesting and stimulating for my listeners.

Tips and ideas

Where do we get our tips from? Throughout the years, it has been very common to receive tips, especially via e-mail and phone calls, both from journalists and the general public upset over the media's handling of a particular issue or event. We have always tried to respond, but it has sometimes been difficult to cope with the flow of what we saw as important tips since we always had to prioritize. We received many ideas and tips from freelance journalists, who wanted to sell a story.

I have produced, edited and presented about 1500 episodes. Well, I can say that most of the ideas and themes that these episodes focused on were obtained from my watch of the media scene in Sweden. I read, listened and watched everything related to the media and asked colleagues with an interest in the topic to tell me about things I was not aware of. There is always something to discuss about the media; its context, content and the way they are presented to the audiences and the stir they might cause. Moreover, because media context, content and responses differ, I did not settle on one particular format or template for my programme. It was the content that determined the format and not the other way round. 'Critical examination of media content' has always been the motto and the driving force of *Publicerat*. 'Critical' not only in the sense of focusing on problems and conflicts, as is the case with most of what we the journalists do. On several occasions, *Publicerat* gave credit to good content and good coverage by the media and highlighted scholarly work with a practical angle.

Publicerat's impact

I remember that at one point we praised the Danish public service television's foreign programme *Horizon*, which we thought was something that our own public television, SVT, could learn from. *Horizon* was a current affairs programme dealing with foreign issues. Swedish Television at that time had quite poor foreign coverage and no programme like Denmark's *Horizon*. The same day we ran the episode on the Danish *Horizon*, SVT's then foreign editor Stig Fredriksson called, commending *Publicerat* and agreeing with our analysis. The result was that SVT started a weekly programme called *Korrespondenterna* or *From Our Correspondents*. The programme is still running and probably it might have been introduced at some point even if we had not run a programme praising the Danish *Horizon*. But we would like to believe that our crediting of the Danish *Horizon* played an important role in SVT's decision to run a similar programme of its own.

Publicerat and academia

What about academia, namely, media and journalism scholars? In the early 1980s, we invited media researchers to serve in an editorial reference board or panel. The board met regularly to discuss the contents of the programme about the media. We met two or three times every four months. Scholars on the editorial board had different backgrounds. Many of them took part in our programmes that involved discussions or debates of controversial media topics or were in need of an expert opinion.

This editorial board disappeared after a few years of consistent meetings and discussions. However, by the time it was dissolved we had already established good contacts with the media and journalism research community in Sweden. I used to attend media and journalism conferences organized by Swedish and Nordic universities. I was regularly invited to symposiums, seminars and Ph.D. defences with a bearing on media and journalism. This gave me a wide-range of topics from which I selected what I saw as the most practical, relevant and useful to my programme.

Getting the academic community engaged in the programme encouraged media professors in Sweden to become increasingly verbal, and open in their handling of the media and press coverage. Therefore, we often received comments on various issues from them. Because of these contacts, we often received ideas, tips on dissertations and papers that their authors or our contacts thought could be of interest to us.

Despite what may seem as good practitioner–academic cooperation, I must say that media academics as a whole could be far more active in presenting their research. There are many in academia who believe that media research, with its sophistication and scientific rigour, is beyond the comprehension of practitioners and, therefore, it should remain beyond the public reach. But we all have to remember – academics and practitioners – it is the taxpayers who pay for a lot of the research; therefore, the public have the right to know whether they will eventually get something in return for their money.

Nick Davies and *Publicerat*

As part of its foreign coverage, *Publicerat* introduced the journalist Nick Davies and his *Flat Earth News* (2009) to the Swedish public. Nick Davies' book, about how the PR industry manufactured a lot of what becomes news in the British media, is an excellent example of how researchers and practitioners can work together. Davies received help from researchers from Cardiff University. Together they showed that most reporters, most of the time, are not allowed to dig up stories or check their facts properly.

The two pillars of the media dynamic – academics and practitioners – are called upon to become engaged in joint ventures like the one that brought Davies and Cardiff University academics together.

Pros and cons

Do the media get better when exposed to criticism by the media? Does it matter or help if someone bashes their own rival? Yes and no. No, because the media – and academics know this better – are known to repeat the same error now and then and find it difficult – like other institutions – to easily break away from their own 'iron cages'.

And yes because some media criticism does make a difference. There are many cases where we can demonstrate how the media take criticisms by other media seriously. We are aware that many of the issues that we raised were on the agenda of media organizations' meetings held behind closed editorial doors. We cannot produce evidence to substantiate such a claim but we have found that, following an interview we had held, some action was taken or a change was introduced. We are aware that many of the topics we presented attracted more attention from the media than issues related to ethics and daily routines.

'Exorbitant' fees

I can draw some concrete cases where the media took some action in response to issues raised in *Publicerat*. One issue that we touched upon several times that drew a lot of attention from the media was related to the massive sums of money that veteran and renowned journalists charged for courses they organized to train industry executives and managers. Should journalists be involved in such things at all?

Bo Holmström was one of the Swedish television public broadcaster's best-known and most influential journalists. He did a lot of training of managers and CEOs on investigative journalism and news production. My own programme, *Publicerat*, interviewed him and other renowned journalists involved in the training of media executives. One of the trainers came from the Swedish Public Broadcasting Corporation, my own employer, and the other from *Sydsvenskan*, the largest distribution newspaper in southern Sweden. We have no problem in Sweden in holding members of our own organizations and their leaders to account.

Following the broadcast of these programmes criticizing media training and the 'exorbitant' fees that the trainers charged, the press began discussing and debating the case of other journalists involved in training. For instance, in the case of *Sydsvenskan*, the discussion in the newspaper's corridors led to new rules, which are applicable even today. According to these rules, *Sydsvenskan* has no objection for its own senior and renowned journalists to lecture public and industrial leaders on various media issues, but they should not become involved in formal training and the lectures that journalists give should take place during working hours. *Publicerat* targeted the Swedish public radio and television who, in response to our criticism, developed their own rules under which all sorts of 'over time' must first be approved by the managers. Today, it is mostly the PR industry that organizes such activities.

There are numerous other examples of positive responses to *Publicerat*. Once, a Swedish editor sent all his journalists to attend a course in statistics following a report by *Publicerat* that found that his newspaper's interpretations of immigration statistics were wrong.

Dagens Nyheter and TT

One of *Publicerat*'s major successes was when we ran a programme defying the authenticity and credibility of an article in Sweden's largest morning newspaper, *Dagens Nyheter*, and the Swedish news agency, TT. We claimed that both had resorted to sensational headlines and sensational journalism to suggest that all Gambians in Stockholm were drug dealers. Both *Dagens Nyheter* and TT alleged to have received their information from a training course that the police had organized in Stockholm. But we challenged the information, prompting the police to set up a commission and carry out their own investigation. Initially, the newspaper and the police insisted that their information was correct. But the investigation, which took six months to complete, disproved the allegations. In a press conference in Stockholm, the commission told reporters that the figures quoted by *Dagens Nyheter* and TT were 'absolutely incorrect' and an apology was issued.

Publicerat under fire

Publicerat's nearly 30 years of broadcasting has had its problems. In Sweden, you can be the target of vetting and scrutiny by various authorities. In our case, as part of the Swedish media scene, there was a special individual who kept an extra eye on us. He was the

Information Director at the Swedish Employers Association, an agency now called Confederation of Swedish Enterprise or Svenskt Näringsliv. The director was unhappy with one of our programmes on *the economics of journalism*, which he felt was one-sided.

Our answer was that *Publicerat* was always open to the other side's ideas and we encouraged the director to come up with a rebuttal. We first asked him to come to our studios in Stockholm for an interview to voice his opinion, but he said he would fly directly to Malmö, the southern Swedish city where *Publicerat* was produced. Sure enough, three hours later he was sitting in our studio, and we recorded his rather short response. Then he flew back to Stockholm again.

A few years later, the same director reacted rather angrily in an op-ed piece he wrote for the Swedish newspaper *Svenska Dagbladet*, one of the two major dailies in Stockholm. He was apparently unhappy with the news that *Publicerat* was getting more resources and close to an hour of airtime. 'It is a scandal', he wrote. He said that over the years, audiences have been indoctrinated with what he called 'the business idea' that made them love 'press subsidies and public service and hate commercial radio and television as well as [Former Italian Prime Minister Silvio] Berlusconi'.

In response, I wrote an op-ed in the same newspaper. I mentioned that I was not aware that we had a 'business idea' in the first place. I said that we had our own 'journalistic ideas' that we have developed through *Publicerat*. I provided statistics to show that the Swedish public service media have received most criticism from *Publicerat*, namely Sveriges Radio and Sveriges Television, rather than the commercial radio and television.

As the programme grew and its impact became felt, the individuals involved in *Publicerat* became the target of scrutiny by the Information Director at the Swedish Employers Association. They appointed a freelance journalist to review and assess all the programmes we had sent out over the years. The result was the publication of a report called *I Åke Petterssons radiosoffa* or *On Åke Pettersson's Radio Sofa* (Svend 1999). As the title suggests, we were criticized for leaning more on discussion rather than investigative journalism. The author of the report was right and I had admitted this fact in my op-ed in *Svenska Dagbladet* in which I attributed the lack of investigative journalism to the lack of resources.

This particular critique aside, the report was quite pleasant reading, and we were given a lot of praise because we often raised issues about freedom of expression, transparency and the problems that Sweden might face if it joined the EU. The programme played a role in bringing about more transparency to these issues, sometimes by revealing what was happening behind the scenes. We actually used downright campaign journalism at the time against the 'transparency minister' – a former judge who refused to talk to us. We reiterated the fact that she was avoiding us in almost every programme and in some of them we aired the recordings we had of the secretaries trying to explain why the minister would not talk to us or answer our calls. Our coverage grabbed front-page headlines like, 'Minister of Transparency declines to answer questions about the future of openness'. Eventually, more and more media began raising substantive issues on the same matters that *Publicerat* had been debating. They openly discussed what would happen if Sweden joined the EU and the aftermath of such a decision.

In the end, the minister relented. She said she would not mind being interviewed by *Publicerat* if the producer promised to air the interview in its entirety. We agreed to devote a special programme for her interview. When asked why she objected to talking to us for so long, she said she feared that we would edit her interview in a manner that might lead to distortions and misinterpretations. But she acknowledged in the interview that it was unwise of her not to agree to discuss in an open and transparent manner the issues that *Publicerat* wanted to talk about with her.

Vetting your own employer

Even in a democratic and free country like Sweden it was not always easy, particularly in the early days of the programme, to criticize our own employer, the Swedish Public Radio. We did not face major problems when trying to hold our own employer to account, but frankly we felt that the bosses were not always so happy with our criticism. But in the course of time, things changed with the directors, executives and editors of Swedish Public Broadcasting Corporation viewing acceptance of criticism as a source of credibility, and we received several awards partly because of this: journalist of the year, radio programme of the year and others.

However, the trend shifted in the past few years or so, with senior editors and directors becoming more sensitive to or even afraid of criticism. About ten years ago, we got a new inexperienced CEO – a politician by the name Peter Örn. The new CEO and the director of programmes he appointed wanted to outsource as much radio production as possible to private production companies as part of new measures to save money. Consequently, a large proportion of the programmes produced by Swedish Radio, and specifically in provinces outside Stockholm, were closed down. It was more difficult to cancel programmes made in Stockholm, where the governors met with the employees daily. The appellation 'Sold Out' was coined in Swedish media in reference to programmes that were closed down.

Threats and protests

Publicerat was under threat despite its success in terms of audience rating. P1, to which the programme belonged, is normally an attraction for old people in Sweden between the ages of 50 and 80 years. In the case of *Publicerat,* it was the opposite. We attracted younger listeners between the ages of 30 and 50 years and in large numbers. But the new management thought that *Publicerat* was part of P1 and as such it had to steer a new path focusing on consumer issues, advertising and computer games, and so on.

We were scared because the new measures meant that everything we had done in the realm of media criticism will come to an end. When rumours that *Publicerat* was under threat of closure spread, there was a spontaneous storm of protest from the public.

A petition was started by a listener in the north of Sweden. In a few weeks, he and a few followers obtained thousands of signatures in support of the programme's continuation. For us, the petition was a good signal because it told us that we at least had been appreciated by thousands of listeners. The organizers of the petition requested an appointment with the radio management in Stockholm to lodge a complaint. In fact, representatives of the protest group from different parts of Sweden flocked to Stockholm and headed for the Swedish Radio headquarters in protest. The popular protest bore fruit and, in the spring of 2007, a decision was taken for *Publicerat* to be relaunched together with a new programme called *Medierna* in Stockholm, produced by a private company. Therefore, the original coverage could proceed and we could forget about testing computer games, consumer-oriented issues and advertising.

To our surprise, we were given access to more resources than before and did not yield an iota in terms of the programme's thrust and approach, although I had to produce a slightly different *Publicerat*, whose job was to examine critically, but more in the form of discussions and conversations, various media issues. The outcome was the opposite of what the managers had in mind for the programme. The whole radio management that initiated the 2007 restructuring, causing such chaos in the Swedish Public Broadcasting Corporation, was sacked a few months later and since then all has been quiet on the Swedish Radio front.

Why target *Publicerat*

There were many reasons for the management's decision to attack the programme in 2007. One main reason probably had been our harsh take on the Swedish Radio, our own employer, and its handling of Digital Audio Broadcasting or DAB. Our criticism was very popular, and later we understood that the bosses would have liked us to highlight DAB's success and not its failures. The DAB project was closed down ten years after its inception despite Swedish Radio's pleas for it to continue. *Publicerat*'s criticism of its own employer proved to be correct because the government felt that it was no use investing more money in it.

The sacked CEO blamed *Publicerat* for 'destroying' the digitization of the radio in Sweden. Later, he wrote a book about his failed leadership, which he titled *Ledare*, or *Leaders* (2010). In it, he wrote that he still could not understand why there was such a storm over the attempt to cancel a 25-year-old programme. 'There were fierce protests when we wanted to shut down the 25-year old media program', he noted. 'This is an example of how one single program managed to undermine the whole management'.

With regard to DAB, he wrote:

> Some employees felt that DAB had taken resources from the editorial work. Some of them opposed DAB simply because they did not like it. DAB was also used as a topic in a large number of radio reports. Some employees even started a fight against the digital technology and the management in their own radio shows.

The CEO was clearly furious in his book of the role that *Publicerat* played not only in undermining his management but also in illustrating how badly DAB investment had been managed.

To be honest, outsourcing of programmes has spared Swedish radio the criticism, which any institution is in need of in a democracy. What you hear today are mainly plaudits of public radio and television. The outsourced programmes centre on how journalism works and overlook structural and critical issues like ownership, media concentration or crises of a controversial nature.

Status quo

In 2013, I started working half-time. At 66, I am now semi-retired. *Publicerat* has come to a halt after more than 30 years of almost non-interrupted broadcasting. There were protests again and I think it is a shame because someone else could have taken the programme over. Now I work part-time as a media commentator/media reporter for the *Culture News* in P1. Today, media issues receive more attention as part of the country's cultural coverage. *Kulturnytt, or Cultural News,* is a short bulletin aired several times a day.

Response from commercial media

So far I have mainly focused on the response to *Publicerat*, namely from the Swedish public service. Let us now move to the reaction that the programme received due to its monitoring, scrutinizing and vetting of both private and public media. Generally speaking, journalists are a very sensitive species. There is probably no person who gets as easily offended as the media people. We are pretty touchy and difficult to interview, although many mainstream journalists are usually available for interviews. However, it would be interesting to see how the power of the people in this particular realm works. When examined thoroughly, one would see that power plays almost the same role in all institutions, and journalists and their organizations are no different. This does not diminish my love for journalism. This is why I will still get upset over bad journalism. My experience with *Publicerat* has demonstrated how important and helpful journalism can be.

Tabloids

Tabloids are a special case. They are often the target of criticism but they can hit back using some of the harshest language one can imagine. Several years ago, we fell out with a major tabloid, *Aftonbladets,* for what we saw as its skewed coverage of the NATO's 1992 bombing of Serbia. This infuriated the then political editor Olle Svenning because we had with us in the programme Phillip Knightley, the famous author of *The First Casualty* (2004), who was critical of the way the media portrayed the bombing of Serbia. The editor thought that it was terrible to listen to *Publicerat*, which had pointed out, in interviews with media researchers, that *Aftonbladet* was most partial in its coverage of the bombing of Belgrade by NATO, along with public radio and television. 'Poor media researchers ... I will never again listen to this awful, disgusting program (*Publicerat*)', he wrote.

Expressen, at the time the largest evening tabloid in Sweden, in an article signed by its then-editor Bo Strömstedt, called me *stiftsjungfru* in Swedish; perhaps the closest English translation would be 'a vicar's maid'. I interviewed Strömstedt for *Publicerat* and asked why he called me *stiftsjungfru*. He said he had picked the pejorative term from his predecessor who thought anyone criticizing the newspaper saw themselves as being superior to others. But as he grew older and quit his position as editor, he started criticizing the tabloids. 'When the devil grows old he turns religious', we say in Swedish. But for the record, I must say that Swedish tabloids and their editors today are more open than counterparts in quality newspapers and even more self-critical. Is this not an interesting development?

More threats

Recently, Hanne Kjöller, a political editor of Sweden's largest morning paper, *Dagens Nyheter*, published a controversial book that was critical of the media. The book concentrated on errors in journalism. I say 'controversial' because the book itself was not immune from many of the errors it pointed out.

In a programme several years earlier, I said that she even gets the spelling of a common Swedish surname wrong. Instead of 'Råstam' she for example wrote 'Råstedt'. My comment on the radio was that she and political editors like her might not consider it so important to get things right. She called me immediately after the programme was broadcast, screaming and shouting. She even reported *Publicerat* to Granskningsnämnden, the state's ethics watchdog, but we were acquitted.

Watchdog

A public service broadcaster like Swedish Television, for instance, with guaranteed income from taxpayer's money – license fee – should really start up some kind of programme that functions like a watchdog, examining their own activities and those of other media. I think that many in Sweden would not think it wise for the media to be without a 'watchdog', in other words another *Publicerat*. There are many important issues to bring up and dicuss, including all the new laws and endeavours that are geared towards restricting the freedom of press. The important issues are not explored sufficiently nowadays. Of no lesser significance are issues related to the blurred boundaries between advertising and journalism, and so on and so forth.

Role of academics

When the media refrain from criticizing the media, then we have no one else to turn to but the media research community – the academia. Therefore, it has become more necessary today than any time before for the media researchers to interact and become actively engaged with media practitioners. It is time that academics made their research available and accessible to the industry.

One positive sign is that current affairs programmes in the radio have shown greater interest in the media and media issues over the past few years. They are quick to pick up and discuss hard and controversial news. The media have also become a centre of discussion by ordinary citizens, whether in blogs or in major social media sites.

Conclusion

In summary, I believe that it is important for the media to examine the media. It increases our credibility. To be a good critic, one has to be aware and knowledgeable of how articles and features are produced. We the media people are the ones who really know how the processes and the technology work and, therefore, are better positioned to judge or review the media as well. Moreover, transparency is an important aspect of the media. It is not a good sign for the media people to be left without someone vetting their output and practices. In the current situation, with structural problems and crises looming, it is understandable that many newspapers and other outlets may not see constructive criticism among their priorities.

But – all in all, the more eyes on the media the better!

References

Dahl, S. (1999), *I Åke Petterssons radiosoffa*, Stockholm: Näringslivets mediainstitut.
Davies, N. (2009), *Flat Earth News: An Award-winning Reporter Exposes Falsehood, Distortion and Propaganda in the Global Media*, London: Vintage.
Knightley, P. (2004), *The First Casualty: The War Correspondent as Hero and Myth-Maker from the Crimea to Iraq*, Baltimore: Johns Hopkins University Press.
Örn, P. (2010), *Ledare*, Stockholm: Libris förlag.

Chapter 6

Bridging the Chasm: Can Theory Help Media and Journalism Practitioners

Leon Barkho

Introduction

The academic-practitioner chasm today is at the centre of discussions in the academy. Media and journalism scholars have become aware of the divide. They realize that practitioners generally shun academic research, its implications and findings and, even, resent academic writing. The chasm is more noticeable today than any time before, thanks to practitioners whose gripes about those investigating them, their profession and institutions have come to the open (Chapters 1, 2, 3, 4 and 16).

This chapter elaborates on the discussion of the divide between the world in which practitioners exercise their daily activities and the world of scholarship, in which academics conduct their research. The chapter's title is dialectical – bridging the chasm – because the issue of the scholar-practitioner divide has been in my mind since I joined the academy after a long career as a journalist. As a practitioner (first with Reuters News Agency and then with the Associated Press), it never crossed my mind that I should read or even consult scholarly publications investigating my profession, or seek a scholar's assistance in my work. Journalism and media studies was not something to talk about and the journals where scholars publish their articles never surfaced in the discussions and editorial meetings we had.

It is worthwhile to point out at the outset that any study of the scholar-practitioner divide would err if it overlooked the contributions some academics have made to media and journalism as practice. There are academics who have responded positively to practitioner aspirations, to have them and their immediate needs in mind when investigating their work and institutions (Chapters 2 and 14). However, the majority still believe that the university is a place of scientific investigation and education based on theories and methodologies that explain the media and journalism as social, cultural and economic phenomena and not a place to meet market needs and expectations. They retort that practitioners of other kinds of university education, like musicology, do not pose the same questions because studying musicology is not supposed to help practitioners to become accomplished players of their violins, pianos, saxophones, flutes or guitars (see Schlesinger 2009; Lederer 2007).

However, practice and relevance are not an issue of concern in sciences like medicine, engineering, law and nursing, among others. One wonders why journalism and mass-communication scholarly literature lacks such relevance. Nicolai and Seidl (2010) attribute social scientists' aversion of practice to the nature of social science knowledge and the way methods and theoretical frameworks they employ produce scientific knowledge.

In his introduction to the special issue of the *Journal of Applied Behavioral Science* on bridging the scholar-practitioner divide, Heracleous (2011: 1) mentions 'persistent barriers' hampering efforts to address challenges facing scholar-practitioner collaboration. Some of the barriers, Heracleous says, are inherent in Western philosophy, which guides social science research. This philosophy, he maintains, privileges thought (scholarship) over action (practice). Others, Heracleous adds, relate the divide to organizational cultures in which universities see themselves as fortresses of thought and knowledge whose job is to train their faculty members and students on knowledge production rather than knowledge practice.

There are scholars who say the chasm separating scholarship and practice is merely a cultural issue. In their seminal study, Barley, Meyer and Gash (1988: 24) demonstrate that academics and practitioners belong to two subcultures. The two cultures have many elements in common, but they diverge in many respects. The authors examine the two subcultures carefully, drawing on 192 organizational culture articles, and subject them to a robust discursive analysis to assess the extent of influence the sides exert on each other's interpretations. They find that scholars have come to realize the importance of linking their theory to practice, but practitioners are unimpressed. The data the authors analyse suggests that over time, academics appear to have moved to the practitioners' point of view, while the latter have been little influenced by the former'.

The literature tackling the scholar-practitioner divide places much emphasis on the difference between the two groups. Highlighting the differences between the sides can have both positive and negative consequences. Knowing about what drives the groups apart might provide an incentive to try to close the gap. However, it could be counterproductive in the sense of each side blaming the other for what they see as an 'unbridgeable' chasm, ignoring the fact that 'both can benefit and even thrive on cross fertilization' (Catterall 1998: 69).

Many academics see practice-based research as futile because they believe the gap between scholars and academics is too deep to bridge. Rynes, Giluk and Brown (2007: 987) say '[t]he gap between science and practice is so persistent and pervasive that some have despaired of its being narrowed'. Media and journalism studies is a late-comer to practice research. The past three decades or so have seen a surge in interest in practice-oriented research in many academic disciplines. In fact, in some fields like medicine, education, psychology, marketing and rehabilitation, scholars have gone a long way in responding to the needs and requirements of those they research. Known as 'evidence-based' research, practice-oriented studies have assumed their position in the academy in these disciplines long before media and journalism scholars began to think seriously about the issue (see Straus et al. 2005; Ford 2005; Law 2002; Southworth and Conner 1999).

Academics are not required to abandon theory and focus only on practice (Chapter 1 and 14). However, practitioners' resentment of academic writing is evident in the conflicts, issues, and concepts and ideas scholars tackle in their research. Academic literature, for instance, is replete with criticism of journalism and the media as a profession and practice. Nonetheless, the criticism, based on intricate methodologies and rigorous scientific investigations, has done little to improve the profession and its management. The situation is different in other established fields like medicine, law and engineering where academic research contributes to improvement and 'progression toward professionalism' (Duncan 1974: 727).

There are numerous reasons for the persistence of the scholar-practitioner divide in the sphere of media and journalism both as practice and research. I have summarized these reasons under the following headings: one-way traffic, language problems, two different worlds, lack of collaboration and not giving 'hackademics' their due.

One-way traffic

To say that traffic is only one direction is an overstatement because, essentially, there is no intellectual traffic between the groups. At present, there is very little traffic of ideas from the academy to media and journalism practitioners, or the other way round. Academics usually ignore practitioners' contribution to their research and practitioners overlook academic research. A two-way intellectual traffic would be beneficial to both sides. Academics, for instance, can strengthen their research if they have access to practitioners' knowledge of their own work and organizations. Practitioners could benefit from academic research by establishing good contacts with universities and inviting scholars to talk to their organizations about research they see relevant to their situations. In fact, both groups could benefit a great deal if they reexamine the taken-for-granted assumptions and prejudices they harbour about each other.

The issue of scholar-practitioner divide has attracted a great deal of attention in many spheres of social science and even humanities. It might be worthwhile to elaborate on the discussions going on in other fields, whose studies, like media and journalism, suffer from the wide divide between theory and practice. Here, I will concentrate on translation studies where, as in media and journalism studies, there is a whooping gap between theory and practice. In 2004, Chesterman and Wagner wrote an important book on the theme with the title: *Can Theory Help Translators: A Dialogue Between the Ivory Tower and the Wordface*, part of which I use as the rubric of this chapter. The book is a dialogue between Andrew Chesterman, a translation studies scholar, and Emma Wagner, a translation practitioner and manager.

The discussion between Chesterman and Wagner is interesting and has a lot of bearing on the current debate between journalism scholars and practitioners on the pages of this book. What is intriguing is the way Wagner depicts the chasm from a practitioner's viewpoint, saying that translation theory is one of few professions still suffering from 'a yawning gap' between theory and practice (Chesterman and Wagner 2004: 1). Wagner provides examples of how translation theory has failed translation practitioners and that she and her colleagues at the European Commission in Luxemburg rarely bother about what translation scholars write because it is of little relevance to their practice.

Wagner's criticism of translation theory and its lack of relevance echoes the complaints practitioners raise in the chapters they have submitted to this book. Like Wagner, Journalism practitioners (Chapters 1, 2, 3, 4, 15 and 16) admire academic research and how it interprets their work and the way their institutions work, exercise power, manufacture news, manipulate truth and frame their themes. However, they question whether the information academic research provides will ever help them become better journalists.

There is discord between media and journalism as an academic discipline and as practice. Their coexistence is hard to achieve because academics try to interpret the world in which the subjects of their research live and provide a deep understanding of their social reality, and the practice of journalism requires mastery of vocational skills. Media and journalism education leans on 'how to do' research and knowledge rather than how to practice. Academic textbooks are more like manuals of what media and journalism scholars consider good practice, and pay little attention to what practitioners see as good practice. The focus of textbooks is on media and communication theories, comparisons between them and the procedures or methods required to analyse media texts in light of the theories learnt (Zelizer 2009).

Practitioners' preoccupation is not with theory building and the toolkits of analysis techniques. Their main concern lies in production of content and improvement of conditions and practical skills. They struggle to preserve their jobs while competing in a highly digitized world. Media and journalism academics are mostly preoccupied with the conceptual and methodological underpinnings of their research. Their main target is to have their academic articles printed in peer-reviewed journals, and preferably the ones with impact factors, which practitioners hardly know about and rarely consult (Chapter 2).

Thus, it is not surprising to see the gap persisting and even widening despite the wealth of remedies, ideas and suggestions on how to close it. Within the academic circles, many scholars openly express their uneasiness with the gap and, at the same time, emphasize that they are prepared to listen to practitioners, investigate their gripes and respond to them. There is no doubt that many in the academy have the willingness and desire to make research and teaching more relevant to the industry. Nonetheless, the gap is still there. One reason could be the system itself, which is built to meet the needs of academics for publishing and promotion. The system, as it stands, does not encourage academics to enter into relationships or do research to serve the practitioner community (see Rynes, Bartunek and Daft 2001; Vermeulen 2005; Markides 2010).

Language problems

There is the issue of language. Academics and practitioners do not speak the same language. Their discourses are different and complaints by practitioners about media and journalism studies highlight the complex, jargon-laden and convoluted nature of the language academics use in their research (Chapters 1 and 3). So long as practitioners find it hard to grasp the jargon, the technical terms and the language scholars employ, any talk of collaboration and the change of research perspective and methodology might remain a hollow construct.

To overcome the language barrier, which for practitioners is almost insurmountable, Barley et al. urge the sides to 'adopt the *symbols* or rhetoric of the other to make their objectives appear palatable' (1988: 26, original emphasis). Though the authors speak of theory-practice correlation in management, organizations and business studies, their recommendation has wider resonance in the sphere of journalism and media studies and its place in and relevance to the world it investigates. The authors urge academics to employ language that is prevalent among practitioners and easily understood by them. Academics, they add, should adopt practitioner language at all levels of their research, starting with the negotiation of access, gathering data and conducting interviews, to the writing up of final manuscripts before sending them for possible publishing by academic journals.

If the language barrier is addressed, Barley et al. believe it could usher in a milestone in collaboration because

> symbolic and conceptual influences alter the use of language, and because language occurs in writing as well as in speech, one may minimize the problems of studying direct influence by examining texts for evidence of symbolic and conceptual change.

> (1988: 27)

When members of two subcultures (academics and practitioners) do not speak the same language, room for mutual suspicion and incomprehension grows, diminishing the prospects for applying the result and outcome of painstaking academic research and analysis and thereby denying the targets of the research the opportunity to alleviate their problems and improve their conditions (Snow 2012).

Is it possible for academics to alter their language and make it palatable to practitioners? This depends on the targets of academic research and its audience. So far, academics mostly target other academics. Journalism practitioners do not write for peers but audiences outside their profession, and use the type of language their readers and listeners can easily grasp. Through their linguistics, journalists exercise tremendous influence on the world around them, including academic scholars (Hadley 1997; Lotman 1990).

If academics want to influence the practitioner community, they will need to alter their language and make it palatable to those they research. In other words, media and journalism academic community should adopt a language that is within the norm and framework of the subculture of the community it represents. Culture is inherently linked to language and language is an inseparable part of culture (Palmer 1996). The linguistic divide between academic and practitioner communities is one of the major hurdles preventing the flow of knowledge from those researching the same culture and those practicing it. Journalists complain about the complexity of an academic language they find hard to understand and unravel. Academics have rarely complained about their inability to understand journalistic language. Their major gibes relate to issues of objectivity and impartiality.

In the hope of narrowing the scholar-practitioner linguistic divide, Barley et al. (1988: 27) call for a two-tier approach to academic research. Each tier, they say, should develop its own 'contextual markers' – concepts, ideas and themes – as well as 'lexical and collocational indicators' – words, phrases and co-occurrence of lexical items. The discourses and narratives commonly used by academics employ linguistic markers and indicators that are different from those prevalent among practitioners. In the first tier, the 'contextual markers' and 'lexical indicators' of the scientific knowledge that is produced for the benefit of practitioners should include content with linguistic elements prevalent among the practitioner community to help in the flow of knowledge and information and mutual influence and reward. In the second tier, scholars will stick to the 'contextual markers' that are common among the academic community. Academic discussion falling within the category of this tier will have academics as targets of research.

However, Barley et al.'s two-tier recommendation, though plausible and in-line with practitioner demands, does not say who will reward academics opting for the first tier as it is not clear whether universities will accept articles of this nature for academic promotion and tenure decisions. Moreover, most top-tier social science journals would frown at submissions written in a language that is common among practitioners and meant to serve their immediate needs. Likewise, there are fears that the two-tier proposal may generate 'double standards in information' and knowledge (Liberati and Magrini 2003).

Two different worlds

Practitioners do not read academic papers and do not bother about the topics they cover. Even if they come across an academic article discussing a topic of interest, the style of writing does not motivate them to read (see Chapters 1–3). Scholars do what they can to gain access to practitioners and their organizations for interviews, observation and data collection. During this important phase of academic research, academics show an interest in the organizations they study and may try to find out what their problems, needs and interests are. However, interaction and cooperation usually end following this stage. As researchers start writing up their papers or dissertations, they forget about the objects of their research.

Practitioners do not hear from academics who interviewed them and observed their daily activities about the problems and obstacles they face and how to address them. Practitioners have no role to play in the conceptualization phase of the research and have no inkling of what the researcher who interviewed them, for instance, will exactly do with the information they provide. Moreover, academics usually fail to answer repeated questions from practitioners on whether they or their organizations will eventually reap any practical benefits from the research.

Media and journalism practitioners write and issue content that is timely and mostly addresses fresh and lively topics. With the digital revolution, it does not take long to issue a news story with related pictures and video and update it several times in the course of 24 hours. Practitioners are quick and compete with rivals in terms of speed, scoops and range of coverage. They are in constant dialogue with their sources and communicate regularly with their audience for information and comment to add a human touch to their writing.

Academics do not work like that. It takes months to write a paper and many years to get it published, if the authors are lucky to have their research accepted for publication by a premier journal. Postgraduate students spend years writing their dissertations, most of which are not published and gather dust on library shelves. Many Ph.D. students produce research with a lot of bearing on relevance and practicality, but the chances for practitioners to have access to their findings and implications are very slim. Practitioners are too busy to read lengthy, convoluted and dense prose that generally characterizes academic writing. Academics do not have the desire and are not willing to change approaches and methodologies of scientific research writing to serve urgent needs of non-academic audiences. Practitioners are interested in studies written specifically to serve some of their immediate needs, addressing the problems they face and, not merely in academic studies, emphasizing how biased, unbalanced, subjective, partial, framed or tendentious their content is.

Media and journalism research is massive and it certainly includes issues of direct interest to practitioners. However, it is hard for practitioners to have easy access to it as we still do not have a system or inventory designed specifically to guide to research they may find relevant. Academics have the time to scour hundreds or even thousands of academic journal pages in search of relevant topics or citations. Practitioners say it is not their job to find research relevant to their practice, simply because there is no way for them to do so. Scholars and their academic journals have not developed means to tell practitioners which material might be of practical use for them.

Practitioners normally have no problem publishing articles from academics or publicizing results of scientific research in their own language. Editors usually subedit articles by academics sent to their outlets for publishing to make them as readable as possible. Academic journal editors rarely rehash or rework the style of an academic paper as newspaper or newswire editors do, for instance, with almost any raw material submitted to them.

Academics operate in ways that do not respond to the needs and aspirations of practitioners as clients. Unlike applied researchers in R&D projects, whose aim is to improve products for clients via new knowledge, academics do not transform, or probably are not willing as outlined above, to transform their knowledge into new insights for the media and journalism industry. Some may even think that rendering theoretical knowledge relevant, practical and useful to practitioners might be a sign of weakness and inability to pursue rigorous research (Porter 1996).

Lack of collaboration

The scholar-practitioner gap will not close if the two groups do not start 'making connections' to place concepts and methodologies within wider contexts, writes Boyer (1990: 18), adding that scholars who deal with large amounts of data and abstract concepts are required to explain, illuminate and teach 'non-specialists' how to apply them and make them relevant to their situations. Boyer's (1990) call for 'making connections [...] illuminating data in a revealing way, often educating non-specialists' is valid and relevant to the current state of media and journalism research activities, ranging from the writing of textbooks to journal articles.

Collaboration means engaged scholarship, a process in which the two groups cooperate at all levels, particularly when analysing the data, summing up the findings and considering the implications the findings may have on the industry. But not all scholars are happy with engaged scholarship in which practitioners are real partners in research. There are academics who have questioned the soundness and plausibility of scholarly research with practitioners as partners and true collaborative researchers. They say that practitioners' main interest lies in discussions of problems that they face and how to address them. Academics, they add, pursue rigorous and scientific investigations that add to current knowledge, which they later produce in a format, style and language that meet academic journal guidelines. In some social science disciplines, like management and organizational sciences, scholars have provided detailed descriptions on how to carry out collaborative or engaged research (e.g. Van de Ven 2007; Kowalski et al. 2003; Shani et al.; Bartunek and Louis 1996; Bartunek 2007), the thing in which media and journalism studies is still lacking.

Not giving 'hackademics' their due

Hackademics or, as Errigo and Franklin (2004: 43) dub them, 'hardy hybrids' are reporters who have moved from newsroom to classroom and whose major task in academia is developing news skills and, to a lesser extent, write papers for academic journals. They are journalists who turned into scholars at some point of their careers. They are probably aware of how disparate and divergent the sides are.

A former practitioner myself, I believe journalists-turned-scholars pass through a dramatic conceptual shift. From being practitioners who work within the limits of the news paradigm (event, news values, interview, inverted pyramid and objectivity), to scholars whose target is to produce knowledge by applying rigorous methodologies (Høyer 2005). As practitioners, they wrote stories of a few hundred words in simple and lucid language about daily events. In the academy, they have to investigate a case rigorously, read related literature, collect data, analyse it, construct hypotheses, raise questions, operationalize theories and apply methodologies as part of an ongoing process of discovery. As practitioners, they wrote and published their stories (articles) on a daily basis. As academics, it may take them a year or two to write a scholarly article, and maybe longer to get it published in a scholarly journal.

Practitioners seem to have penetrated 'Fortress Academia' (Chapter 2) and, in some universities, particularly in the United Kingdom, Ireland, the United States, New Zealand and Australia, they may comprise a good portion of the faculty. As part of journalism or mass communication faculty, students, particularly undergraduates, have found their teaching practical, useful and relevant to the demands of an industry they hope to join in the future (Greenberg 2007). But the move has been one-sided with only practitioners 'barging' the walls of 'Fortress Academia'. One wonders whether 'Fortress Journalism' would allow academics to occupy a desk in the closely-guarded confines of the newsroom. If practitioners are not happy with the way academics conduct their research, academics, in their turn, criticize journalists for making access to their organizations, even for purely research purposes, rather difficult. Interviewing journalists and observing their organizations 'is still not an easy task', and their responses to surveys are decreasing while 'newsroom observation studies are perhaps the most difficult of any journalism studies' (Loffelholz and Weaver 2008: 6).

The presence of practitioners as part of university faculty in many journalism departments is a welcome move, but it remains to be seen whether the academic research these 'hackademics' produce will usher in new methodologies that will make their writings palatable to reporters. Journalists-turned-academics' tasks at universities are not confined to teaching. As academics, they must write scholarly papers in peer-reviewed journals to boost their academic standing and climb the academic ladder. Of the 65 'hackademics' interviewed by 'Harcup' (2011) in the United Kingdom, only 18 had printed a paper in a peer-reviewed journal. We still do not have studies investigating the nature of research done by hackademics and its impact on journalists and their organizations, despite predictions by Machin and Niblock (2006) that such research would provide good knowledge on how journalists and their newsrooms work, their practical needs, and how academics and practitioners can work together to bridge the current gap. While the authors acknowledge that both academics and practitioners have grown to suspect and dislike each other, the presence of hackademics, and in increasing numbers among faculty ranks, they say, holds the potential of reducing tensions and boosting mutual understanding. Other scholars agree. Greenberg (2007) suggests that practitioner-turned scholars have the opportunity of turning journalism research around: instead of coming up with theories interpreting journalists and their organizations, they can add a new dimension – operationalizing theory to meet workplace requirements. Duffield (2009) says academics who had worked as reporters may employ their practical experience to advance theory and methods of journalism research.

Conclusion

Perhaps journalism and media studies is one of the few academic disciplines where the transfer of knowledge between scholars and practitioners is extremely hard to come by. It is the field exhibiting great potential for misunderstanding and miscommunication when it comes to scholar-practitioner interaction. Practitioners want research not only to be relevant to their practice but also written and carried out in a manner and language they can access, follow and understand. The two parties' criteria for acceptable research differ and have little in common.

For academics, as Gouldner argues, 'the process of theory development is quite different from the process of theory utilization' (1956: 169–81). Scientific and practical orientation is the driving force for media and journalism academics, who see theory and methodology as ends in themselves. Practitioners' views of theory and methodology rest on how practical, useful and relevant they can be to their work, activities and requirements. Each party stems from its own concerns and evaluates the other in the light of their interests. Shedding light on concerns like these may be crucial in determining the path for interaction between the parties.

Academics need to highlight the problems of those they investigate, the manner in which they carry out their investigations, the role of practitioners in the investigation and the implications their research may have for the industry. In other words, practical perspectives and realities should determine the aspects of scientific research in consultation and follow in-depth conversation with practitioners and their views of what is genuinely valuable, useful and practical.

The interface between research and practice does not mean that academics compromise methods of rigorous inquiry. In addition, it does not mean that practitioners should accept academic research as it is even if they find it difficult to follow and grasp its language, and see it as impractical and irrelevant to their profession. The interface, as Shlesinger (2009: 1) notes, can only be meaningful when the academy gives practitioners the chance to include their 'intuitions … into the research setting'.

The nature of the jobs the two sides do and the type of cultures and institutions they belong to shows that change is not easy in systems that are set up to serve their members well. Such systems only change in response to pressure. Pressure on the academy to change may come from research councils and philanthropists offering grants for media and journalism studies. Journalism and media studies is a growing business at universities. There has been a noticeable surge in the number of university faculties and departments offering media and journalism studies courses at both undergraduate and graduate levels along with the number of students enrolling in these programmes. In the face of high demand, academics find no reason to change the system because, economically, it is viable and, academically, it provides a relatively easy path to climb the academic ladder, which in turn increases the spiral up the financial ladder. The system will only change when issues related to promotion and research grants are addressed and there is a sudden slump in demand for media and journalism studies (Oviatt and Miller 1989).

There are numerous areas where scholars and practitioners share common goals and interests. It is important to examine both the differences and commonalities between the two groups if we are to obtain some insight into the type of praxis-based research academics should carry out. Academics need to agree among themselves about the requirements of practice research and the conditions necessary to make it relevant and useful to the society. Media and journalism academy has yet to develop a practice-based brand of media and journalism research specifically geared towards the practical needs of the industry.

References

Barley, S. R., Meyer, G. W. and Gash, D. C. (1988), 'Cultures of culture: Academics, practitioners and the pragmatics of normative control', *Administrative Science Quarterly*, 33, pp. 24–60.

Bartunek, J. M. (2007), 'Academic–practitioner collaboration need not require joint or relevant research: Toward a relational scholarship of integration', *Academy of Management Journal*, 50: 1323–1333.

Bartunek, J. M. and Louis, M. R. (1996), *Insider/Outsider Team Research*, Thousand Oaks, CA: SAGE.

Boyer, E. L. (1990), *Scholarship Reconsidered: Priorities at the Professorate*. Princeton, NJ: Carnegie Foundation for the Advancement of Teaching.

Catterall, M. (1998), 'Academics, practitioners and qualitative market research', *Qualitative Market Research: An International Journal*, 1: 2, pp. 69–76.

Chesterman, A. and Wagner, E. (2004), *Can Theory Help Translators?: A Dialogue Between the Ivory Tower and the Wordface*, Manchester, UK: St Jerome.

Duffield, L. (2009), 'A news story as big as a doctoral thesis? Deploying journalistic methodology in academic research', http://www.cpe.qut.edu.au/conferences/2009/anzca/proceedings/Duffield_ANZCA09.pdf. Accessed 19 April 2010.

Duncan, W. J. (1974), 'Transferring management theory to practice', *Academy of Management Journal*, 17: 4, pp. 724–38.

Ford, K. (2005), *Brands Laid Bare: Using Market Research for Evidence-based Brand Management*, Chichester, UK: Wiley.

Gouldner, A. W. (1956), 'Explorations in applied social science', *Social Problems*, 3: 3, pp. 169–81.

Greenberg, S. (2007), 'Theory and practice in journalism education', *Journal of Media Practice*, 8: 3, pp. 289–303.

Hadley, G. (1997), 'Lexis and culture: Bound and determined?', *Journal of Psycholinguistic Research*, 26: 4, pp. 483–496.

Heracleous, L. (2011), 'Introduction to the special issue on bridging the scholar-practitioner divide', *Journal of Applied Behavioral Science*, 47: 1, p. 5.

Høyer, S. and Pöttker, H. (2005), *Diffusion of the news paradigm 1850–2000*, Gothenburg, Sweden: Nordicom. pp. 123–36.

Kowalski, R., Harmon, J., Yorks, L. and Kowalski, D. (2003), 'Reducing workplace stress and aggression: An action research project at the U.S. Department of Veterans Affairs', *Human Resource Planning*, 26, pp. 39–53.

Law, M. (ed.) (2002), *Evidence-based Rehabilitation: A Guide to Practice*, Thorofare, NJ: Slack.

Lederer, M. (2007), 'Can theory help translator and interpreter trainers and trainees?', *The Interpreter and Translator Trainer*, 1: 1, pp. 15–35.

Liberati, A. and Magrini, N. (2003), 'Information from drug companies and opinion leaders: Double standards in information for medical journals and practitioners should go', *British Medical Journal*, 326: 7400, p. 1156.

Loffelholz, M. and Weaver, D. (eds) (2008), *Global Journalism Research: Theories, Methods, Findings, Future*, Oxford: Blackwell.

Lotman, Y. (1990), *Universe of the Mind: A Semiotic Theory of Culture* (trans. A. Shukman), Bloomington: Indiana University Press.

Machin, D. and Niblock, S. (2006), *News Production: Theory and Practice*, London: Routledge.

Markides, C. (2010), 'Crossing the chasm: How to convert relevant research into managerially useful research', *The Journal of Applied Behavioral Science*, 47: 1, pp. 121–134.

Nicolai, A. T. and Seidl, D. (2010), 'That's relevant! Different forms of practical relevance in management science', *Organization Studies*, 31, pp. 1257–1285.

Oviatt, B. M. and Miller, W. D. (1989), 'Irrelevance, intransigence, and business professors', *Academy of Management Executive*, 3, pp. 304–312.

Palmer, G. B. (1996), *Toward a Theory of Cultural Linguistics*, Austin, University of Texas Press.

Porter, M. E. (1996), 'What is strategy?', *Harvard Business Review*, 74: 6, pp. 61–78.

Rynes, S. L., Giluk, T. L. and Brown, K. C. (2007), 'The very separate worlds of academic and practitioner publications in human resource management: Implications for evidence-based management', *Academy of Management Journal*, 50, pp. 987–1008.

Rynes, S. L., Bartunek, J. M. and Daft, R. L. (2001), 'Across the great divide: Knowledge creation and transfer between practitioners and academics', *Academy of Management Journal*, 44, pp. 340–55.

Shlesinger, M. (2009), 'Crossing the divide: What researchers and practitioners can learn from one another', *Translation & Interpreting*, 1: 1, pp. 1–14.

Snow, C. P. (2012), *The Two Cultures*, Cambridge, UK: Cambridge University Press.

Southworth, G. and Conner, C. (1999), *Managing Improving Primary Schools: Using Evidence-based Management and Leadership*, New York: Routledge.

Straus, S. E., Richardson, W. S., Glasziou, P. and Haynes, R. B. (2005), *Evidence-based Medicine: How to Practice and Teach EBM*, 3rd edn., Edinburgh: Elsevier.

Van de Ven, A. H. (2007), *Engaged Scholarship: A Guide for Organizational Research*, Oxford: Oxford University Press.

Vermeulen, F. (2005), 'On rigor and relevance: Fostering dialectic progress in management research', *Academy of Management Journal*, 48, pp. 978–982.

Zelizer, B. (2009), 'Journalism and the Academy', in K. Wahl-Jorgensen and T. Hanitzsh (eds), *The Handbook of Journalism Studies*, Routledge: New York and London, pp. 29–41.

Part II

What Media Academics Say

Chapter 7

Towards a Praxis-based Media and Journalism Research

Leon Barkho and Ibrahim Saleh

Introduction

What is central for media and journalism research? Is it practice or theory? Which of the two themes should be given more prominence and space? Should the two concepts be given the same degree of importance? Which of the two themes should receive more attention from media scholars today? Are media scholars under any obligation to relate their theories to practice? Is theorizing sufficient to explain the social reality of the media? How attached should media scholars be to the subjects and the organizations they investigate? What views and attitudes do these subjects have about research findings with a bearing on their work? Why do media practitioners generally discard or distrust these findings?

These are some of the essential questions that are raised when discussing issues pertinent to the relationship between the media as theory and the media as praxis or practice. Media research landscape has hitherto primarily focused on raising questions on the nature of subjects being investigated and what constitutes their organizations' social reality, and the knowledge that can be gleaned from the way they organize themselves. The information and knowledge media researchers gather is supposed to change the lives of their subjects and their institutions for the better, because it aims to reveal social reality constructions they are either unaware of or they intentionally ignore.

But have we, as media researchers, theorists or analysts, succeeded in bridging the gap that separates us from the subjects of our studies and investigations? Before addressing questions like these, let us first start with some explanation of the key terms that are the focus of this chapter: theory and praxis.

Praxis, practice, applied

'Praxis' as a term is less known than 'practice' or 'applied' in media scholarly jargon. The three terms, though orthographically and phonetically different, are often used interchangeably because they express almost the same thing: the practical application of knowledge. The word 'praxis', the doing of something, is usually used in the literature in opposition or contrast to 'theory', the interpretation of something. Theories provide knowledge and rules. In praxis, we apply these rules in order to solve the problems we face and change our life for the better. The media as a social science discipline has traditionally been more concerned with theory building than practical application: hence the gap that separates theorists from the institutions they investigate.

Praxis as a philosophical concept is as old as Aristotle for whom the investigation of disciplines, through which thinkers attempt to interpret our world, must have a three-tier categorization, each with its own *telos*, or purpose. Aristotle and other Greek philosophers, according to W. Carr and S. Kemmis, believed that:

> The purpose of a theoretical discipline is the pursuit of truth through contemplation; its telos is the attainment of knowledge for its own sake. The purpose of the productive sciences is to make something; their telos is the production of some artefact. The practical disciplines are those sciences which deal with ethical and political life; their telos is practical wisdom and knowledge.
>
> (1986: 32)

Aristotle's threefold classification, though implicitly envisaging three separate and independent disciplines, is coherent, and has been taken as the foundation for how to relate theory and the pursuit of truth via 'contemplation' to the well-being of the society. Thus 'praxis' as a discipline is not easy. It may demand more rigour and sophistication than theory because it directly deals with human beings and the way they go about their lives. An 'error' in praxis may have far more grave consequences than an 'error' in theory. Thus, as Carr and Kemmis (1986: 190) remind us, the application of knowledge and theoretical rules demand 'wise and prudent practical judgment (on) how to act' in particular situations.

Praxis requires 'wise men' with the right experience, knowledge and capacity to communicate and enter into 'wise' deliberations and dialogue with the subjects and institutions they are investigating. Praxis will not materialize if those meant to benefit from it cannot see in practical terms how it is going to change their life by solving the problems they are facing. Aristotle, in his *The Nicomachean Ethics,* relates praxis to 'prudent man' because the rules that will be applied on the society should contribute to the 'good life generally':

> The mark of a prudent man [is] to be able to deliberate rightly about what is good and what is advantageous for himself; not in particular respects, e.g. what is good for health or physical strength, but what is conducive to the good life generally.
>
> (2004: 209)

The call for a praxis-based research is not new. It is as old as Greek philosophy, and particularly those theorists who have sought to carve a conceptual and methodological path that does not mimic empirical and analytical disciplines, and it is explicitly highlighted in the mainstream social science. Isaiah Berlin provides a solid theoretical framework:

> The first step to understanding men is the bringing to consciousness of the model or models that dominate and penetrate their thought and action, and the second type is

to analyze the model itself, and this commits the analyst to accepting or modifying or rejecting it, and in the last case, to providing a more adequate one in its stead.

(1962: 19)

Media research needs praxis

Media research is in need of a turn that shifts focus to the needs of media practitioners, employing theory in the service of practice by conducting research with a critical angle to not only explain the social reality of the media but provide alternatives to help them pursue 'rational' policies. Social science thinkers underscore the importance of praxis and how it should be related to theory. R. J. Bernstein, for instance, advices social science analysts to get engaged in investigations 'penetrating understanding of what had gone wrong, of how the straitjacket of established thought had come to dominate human life'. His call to liberate science from 'the straitjacket of established thought' is more relevant and applicable to today's world of media systems. What we need today 'is a critique that aims to get at the roots; a rethinking of what it means to live a rational life; and a relating of theory to practice' (Bernstein 1976: xxiii).

The need for praxis does not mean that media researchers abandon their highly-pursued goals of disinterestedness and detachment. Detachment and disinterestedness are qualities highly admired by both media theorists and practitioners. But these two valuable research notions are related to our efforts as researchers to not include our subjectivity, as far as possible, into our research processes. For our research to be of practical value, we need to be attached to and interested in the institutions we investigate and engage with their subjects through dialogue, debate and mutual understanding if we are to bridge the gap between theory and practice.

Praxis and media studies

Praxis research is an attempt to bridge the gap between media theory and practice and how to apply our research findings to the practical problems media practitioners and their outlets face. This is not an easy task for several reasons, most prominent among them is the fact that media scholars do not approach their research from a unified social reality view-point. There are differences among media scholars and theorists about their understanding of theory and its relation to practice. The supremacy of theory in media studies has relegated praxis to the receiving end, thereby alienating practitioners and their institutions.

One reason for this alienation might be the result of the preoccupation of social science with postmodernism and its heavy emphasis on fallibilism, shoring up the scepticism and suspicion practitioners and their institutions have developed towards media scholarly research and its findings. To dispel at least some of these suspicions, praxis-based research follows the line of Jürgen Habermas, Paul Taylor and Bernstein among others for the need of objective validity for the praxis-based media research. The appeal to objectivity is intersubjective in the sense of directing research towards change; a change that justifies for practitioners and their institutions, through open debate and argument, the validity and importance of the social or discursive practices we want them to dump, revise or introduce. We need debate and argument throughout our praxis-based research because, as Bernstein (2010: 170) teaches us, '[t]here is no way of analyzing concepts and judgments without reference to language. And we cannot understand language and speech acts except in the context of social and communal practices'. For these thinkers, social science research has to aim at some degree of objectivity and seek constant dialogical communication with its subjects if it is to be taken seriously by media institutions. Media institutions are not isolated islands. They develop their own cultures whose understanding requires a grasp of their daily operations (Dewey 1998).

Research with applied and practical intention should not dichotomize social science into stark and uncompromising categories. We believe there is much in common between theories in both empirical and social sciences as they both aim at explicating and formulating 'relations between a set of variables in terms of which a fairly extensive class of empirically ascertainable regularities' can be explained. But there is a difference in the scope and the universality of the 'regularities', which empirical and social scientists come to determine in their investigation. Regularities in social science, of which the media is a discipline, are far more restricted and much less extensive in their scope in terms of prediction and universality (Schutz 1962: 52).

The media milieu and reality have their own social and discursive characteristics, which researchers attempt to fathom, understand and interpret. In his practical philosophy, Emanuel Kant attaches a rational role to human beings as agents with rules guiding their social concepts, whether theoretical or practical (1819). The path to build a theory passes through Praxis because the 'theoretical route is […] made available from what people *do* to what they *mean*, from their *practice* to the *contents* of their states and expressions' (Brandom 1994: 134, original emphasis). Alfred Schutz has a good word of advice to social science analysts, with which praxis researchers concur. Media analysts of different theoretical persuasions aim at conclusions. For these conclusions to have a practical implication, they must have some claim to objectivity and normative application to be accepted by practitioners and institutions yearning for change. The 'objectivity', we strive for when drawing our conclusions and findings, no matter how solid, should eventually be related to the subjects and their institutions where subjectivity and not objectivity is the norm. Our media theories and research, for them to be useful to the community, will have to be reduced to and relevant 'to the human activity which has created' them (Schutz 1964: 10).

No absolutism, no mutual exclusiveness

Practice and theory have not always been two categorical and mutually exclusive distinctions. Ancient Greek philosophers saw practice as the primary aim of their *bios theoretikos*, the mental and intellectual activity that accompanied their classical thought. They realized that a life of contemplation and theorizing alone will not result in an understanding of human beings and their place in the world and its social reality, unless it is accompanied with practical efficacy (Uždavinys 2004; Eriksen 1976). Greek philosophical thought and subsequent thinkers up to the twentieth century, in which Husserl's phenomenology had far-reaching influence on almost all social science disciplines, emphasized the connection between theory or *theoria*, and practice or *kosmos*. But what is it that caused a departure between *theoria* and *kosmos* or *mimesis* and *biostheoretikos*? Habermas is the philosopher who provides the most succinct answer:

> What was once supposed to comprise the practical efficacy of theory has now fallen prey to methodological prohibitions. The conception of theory as a process of cultivation of the person has become apocryphal. Today it appears to us that the mimetic conformity of the soul to the proportions of the universe, which seemed accessible to contemplation, had only taken theoretical knowledge into the services of the internalization of norms and thus estranged its legitimate tasks.

(1971: 304)

Habermas is not alone in pointing out the dangers of relying solely on our theories and 'methodological prohibitions' to provide rational explanations of our social world, its individuals and institutions. A praxis-based media research cannot and should not have as its basis any form of absolutism in the sense of approaching social reality from the viewpoint of stark dichotomies and divisions, and binary conceptual characterizations. Practice has a bearing on the pragmatic school of thought as expounded by thinkers like John Dewey, Charles Peirce, William James, Richard Rorty and Hilary Putnam, who reject stark divisions of epistemologies and seek instead practical solutions to our daily problems. These pragmatist philosophers emphasize the role of relating our theories to practice and the futility of insistence on *theoria* as a basis of human rationality (Menand 2001).

With these issues and points in mind, let us now move to the conceptual underpinnings of praxis research and its position in the schools of thought that have characterized research in social science.

Conceptual and methodological considerations

Two schools of thought have traditionally characterized social science research and have directly impacted the media. The first relates to those who still believe that it is possible to explain and analyse the social and discursive structures of the media within the same degree of exactness that is required for empirical sciences. The knowledge we gain from our analyses, these researchers claim, can be used to socially 'engineer' the situation and the reality of the media. In other words, media research has the ability to 'manipulate' or 'orchestrate' for practitioners the how and why of their daily practices; not only what the social reality of the media is, but what it ought to be. Theorists and analysts following this line of thought draw heavily on philosophers like Philip M. Hauser and his views of social science as qua science, with the ability to prescribe for social institutions and their practitioners what approach they should follow to solve their problems. Social and empirical scientists who, according to Hauser, both rely on the same processes, analyse and examine the data they collect in the same manner. The knowledge they derive can be used as the foundation for the adoption of social, cultural and political policies of the systems and 'administrators of an organization or a program' they investigate (Hauser 1969: 15). For Hauser and social science analysts pursuing his line, social science is science and, as such, it has a 'mechanical, manipulative, orchestrating or engineering' role in our social reality.

Another oft-cited philosopher in social research pursuing the 'exactness' of empirical sciences is Karl Popper and his defence of 'social engineering'. But a close reading of Popper would reveal that his philosophy views social science from a different perspective by the virtue of his call for a cautious and step-by-step approach in which analysts take into account conditions in the social institutions they are investigating, their needs and their social realities. Popper is not Habermas, for whom the explication of a communicative event is a matter of dialogue, understanding and agreement between analysts and practitioners. However, he explicitly rejects the wholesale imposition of normative findings and practices on institutions and their practitioners. A scientist, according to Popper, should 'make his way, step by step, carefully comparing the results expected with the results achieved, and always on the look-out for the unavoidable unwanted consequences of any reform' (1972: 67).

The second school places more emphasis on praxis. It is prominently highlighted in the writings of Schutz (1964), who attempted to relate Husserl's phenomenology and thought to social sciences and our social world. For him, social scientists are under obligation to be detached and disinterested in the formulation of theory, but at the same time they must be interested in practice not only as represented in the social life of practitioners and their institutions but also in the fact that they, as human beings, are part of social reality. Schutz defends the role of a theorist or researcher as a disinterested and detached observer but this does not mean being detached from the social reality or the subjectivity of the topics investigated. The knowledge the theorist obtains must be geared towards serving the community and its institutions. It should not be kept in the confines of the murals of academia. The relation the theorist builds with subjects should not terminate with the stage of data collection.

Bernstein (1976: 173), more than any other thinker, relates his philosophy to praxis, which he sees as paramount for the work of the theorist. He defends the paradigm of 'self-corrective, open inquiry which is subject only to the critical norms of intersubjective discourse'. An approach that relates theory to practice rejects, according to Bernstein (1976), categorical distinctions of subjectivity versus objectivity, fact versus value, or theory versus practice. For him, these categories are 'closely related' rather than being distinct and separated. 'The search for empirical correlations, the task of interpreting social and political reality, and the critique of this "reality," are not three distinct types of inquiry. They are three internal moments of theorizing about social and practical life' (Bernstein 1976: 174).

Within the same conceptual framework neatly fits hermeneutics, the philosophy that takes the understanding and interpretation of social reality, linguistic or non-linguistic, as one of its main objects. The interplay between the end and means and the intertwinement between theory and practice is at the heart of the methods H. G. Gadamer recommends for the attainment of truth. Aristotle's three-tier categorization of theory, production and practice and his reciprocity of contemplation and practical wisdom are for Gadamer part of a process of action and reaction between knowledge and practice. He writes:

> As we think about what we want to achieve, we alter the way we might achieve that. There is a continual interplay between ends and means. In just the same way there is a continual interplay between thought and action. This process involves interpretation, understanding and application in 'one unified process'.
>
> (Gadamer 1979: 275, original emphasis)

The dialogic nature of praxis – communication between the theorist and the subjects of investigation – is necessary for the three stages of Gadamer's 'unified process' of research. But the dialogism becomes of paramount importance particularly at the last stage, namely application, as the well-being, the health and the security of the subjects and their institutions come into being due to their persistent aspiration for change and search for solution of problems. A theorist should not be satisfied with just working with subjects and their institutions through data-collection methods. It requires, as Taylor tells us, more creative work and relentless pursuit of dialogue:

> We can say that word and action, action and reflection, theory and practice are all facets of the same idea. This action is not merely the doing of something, what Freire describes as activism and Aristotle as *poiesis*. Poiesis is about acting upon, doing to: it is about working with objects. Praxis, however, is creative: it is other-seeking and dialogic.
>
> (Taylor in Smith [1999] 2011, original emphasis)

Praxis attains more prominence and occupies the centre of social science deliberations with the advent of critical studies. The remainder of this section focuses on three major thinkers of critical thought: Horkheimer, Marx and Habermas. These thinkers have left their indelible marks on research with a critical or practical intent.

Horkheimer and praxis

The first major school of thought to deplore the gap between theory and praxis was the Frankfurt School and its leader Horkheimer. This gap was a major point of its criticism of the state of social science research. The proponents of this school accepted most of the conceptual notions of phenomenological thinkers like Wilfrid Sellars, Martin Heidegger, Edmund Husserl and Schutz, and shared their interpretation and analysis of the crises of modern societies. They adopted Husserl's critique of methodological and analytical constraints positivist thinkers had imposed on social science research but, at the same time, they found their phenomenology insufficient to provide a framework for bridging the gap between theory and practice and using theoretical findings as a means of social change (Horkheimer 1972a, 1972b).

For the Frankfurt School, praxis comes into being through a critique of the society, a function that theory-based research pays little attention to. Horkheimer and other Frankfurt School thinkers wanted to add a rational angle to the traditional theory and its application to social reality; a base that will help us rationally critique the realities that we unthinkingly and habitually adopt. The basis of critical theory is its practical intent and Horkheimer clarifies how it can be related to practice: 'By criticism, we mean that intellectual, and eventually practical effort which is not satisfied to accept the prevailing ideas, actions, and social conditions unthinkingly and from mere habit' (1972a: 270).

Frankfurt School's critical theory has practice as a major interest because it sees theory as groundless if it does not improve our existence and help us understand the conditions and the realities of the world we live in. A praxis-based theory, according to Horkheimer, seeks to

transform existence so that mankind will for the first time be a conscious subject and actively determine its own way of life [...] There is a human activity that has society itself for its object. The aim of this activity is not simply to eliminate one or another abuse, for it regards such abuses as necessarily connected with the way in which the social structure is organized.

(1972a, 1972b: 206–207)

It should be noted here that there is a fundamental distinction between the practice-based theory the Frankfurt School formulates and the critical, or practice-based theory of critical discourse analysis (CDA), as developed by two of its most prominent theorists – Norman Fairclough and Teun van Dijk. CDA analyses and investigations mainly focus on the 'negative' attitudes of human existence and emphasize the social and discursive patterns they see as harmful to the society. For Horkheimer, being a critical theorist or analyst does not mean having negative views of existence or gearing our analyses solely towards its negative aspects. Horkheimer writes: The 'theoretician and his specific object are seen as forming a dynamic unity with the oppressed class, so that his presentation of societal contradictions is not merely an expression of the concrete historical situation but also a force within it to stimulate change' (1972a, 1972b: 215).

Marx and praxis

Among the philosophers who influenced critical thinking and its emphasis on praxis, Marx occupies a prominent position. For Marx, a theory is useless if it cannot be proved and applied in reality. Theories will remain unsustainable and part of 'mystics', he says, if they fail to show us better alternatives that, once applied, will contribute to our emancipation. He writes:

Man must prove the truth, i.e. the reality and power, the this-sidedness of his thinking in practice. [...] All social life is essentially practical. All mysteries which lead theory to mystics, find their rational solution in human practice and in the comprehension of this practice. [...] The philosophers have only interpreted the world, in various ways; the point is to change it.

(Marx 1998: 143)

In contrast to Marx's praxis-based theory, Horkheimer's critical and practice-based approach is not revolutionary and radical. Nonetheless, some critical studies in general and CDA in particular, specifically those driven by Marx, have made the issue of exposing those in power and helping out those who are exploited by it in the society the centre of their research and its practical intent. For them no interpretation and account of the society's reality is sound without us being made fully aware and conscious of this historical situation. For them, as Bernstein (1976: 183) points out, a position like this becomes 'a central issue – some might say, their *Achilles heel* – to determine who is or will become this revolutionary class, who are the subjects to whom critical theory is addressed'.

Habermas and praxis

Habermas highlights the problem of a social science that gives primacy to theory over practice. He sees the absence of a theoretical framework on how to relate research to the society and enter into debate and dialogue with its institutions to bring about change as one of the most urgent issues for scientists to tackle. While emphasizing the importance of scientific rigour of the research, Habermas (1973) recommends a shift towards helping the society to pursue a better way of life. Scientific knowledge in terms of theory building is vital for social science research, he says, but adds that so long as this scientific knowledge remains out of the society's reach it will be of limited use. Hence, his call for a compromise in which praxis takes its due place in scientific research.

Habermas adopts a much more ambitious critical and practical approach to the analysis of the society than Horkheimer and Marx. Outlined in detail in his *Knowledge and Human Interests* (1971), Habermas traces the notion of praxis as interpreted by Aristotle and until the modern age. His approach is a 'historically oriented attempt to reconstruct the prehistory of modern positvitism with the systematic intention of analyzing the connections between knowledge and human interests' (Habermas 1971: vii).

A praxis-based research in the Habermasian sense must have certain characteristic features. Maintaining the rigour and sophistication that are part of scientific investigation is one of them. The other is rendering theory and its findings practical and possible without relinquishing the research's objective orientation. Habermas raises some crucial issues about praxis-related research which still are not fully addressed, a gap which praxis-based research wants to bridge. Here are some of his questions in paraphrase: How can researchers clarify that their investigations and their outcome can have some practical application? How can we rationally justify that the praxis part of our research is the right thing for the practitioners to follow? How to address the problems the society faces and at the same time preserve the rigour through which we gather our data and conduct our scientific research? The final question, which is the most important, relates to the design of a sound methodological and conceptual framework for a praxis-based research that we hitherto do not have (Habermas 1973). Praxis-based media research will have to address these questions from two different but related angles: First, designing the right theories and methodologies and how to have them operationalized, and second working out a formula that will eventually reduce and bridge the current gap between media scholarship and media institutions and industry.

Another relevant notion is the differentiation Habermas draws between 'practical' and 'technical', a distinction that we believe to be crucial to the realm of praxis-based media research. Empirical sciences are driven by technical power and technological forces that aim at exactness, providing rigid frames for our existence often regardless of their being rational or suitable for the society's aspirations for change and the provisions of humanely acceptable conditions. Thus, Habermas warns against a praxis-based research that controls or changes the society in order to meet its own technical intentions. Praxis-based research has to be practical and not technical; it has to be rational in responding to the practical and human needs of the society and addressing the issues it faces. Here is how Habermas clarifies the differences between 'technical' and 'practical'.

> The real difficulty in the relation of theory and praxis does not arise from this new function of science as technological force, but rather from the fact that we are no longer able to distinguish between practical and technical power.[...]. For then no attempt at all is made to attain a rational consensus on the part of citizens concerned with the practical control of their country. Its place is taken by the attempt to attain technical control over history by perfecting the administration of society, an attempt that is just as impractical as it is unhistorical.
>
> (Habermas 1973: 255)

The critical aspect of Habermas' praxis does have an emancipatory element, but it should not be seen in Marx's revolutionary or radical critique. Praxis for Habermas is a means for liberation, e.g. from ideological mystifications, but at the same time he warns against attempts that confine the concept to criticism and the uncovering of what theorists see as the negative and harmful practices of the institutions they examine. The other point that Habermas stresses is perseverance on the part of theorists not to give up relating their investigations to practice in case they initially fail to transform and 'liberate' practitioners and their institutions. To bridge the gap between theorists and practitioners, he suggests three primary conceptual platforms worth investigating by media academics and scholars willing to engage in praxis-based research. Although so far viewed as non-reducible, Habermas believes these three different cognitive approaches should not be treated in isolation from each other; hence his call for a communication-based intersubjective approach that subjects the subjectivity of social science to objective examinations. Here are Habermas' three conceptual distinctions each related to a distinctive type of science or discipline: 'The approach of the *empirical–analytical* sciences incorporates a technical cognitive interest; that of the *historical-hermeneutic* sciences incorporates a practical one; and the approach of critically oriented sciences incorporates the *emancipatory* cognitive interest' (1971: 308, emphasis added).

Habermas rejects the notion of adopting any of the three cognitive approaches to the study of sciences and disciplines as the only legitimate type of knowledge available to explain and interpret our social reality.

> On the contrary, I regard as abortive, even reactionary, the attempts which characterized the old methodological dispute, namely, attempts to set up barriers from the outset in order to remove certain sectors altogether from the clutches of a certain type of research.
> (Habermas 1974: 218)

Habermas is much influenced by Aristotle. He sees his ancient philosophy as still relevant particularly in relation to praxis and the importance of communication, dialogue and self-reflection in the building of knowledge. Human knowledge, according to Habermas, must be constructed through communication and intersubjectivity and not technical control. However, Habermas is quick to note that conditions for authentic communication and dialogue might not always be available. The various and conflicting concepts our modern world and its political and social institutions have developed about basic notions such as democracy, objectivity, impartiality, justice and freedom are a good case in point. Bernstein (2005) stresses this point when referring to how our modern world has become a victim of knowledge claims backed by technical interest and technological force, a world where chances for genuine praxis, dialogue and communication are diminishing.

Conclusion and implications

The conceptual platform for praxis-based research that media and journalism studies can benefit from should be akin to how Habermas (1971) clarifies and conceptualizes the term. Praxis-based media investigations should seek to uncover first the resistances institutions have to change. Second, they should be solid enough not only to tell practitioners what they do not know about themselves, or what they want to hide from others but also persuasive enough to be adopted by them. Media researchers should not attempt to impose their knowledge or theoretical models on the institutions they examine. They should work in tandem with institutions mainly through dialogue and communication until they reach a level of self-reflection in which they accept the analysis, its findings and the alternatives it suggests to change and improve conditions. If change does not come about 'there is still an alternative: either the interpretation is false (that is, the theory or its application to a given case) or, to the contrary, the resistances which have been correctly diagnosed, are too strong' (Habermas 1971: 266).

In a praxis-based media research, there are two essential approaches that we need to consider. First, enabling our subjects and institutions to have a clear understanding and interpretation of their social reality – the historical conditions and situations they find themselves in; second, offering suggestions, alternatives and proposals that will motivate practitioners, through dialogue and communication, to bring about change. In Habermasian vocabulary, praxis in this context should help institutions and the society first to spot and then remove traces of distorted communication that prevent the creation of a community that is fully aware of the why and how of its conditions.

The central issue of a praxis-based media research is building a theory with practical implications. But this research should not have as its sole focus the 'emancipation' of the society – a radical and revolutionary change as stipulated by Marx. Change comes through dialogue, understanding and motivation. Developing a critique of how ideology sweeps modern societies and their media and how the powerful suppress practical and rational discourses is important for any praxis-based media research. However, the research should not have as its sole target exposing and demystifying media ideologies merely to identify their faults, errors or negative sides.

It is wrong to assume that there will ever be a time we can reach an ideal situation in which media structures and institutions shall live without crises and problems. Crises, conflicts, controversies and contradictions will be part of our life. Therefore, it is not sufficient to confine our research to exposing, demystifying and uncovering of these conflicts and their ideologies. What is more important is the how and why of these conflicts and the ways, alternatives or suggestions we can advance to ameliorate and alleviate their adverse impact on the society.

Our modern societies, though under the spell of technical and technological and law-like forces, are so diverse that it will be naïve to assume that the praxis-related theories we construct will have global implications. Even a principal notion such as 'objectivity', which is crucial for media and journalism research, can have diverse interpretations and applications (Maras 2013).

Bridging the gap between theory and practice requires further understanding of media's social reality in search of not only regularities and correlations to build a theory but also of the different social variables and the way they act and interact in real-life situations. An understanding like this is a crucial and an indispensable step for the application of the knowledge we gather and the alternatives we provide for change and solution of problems.

References

Aristotle (2004), *The Nicomachean Ethics* (trans. J. A. K. Thomson), London: Penguin.
Auchard, E. (2013), 'What are the new rules for reporting, sourcing, verifying, editing and publishing a social media world?', *Journal of Applied Journalism and Media Studies*, 2: 1, pp. 65–76.

Berlin, I. (1962), 'Does political theory still exist?', in P. Laslett and W. G. Runciman (eds), *Philosophy, Politics and Society*, Oxford: Basil Blackwell, pp. 1–33.

Bernstein, R. J. (1971), 'Herbert Marcuse: An immanent critique', *Social Theory and Practice*, 1: 4, Fall, pp. 97–111.

————— (1976), *The Restructuring of Social and Political Theory*, London: Methuen.

————— (1983), *Beyond Objectivism and Relativism: Science, Hermeneutics and Praxis*, Oxford: Basil Blackwell.

————— (2005), *The Abuse of Evil: The Corruption of Politics and Religion Since 9/11*, Cambridge: Polity Press.

————— (2010), *The Pragmatic Turn*, Cambridge: Polity Press.

Brandom, R. (1994), *Making It Explicit*, Cambridge: Harvard University Press.

Carr, W. and Kemmis, S. (1986), *Becoming Critical: Education, Knowledge and Action Research*, Lewes: Falmer.

Dewey, J. (1998), *The Essential Dewey*, vols 1 and 2, Bloomington: Indiana Press.

Elstein, D. (2013), 'Press freedom in the UK and the Leveson inquiry', *Journal of Applied Journalism and Media Studies*, 2: 1, pp. 19–31.

Eriksen, T. B. (1976), *Bios Theoretikos: Notes On Aristotle's EthicaNicomachea X, 6–8*, Oslo: Universitetsforlaget.

Fielden, L. (2012), 'Lara Fielden of the Reuters Institute for the study of journalism on press regulation in an era of blended media', *Journal of Applied Journalism & Media Studies*, 1: 2, pp. 173–180.

Gadamer, H.-G. (1979), *Truth and Method*, London: Sheed and Ward.

Gadotti, M. (1996), *Pedagogy of Praxis: A Dialectical Philosophy of Education*, New York: SUNY Press.

Habermas, J. (1971), *Knowledge and Human Interests* (trans. J. J. Shapior), Boston, MA: Beacon Press.

————— (1973), *Theory and Practice* (trans. J. Vietel), Boston, MA: Beacon Press.

————— (1974), 'Rationalism divided in two: A reply to Albert', in A. Giddens (ed.), *Positivism and Sociology*, London: Heinemann Educational, pp. 195–223.

Hamilton, E. (2012), 'The CEO of Sweden's Public Broadcasting Corporation (SVT), Eva Hamilton, on benefits of expanding ties between content industry and the state in the digital age', *Journal of Applied Journalism & Media Studies*, 1: 1, pp. 25–31.

Hauser, P. M. (1969), 'The chaotic society: Product of the social morphological revolution', *American Sociological Review*, 34: 1, pp. 1–18.

Horgan, J. (2012), 'Ireland's press ombudsman, John Horgan, on accountability, regulation and redress: Where do press councils stand?', *Journal of Applied Journalism & Media Studies*, 1: 2, pp. 201–207.

Horkheimer, M. (1972a), *Critical Theory*, New York: The Seabury Press.

————— (1972b), 'The latest attacks on metaphysics', *Critical Theory*, New York: The Seabury Press, pp. 132–187.

Kant, E. (1819), *Logic*, London: W. Simpkin and R. Marshall, http://philpapers.org/s/Immanuel%20Kant. Accessed 28 August 2016.

Maras, S. (2013), *Objectivity in Journalism*, Cambridge: Polity Press.

Marsh, K. (2012), 'Kevin Marsh, ex-executive editor, BBC College of Journalism, on issues of impartiality in news and current affairs', *Journal of Applied Journalism & Media Studies*, 1: 1, pp. 69–78.

Marx, K. (1998), *The German Ideology: Including Theses on Feuerbach and an Introduction to the Critique of Political Economy*, Amherst, MA: Prometheus Books.

Menand, L. (2001), *The Metaphysical Club: A Study of Ideas in America*, New York: Farrar, Straus and Giroux.

Popper, K. R. (1972), *The Poverty of Historicism*, rev. ed., London: Routledge & Kegan Paul.

Purvis, S. (2012), 'Managing Murdoch': How the regulator that became a problem then became a solution', *Journal of Applied Journalism & Media Studies*, 1: 2, pp. 143–55.

Schutz, A. (1962): *The Problem of Social Reality: Collected Papers I*, The Hague: Martinus Nijhoff.

—— (1964), *The Social World and the Theory of Social Action: Collected Papers, Vol. II: Studies in Social Theory*, The Hague: Martinus Nijhoff.

Smith, M. K. ([1999] 2011), 'What is praxis?', in *The Encyclopaedia of Informal Education*, http://www.infed.org/biblio/b-praxis.htm. Accessed 12 March 2013.

Taylor, P. (1993), *The Texts of Paulo Freire*, Buckingham, UK: Open University Press.

Tucker, R. C. (1978), *The Marx-Engels Reader*, New York: W. W. Norton & Company.

Uždavinys, A. (2004), *The Golden Chain: An Anthology of Pythagorean and Platonic Philosophy*, Bloomington, IN: World Wisdom Books.

Chapter 8

From the High Ground to the Swamp: A Model for Immersive Journalism Research

Sarah Niblock

Introduction

Philosopher Donald Schön, who made a remarkable contribution to the theory and practice of learning, urged that 'in the varied topography of professional practice, there is a high, hard ground overlooking a swamp' (1987). For Schön, academics tend to view their research as on the high ground – authoritative, linear and logical – and assume that publishing their findings in a journal or book will somehow filter down to the swamp and transform practice. Despite increasing numbers of journalists moving from newsrooms into the academy in recent years, the news industry continues to voice its wariness, at best, of the relevance of academic research to daily news production. Unlike so many other occupational areas such as law, engineering and medicine, journalists and academics continue to struggle to find a common purpose and shared critical vocabulary. Alvesson and Skoldberg (2000) warn that the 'high ground' approach to research, where academics examine the processes and products of journalism from the outside (Niblock 2007), leads to a one-way street whereby research subjects are unable to feed back on whether the study is useful. Contextualization of research findings to the practitioner world is essential (Wood, Ferlie and Fitzgerland 1998) or the research/researched relationship becomes elitist. As Foucault (1980) observed, those with knowledge tend to assume positions of power and define what is to count as valid knowledge in a self-perpetuating cycle. The challenge for journalism researchers is to push forward the barriers in research; to define, test and further develop methods of investigation that are appropriate to the needs of funding bodies but which, crucially, also meet the needs of media practitioners.

It is essential for journalism researchers to leave the high ground inhabited by academics and go down to the 'swamp' where practitioners go about their daily work, to 'enter a milieu where it is inappropriate to follow the formally agreed method of writing up research as a logical, linear process as objective and uncontaminated by the real-world of practice' (Freshwater and Rolfe 2001: 527). Journalism research methods that are interactive, iterative and rest on a dynamic communicative partnership between academics and practitioners, offer the best way for understanding change in our dynamic field. This permits the researcher to coalesce and indeed strengthen their identity as a practitioner-academic and develop research projects that are mutually beneficial for advancing scholarship and practice. Drawing on scholarship in reflexive methodologies in the human sciences, such as hermeneutics, cybernetics and constructivism, this chapter envisions an immersive approach embracing phenomenology and Gestalt as a fully reflexive method of data collection.

Reflexivity: A multidisciplinary approach

One of the roadblocks for closer working ties has been the sense – rightly or wrongly – that theories of journalism and media are too divorced from the reality of editorial and media processes or use obscure language (Mair 2013; Eltringham 2013). Susan Greenberg (2007: 292–93) nails the tension and explains why theory vexes journalism and media practitioners far more than it does practitioners in other professions such as law, medicine and teaching. She sees a 'clash of underlying philosophy' between the two disciplines that inform journalism studies. Communication studies has been accused of focusing too much on media control and power rather than strategies for engaging citizens. While cultural studies problematizes concepts such as 'truth' and 'reality', which of course journalism relies on for its lifeblood, reflexivity emanates from a different philosophical position, one that synthesizes theory with practice via praxis.

Barkho and Saleh 2013 provide a detailed explanation of praxis, including its manifestation through the work of several abiding sociologists of media and the public sphere, which highlights the need for reflexive approaches. First they describe how praxis means 'the doing of something' (Chapter 7) in contrast to theory, described as 'the interpretation of something' (Chapter 7). They draw on the theoretical framework of Isiah Berlin, who writes:

> The first step to understanding men is the bringing to consciousness of the model or models that dominate and penetrate their thought and action, and the second type is to analyze the model itself, and this commits the analyst to accepting or modifying or rejecting it, and in the last case, to providing a more adequate one in its stead.
>
> (1962: 19)

Reflexive research is a meta-methodology, whose object of study is itself. This reflexive notion of the researchers also being the subject of their own research was first suggested by Heron (1981), who referred to it as experiential research, and was later developed by a number of action researchers (Stenhouse 1985; Elliott 1991; McNiff 1993). Though rather than turning inwards, the research can be explored as part of wider engagement that goes beyond the researcher/subject relationship, and becomes instead cooperative enquiry (Reason and Rowan 1981). A reflexive researcher can work *with* their dualistic thought processes – as an educator who is identified and evaluated on their 'insider knowledge' by students and industry colleagues, and as someone whose academic value is formally measured via research assessment exercises and performance-related markers including research grants and publications. There is tremendous scope for practitioner-academics to forge a strong professional identity that *coalesces* their professional/practical and scholarly leanings. This is a far preferable situation than being associated with one 'side' or the other and not being able to fulfil that role fully due to the demands of the other.

To reach this position requires revising the prevailing view within journalism studies that research is delimited by formats and outcomes and to envision journalism research as the articulation of a process. Work in disciplines such as education, nursing and arts, such as Niedderer and Roworth-Stokes' analysis of creative practice, makes clear the benefits of understanding practice as scholarship 'from the insider's point of view with the context of their own language' (2007: 4).

Schön (1983: 36) argues that it is wrong to separate thinking from doing because reflection is complementary to action and part of it. In this way, critical reflection should not be seen as a threat to journalistic immediacy and rigour, according to Sheridan Burns:

> Instead of relying on theoretical knowledge to explain everything, the reflective practitioner is constantly testing ideas against practical experience. Instead of making problems fit existing categories, the reflective practitioner constructs the categories that will enable him or her to find a suitable response.
>
> (2003: 13)

This practice-led approach, whereby reflection is implicit in action, is helpful in exposing how the practical act of 'thinking on your feet' in a journalism setting is in fact the enactment of a sophisticated process of judgement borne out of experience. It assists by countering any suggestion that the journalist does not 'think', they just 'do'. Sheridan Burns takes the notion of reflective practitioner a step further by positing that journalists need to be mindful of the wider context within which they report: 'Reflection is also the process by which journalists learn to recognize their own assumptions and understand their place in the wider social context' (2003: 33). This runs in parallel with academics seeking to forge mutually beneficial and illuminating research relationships with media partners.

Making sense of our work as journalism practitioner-academics requires the integration of varied experience into a coherent narrative. Academic parlance requires mediated experience because uninterpreted raw experience – or 'thinking on your feet' as editors often label split-second in-the-moment judgement – would be deemed unintelligible. However, experience and perception occur side by side in routine, daily journalism work. The journalistic mind does not passively employ editorial skills to a given scenario; it actively receives cues from the culture of the newsroom and from past experience in similar scenarios, which are distilled into action at any given moment. So it is with the academic researcher seeking to develop critical narratives of journalistic behaviour, whether analysing practice or deconstructing meanings within products of editorial split-second judgement. We automatically construct meaning from what we perceive, yet as we reflect we realize that in most cases there is more than one construction available. The process of reflexive praxis-based research is a dialogue through which new meanings and constructions may emerge.

Research should be an interactive, reflexive process, cognizant of the researcher's own background, experience, gender, class, ethnicity and what that brings to the moment of analysis of relationships and tensions in the social worlds and texts under scrutiny. It is akin to the use of autobiography employed by artists as a means of linking theory work to their life (Stewart 1996: 38) Taking journalism studies forward means embracing practitioner perspectives but always in the knowledge that the researcher, however much they might align themselves with professional practice, is at one and the same time employed in higher education or research as their habitus. This does not mean an outright capitulation to formative notions of academic 'value'; by being reflexive, the researcher does more than produce outputs, they also develop the ontology and epistemology of the subject area so as to improve practice. Mezirow states critical reflexivity is transformative for practice:

> Transformative learning involves an enhanced level of awareness of the context of beliefs and feelings, a critique of their assumptions and particularly premises, an assessment of alternative perspectives, a decision to negate an old perspective in favour of a new one or to make a synthesis of old and new, than ability to take action on the basis of the new perspective, the desire to fit the new perspective into the broader context of one's life.
>
> (1991: 161)

This describes a learning process of 'becoming critically aware of one's own tacit assumptions and expectations and those of others and assessing their relevance for making an interpretation' (Mezirow 2000: 4). This conceptualization draws useful parallels with Gadamer's dialogical view of hermeneutics. Hermeneutics promotes understanding the meaning of language to expand the infinite possibilities of human thought (Palmer 1969). What is significant about Gadamer's hermeneutics is his ontological focus (Being) and capacity to interpret not only human understanding but also misunderstanding as a mechanism for effective communication.

In his analogy of research as a translation process, Steier ([1991] 1992) argues that researchers of human systems must acknowledge their contributions to the phenomenon under scrutiny that in turn contribute to the construction of the system being investigated. This bridge-building system is as much an artefact of the theoretical conversations guiding the researcher's actions as it is of the participants' actions and orientations. Reflexivity is in this case not based on theories; it is a meta-theory as theories are products of one's own culture. Rather, subjects must be analysed in context of time and place so as to be self-conscious of our theories and assumptions and to move towards deeper understanding (Becker 2000: 254).

Reflexivity is not viewed only as a tool for learning or for discovering the knowledge embedded in experience (Schön 1987). In 2007, this author wrote a keynote article for the first edition of *Journalism Practice* exploring the synthesis of theory and practice in journalism, drawing on work on reflection and reflexivity by Schön (1983), Ryle (1949) and others (Niblock 2007). The paper was published around the time of similar work by journalism practitioner-academics such as Barbie Zelizer (2004) and Wendy Bacon (2006) who, respectively, examined the tacit scholarly behaviour within editorial judgement and the status of journalism practice within research. The debate has subsequently gained momentum in the United Kingdom, New Zealand and Australia in particular as pressure mounts from universities for all academics, including practitioners, to be 'research active'.

However much of the literature, while arguing from a methodological standpoint, has not examined actual or potential research methods.

A reflexive method of data gathering for praxis-based research advances our knowledge, awareness and understanding of editorial practice in a transparent fashion that simultaneously demystifies research. Praxis is a particular philosophy used to guide and conduct research, which engages an individual or group under study in the research process (Tierney and Sallee 2008). One of the useful characteristics of praxis-based research for journalism researchers from an industry background is that it uses personal reflection as a key data source (Mayo 2006). When a researcher is in dialogue with practice, the material that emerges may be novel to both even though both parties were already familiar with the 'facts'. A reflexive approach involves making explicit the tacit knowledge or theory that underpins all practice, even in split-second editorial decisions. It aims to improve future practice through a better understanding of how context, experiences and history can impact quite profoundly on journalism and media production at any given moment. In that way, praxis is empowered by seeing research and practice on the same pathway. Just as a journalist aspires to a liminal role, not identified as part of the status quo so as to be perceived as neutral, so does the practitioner-academic working within and between competing and overlapping perspectives.

While news journalists are accustomed to swift output, praxis-based research is not for those interested in quick data collection and output. It is a lengthy process requiring academics to establish mutually beneficial relationships with industry partners. Stewart (2001) believes innovative thinking is often triggered by co-joining seemingly dissimilar phenomena, and I would also apply that to people. This is a key argument for reflexivity – looking beyond the parameters of our own habitus and incorporating fresh ideas into our work. In this way we can deepen our awareness of how, within practice, we find embedded cultural influences, personal experiences and aspirations (Hawke 1996: 35; Jeffries 1997: 5, in Stewart 2001). Thus, the approaches to research are as limitless as the mindsets of different practitioners in the field – what we need is a deeper sense of the underlying structures and ethical frameworks on which practice happens.

In the development of my own reflexive research/practice interface, praxis is the obvious next stage. In accordance with Barkho and Saleh's (2013) call for research to be of service to practice, the next stage is to create research partnerships and communities of practitioners and academics to engage in reflexive dialogue and, as Gadamer suggests, engage in the 'continual interplay between ends and means' (1979: 25, in Barkho and Saleh 2013).

Phenomenology in journalism praxis

Having illuminated theoretical processes embedded within practice, the next stage is to subject them to scrutiny to identify areas for development or improvement of practice. Barkho and Saleh assert that media research needs praxis as 'theory in the service of practice' and to 'provide alternatives to help [media practitioners] pursue "rational" policies' (Chapter 7). A phenomenological approach to media research would seem to assist in this endeavour. As opposed to a distanced, scientific objective approach to research, Barkho and Saleh assert:

> For our research to be of practical value, we need to be attached to and interested in the institutions we investigate and engage with their subjects through dialogue, debate and mutual understanding if we are to bridge the gap between theory and practice.
>
> (2013: 6)

The practitioner voice enhances that bridge-building, whether that of the practitioners we engage with as researchers or our own as practitioner-academics, by revealing the specific social and discursive characteristics of the 'media milieu'.

Phenomenology is probably the most significant philosophical movement of the twentieth century as far as the social sciences are concerned. Founded in the early twentieth century by Edmund Husserl phenomenology was, in origin, a reaction to the fact that science has traditionally only concerned itself with what is objective and measurable. The movement's development in the human sciences is greatly influenced by the approach of French phenomenologist Maurice Merleau-Ponty, particularly his 1945 work *Phenomenology of Perception*. Phenomenology draws attention to the fact that every perception owes as much to the mentality of the perceiver as it does to the structure of the object. 'Phenomenology is a transcendental philosophy which indeed suspends the affirmations characteristic of the natural attitude. But it does so only in order to shed light on them [...]' (Merleau-Ponty 1945: preface). In his work, Merleau-Ponty prioritizes our experiences in the moment as the most reliable data for understanding the world and our relationship with it. This is quite different from a scientific approach that assumes an already experienced perceptual world (Gallagher 2010: 183).

Phenomenology is one of the most relevant techniques for immersionist or reflexive approaches to journalism research, as being in the moment is the way most practice is conducted. It is a method for identifying the agency that journalists have in any given moment in the editorial process. Gallagher notes: '[...] consciousness is embedded in the physical world, the social world, in time, in history, and such insights force us to rethink the large concepts of intentionality, language, and rationality [...]' (2010: 184). In this sense, the researcher and the researched are in the same position, engaged in a relational dialogue with themselves, one another and the world in any given moment. This opens a potentially positive and productive space of conceiving of the journalist as an agent rather than only as a passive practitioner, subject to external forces (Curran and Seaton 1997). Phenomenological researchers generally agree that their central concern is to return to embodied, experiential meanings by rich descriptions of a phenomenon as it is concretely lived. It is necessary to understand the meaning attributed by persons to the activities in which they engage in order to understand their behaviour. As Wertz writes: 'Phenomenology is a low-hovering, indwelling, meditative philosophy that glories in the concreteness of person-world relations and accords lived experience with all its indeterminacy and ambiguity, primacy over the known' (2005: 175). Giorgi (1989) states that four core characteristics hold over all variations of phenomenology: the research is descriptive, uses phenomenological reductions, explores the intentional relationships between persons and situations, and discloses the essences or structures of meaning in human experience. Typically this research starts with concrete descriptions of lived situations, often first-person accounts (Finlay 2009: 10) set down in everyday language and avoiding abstract intellectual generalizations. The researcher then proceeds to identify general themes about the sequence of what has been observed, aiming to go beneath surface expressions so as to read between the lines and capture implicit dimensions.

This interpretative phenomenology has emerged from the work of hermeneutic philosophers including Heidegger, Gadamer and Ricoeur who assert the inescapable historicity of all understanding and our embeddedness in the world of language. 'The meaning of phenomenological description as a method lies in interpretation' wrote Heidegger ([1927] 1962: 37). Gadamer (1975) describes this process in terms of being open to the other while recognizing biases. Placing himself within his work, he argues that knowledge in the human sciences always involves self-knowledge:

This openness always includes our situating the other in relation to the whole of our own meanings or ourselves in relation to it [...] This kind of sensitivity involves neither 'neutrality' with respect to content nor the extinction of one's self, but the foregrounding and appropriation of one's own fore-meanings and prejudices. The important thing is to be aware of one's own bias, so that the test can present itself in its otherness and thus assert its own truth against one's own fore-meanings.

(1975: 268–269)

Applying the method

The aim of a journalism practitioner-researcher using the phenomenological approach is to engage the subject in as thorough an exploration or description of the topic or practice under scrutiny. This might be news selection criteria or target audience choice of vocabulary, for instance. This close engagement is likely to reveal statements, beliefs or observations that the journalist or news organization holds about their role, about others such as sources, audiences or rivals, and about their world or field in general. How these three areas intersect in editorial decision-making is particularly interesting to the status of the researcher, potentially in its unveiling of discrepancies, contradictions or paradoxes. There are three 'rules' of investigating the journalist's or organizations' viewpoint or editorial approach using the phenomenological method.

Bracketing

This refers to the researcher's attitude of setting aside any initial biases and prejudices and my efforts to suspend, or bracket, all expectations and assumptions regarding the journalist's statements and any implicit meaning. A researcher must remain open to any number of alternatives, setting aside any immediate personal predispositions or preferences towards any particular meaning or explanation. Gadamer suggests all interpretations are derived from a basic level of understanding or pre-judgement, because in 'view of the finitude of our historical existence, it would seem there is something absurd about the whole idea of unique, correct interpretation' (1975: 118). Understanding is ultimately self-understanding and any unchallenged presuppositions will only serve to maintain a restrictive interpretation (Gadamer 2004b: 251).

Description

The phenomenological approach rejects focusing attention on theoretical explanations of what the journalist presents, in favour of simple and concrete description of their experience in the moment. The essence is: 'Describe, don't explain'. For example, a journalist in an observation might express a strong negative view about giving airtime to a particular story. As a researcher, one might assume this aversion is representative of embedded institutional or individual bias, thus proving a specific theoretical principle. From a phenomenological perspective, however, the focus would be on how that negative view was experienced and expressed, not what may have caused it. Is the negativity consistent or does it depend upon the context in which the story arises? How is the concern voiced in terms of tone and vocabulary? What does the negative perspective prevent for the journalist? Or enable? How might it be different for the newsroom if the negativity subsided?

Horizontalization

This refers to the act of treating all the researcher observes with equal value, and not assuming any one thing to be more important than another. Typically, a researcher might go in with a particular quest and ignore other fascinating and revealing statements and events. The rule of horizontalization challenges the researcher to avoid making judgements about which statement is of greatest significance. Instead, a researcher might reflect back to the journalist, '[i]f you were in my position, which one of these aspects of your work would make the best sense to explore further'. In this approach it is the 'lived experience' (Husserl 1925) of the journalist or newsroom that matters and there is a radical rejection if mechanistic approaches in favour of a genuinely two-way encounter and dialogue (Kirschenbaum and Henderson 1989; Friedman 1986). The author's immersionist work in news organizations typically involve witnessing and describing what she sees as well as interactions with members of the staff team. Those interactions are usually in the form of semi-structured interviews aimed at deeper reflection on events witnessed. To beckon deeper reflection she asks open-ended questions to encourage elucidation. These questions might include:

What exactly did you mean when …? How did you reach that decision …? Who benefits from this …?

What options were available to you …? How do you know this …?

Can you give me an example …? What would happen if …?

What evidence is there to support what you are saying? What are the consequences …?

What alternative ways of looking at this are there …?

Another way of looking at this is …, does that seem reasonable?

An immediate question this poses is how researchers can test phenomenological data for its veracity. Just as phenomenology is not guided by specific theoretical models, nor is it a hypothesis testing model per se. Criteria such as validity and reliability persist as a legacy of the scientific method, note Koch and Harrington (1998), who argue that evaluation criteria can be generated within the research project itself through detailed writing up and overt reflexivity in presenting the research process. Giorgi supports the need to have a 'certain openness and flexibility' (2008: 42) when it comes to applying the method; he insists that criteria associated with scientific rigour need to be completely respected. Any discerned meanings that come out of the research need to be seen as based on data and achieved through a systematic process of free imaginative variation that allows a kind of internal validity check. Halling (2008) suggests a slightly different version of this free imaginative variation, which he calls 'empirical variation'. Here, emphasis is placed on working collaboratively with others where the group members dialogue about their various perspectives, allowing the phenomenon to show itself in new ways. In adopting such an approach, Halling is engaged in a distinctly scientific project. However, he also acknowledges something of the art within the process: 'The process is an intermingling of receptivity and creativity, of discovering truth and creating truth' (2008: 168), though it may produce data that can be tested via other means. A great deal of human experience is non-repeatable. It is not uncommon for humanities researchers to team up with scientists to examine their findings, and journalists and media researchers need to do the same.

The phenomenological method lends itself well to journalism praxis-based research as it is so similar to the journalistic mentality; it involves approaching phenomena with a fresh, open and welcoming mind, as coming upon something new, wonderful and strange. It requires a willingness to welcome what is unfamiliar and to be able to regard what is familiar with the same freshness as one perceives what is new. This method of enquiry is initially descriptive, allowing events or things to speak for themselves. The process of immersionist research in a journalistic environment is therefore a dialogue from which new meanings emerge. These may come from a change of perspective. This becoming immersed in the journalist's world sets up a resonance between the researcher and subject such that the researcher begins to experience in a way that parallels the experience of the journalist subject. It becomes a joint effort. The signal from the journalist is amplified as the researcher recognizes and resonates with it. In this way, between the two, a great deal more of the journalist's experience and intuition is brought to light.

Occupational challenges

Nonetheless, this way of working presents occupational challenges to the mindsets of both academic researchers and journalists. The term 'journalism research' suggests a united whole with a shared problematic. 'Journalism research' becomes unquantifiable as it spans an unlimited array of quests and contexts, including the technical, methodological, political, sociological, semiotic and ethical. Immediately, this points to the fact that 'journalism research' is multidisciplinary that makes it hard to identify any one voice, such as that of the practitioner or the pure academic, as essential or prioritized.

Traditionally, the format of the output has to a large part defined whether or not it is to be deemed research and academics regularly encounter conflicting accounts of what 'good' research is within and between institutions. Research, as it is widely understood in universities where many lecturers have followed a more academic route into teaching foregrounds declarative or propositional knowledge as it is based on clear explication through language or text (Ryle 1949; Stanley and Williamson 2001). Practice-as-research is an opportunity to interrogate and expand the epistemology of Journalism journalism studies, though 'appropriate' practice-as-research needs some delineation. Whereas in art and design where the emphasis is on creative output (Piccini 2004), in areas such as education the focus is on the processes of learning (Kolb 1984). Many believe that long-term journalism projects offering fresh insights or new knowledge are best placed to constitute research outcomes. For example, Bacon (2011) makes a strong case for the research-led nature of investigative journalism. But in such a diverse and dynamic occupation, research is urgently needed on more rapid forms of editorial judgement and thinking-in-action as well as 'infotainment'.

Tacit knowledge can be verified within and through action and its result, where every action constitutes a critical judgement over appropriate action. From one perspective, this might be viewed as evidence of a detrimental shift away from critical academic enquiry. From another perspective, that moment of editorial judgement might be extrapolated as highly critical, by beckoning close examination and justification of choices made. In this way, practice is validated because the act of abstraction deems knowledge to be inherent. It is this underlying notion of the great potential for reflexive research that drives my ideas about methodology.

If research work poses such challenges to a practitioner-academic, it is not hard to see why industry practitioners and those new to scholarship might be wary of involvement. Practice-based university modules are intensively delivered with large class contact hours and the expectation of employability. This can be a significant obstacle in practitioner-academics undertaking research degrees and developing their own scholarship. The time it takes for research to reach the publication stage is a huge deterrent to academic endeavour, with many in the industry arguing that scholarship targeted purely at academic peers is of little use beyond the ivory tower. Occupationally, journalists who work 'intuitively' feel very challenged by the idea that they must stand back from what they do and discuss methodology (Niblock 2007). Putting themselves in their research when all their professionalized training and experience tells them to be 'neutral' presents a significant cognitive barrier.

News organizations are understandably wary of allowing individuals or teams of researchers into busy newsrooms. It may at best be inconvenient but at worst it may be seen as serving little or no purpose for the organization. For researchers to be welcome, their work must be seen to have use value to the host. This is why a mutual partnership takes a great deal of time and discussion to broker, a fact that must be acknowledged by universities when allocating teaching loads and research budgets to industry-facing departments. Newsrooms need to grasp the benefit of entering into unknown territory or they will, understandably, see no reason to allow academics access.

Conclusion: Creating opportunities for praxis

People in everyday life suspend their doubts in order to turn their world into a safer one (Schutz 1976). Mainstream journalists harness statements such as 'gut instinct' and a 'nose for news' as an indicator of the permanence of certain everlasting 'truisms' in their occupation. Such an attitude assumes a reliable premise in the permanence of the structures of the world: one trusts that the world will remain the same. Reflexive immersionist research questions the basis of this familiarity with social reality, and suggests certain organized standards of routine (Schutz 1976: 108) are learned from this knowledge of typical behaviours, such as standard newsroom protocols like writing style, use of quotations and headline-creation methods. It explores whether editorial judgement is constructed out of the socially available stock of knowledge at hand and is applied in the actual interpretative process of daily news routines on the basis of practical purposes of the journalist. As Tuchman, closely following Schutz, reminds us, social action is carried out in the future perfect tense: 'Action is cast into the future in order to accomplish acts that will happen should everything go as anticipated' (Tuchman 1978: 41). In the face of each news situation, the journalist will look for similar past events from their own experience and act in a similar way as before, following principles that things will remain the same. This research has the great potential to make manifest meanings and alternatives not previously known to either side in the dialogue and can be mutually beneficial.

Cultivating these research relationships, however, takes time and these are some initial suggestions. There is an urgent need to reduce the physical split between media practice and the academy. Bridges can be built by introducing journalists-in-residence to university newsrooms to work with scholars as well as students. This already works well at several universities. Universities might also bring journalists in to teach research methods. Investigative journalists are well placed to work with research academics as well as students on search, interviewing and other modes of data collection.

It is important that the next wave of Ph.D. students is sufficiently equipped with the skills to be ethically immersed. Ph.D.s and mid-career professionals-turned-academics face many tests of their research ethics when they go back to study their former newsrooms. Journalists could do much to brief and socialize prospective researchers about newsroom protocols as a key part of a programme of research methods training. Issues faced by my own Ph.D. students have included pressures to withhold certain data, knowing when and how to assert professional distance in familiar newsrooms and securing a sound methodology for semi-structured interviews with staff.

The phenomenology-based methodology outlined above would seem to offer a transparent and feasible solution to many of these issues. Beckoning a reflexive approach on the part of the researcher and the academic allows them to enter into a mutually beneficial working dialogue free of prior expectations, values or preconceptions so as to identify and analyse previously unknown details about the news-making process. Forging such relationships between researchers and the journalism industry is a crucial and urgent step if we are to realize our shared aims of taking practice forward.

References

Alvesson, M. and Skoldberg, K. (2000), *Reflexive Methodology: New Vistas for Qualitative Research*, London: SAGE.

Bacon, W. (2006), 'Journalism as research?', *Australian Journalism Review*, 28: 2, pp. 147–57.

——— (2011), 'Investigative journalism in the academy – Possibilities for storytelling across time and space', *Pacific Journalism Review*, 17: 1, pp. 45–66.

Barkho, L., & Saleh, I. (2013), 'Towards a praxis-based media research', *Journal of Applied Journalism & Media Studies*, 2: 1, pp. 3–18.

Barthes, R. (1995), *Roland Barthes by Roland Barthes*, London: Macmillan.

Becker, A. L. (2000), *Beyond Translation: Essays Toward a Modern Philology*, Ann Arbor, MI: University of Michigan Press.

Berlin, I. (1962), 'Does political theory still exist?', in P. Laslett and W. G. Runcimann (eds), *Philosophy, Politics and Society*, Oxford: Basil Blackwell, pp. 1–33.

Curran, J. and Seaton, J. (1997), *Power Without Responsibility*, London: Routledge.

Elliott, J. (1991), *Action Research for Educational Change*, Milton Keynes, UK: Open University Press.

Eltringham, M. (2013), 'Journalists and academics: Trade your "fortresses" for practical partnership', http://www.bbc.co.uk/blogs/blogcollegeofjournalism/posts/Journalists-and-academics-trade-your-fortresses-for-practical-partnership. Accessed 29 May 2014.

Finlay, L. (2009), 'Debating phenomenological research methods', *Phenomenology and Practice*, 3: 1, pp. 6–25.

Foucault, M. (1980), *Power/Knowledge; Selected Interviews and Other Writings 1972–77*, Brighton, UK: Harvester.

Freshwater, D. and Rolfe, G. (2001), 'Critical reflexivity: A politically and ethically engaged research method for nursing', *Nursing Times Research*, 6: 1, pp. 526–36.

Friedman, M. (1986), 'Carl Rogers and Martin Buber: Self-actualization and dialogue', *Person-Centered Review*, 1: 4, pp. 409–35.

Gadamer, H. G. (1975), *Truth and Method*, London: Sheed and Ward.

——— (1979), *Truth and Method*, London: Sheed and Ward.

——— (2004a), *Truth and Method*, London: Sheed and Ward.

——— (2004b), *Philosophical Hermeneutics* (ed. and trans. D. E. Linge), 2nd edn, Berkeley: University of California Press.

Gallagher, S. (2010), 'Merleau-Ponty's phenomenology of perception', *TOPOI*, 29: 2, pp. 183–185.

Giorgi, A. (1989), 'One type of analysis of descriptive data: Procedures involved in following a phenomenological method', *Methods*, 1: 2, pp. 39–61.

——— (2008), 'Concerning a serious misunderstanding of the essence of the phenomenological method in psychology', *Journal of Phenomenological Psychology*, 39: 1, pp. 33–58.

Greenberg, S. (2007), 'Theory and practice in journalism education', *Journal of Media Practice*, 8: 3, pp. 289–303.

Halling, S. (2008), *Intimacy, Transcendence, and Psychology: Closeness and Openness in Everyday Life*, New York: Palgrave Macmillan.

Heidegger, M. ([1927] 1962), *Being and Time* (trans. J. Macquarrie and E. Robinson), San Francisco: Harper and Row.

Heron, J. (1981), 'Philosophical basis for a new paradigm', in P. Reason and J. Rowan (eds), *Human Inquiry*, Chichester: Wiley, pp. 19–36.

Husserl, E. (1925), *Erste Philosophie. Erster Teil: Kritische Ideengeschichte/First Philosophy Vol 1: Critical History of Ideas*, The Hague, Netherlands: Martinus Nijhoff.

Jefferies, J. (1997), 'Autobiographical patterns', *N. Paradoxa*, 4, pp. 1–6.

Kirschenbaum, H. E. and Henderson, V. L. E. (1989), *Carl Rogers: Dialogues: Conversations with Martin Buber, Paul Tillich, BF Skinner, Gregory Bateson, Michael Polanyi, Rollo May, and Others*, Boston, MA: Houghton, Mifflin and Company.

Koch, T. and Harrington, A. (1998), 'Reconceptualizing rigour: The case for reflexivity', *Journal of Advanced Nursing*, 28: 4, pp. 882–890.

Kolb, D. (1984), *Experiential Learning: Experience as the Source of Learning and Development*, Englewood Cliffs: Prentice Hall.

Mair, J. (2013), 'Sadly too many journalists seeking academic credibility can't write', http://www.theguardian.com/media/greenslade/2013/aug/27/journalism-education-newspapers. Accessed 29 May 2014.

Mayo, E. (2006), 'Researching together: Praxis-based research among practitioners', in C. Mutch (ed.), *Challenging the Notion of 'Other'*, Wellington: NZCER Ministry of Education, pp. 119–139.

McNiff, J. (1993), *Teaching as Learning*, London: Routledge.

Merleau-Ponty, M. (1945), *Phenomenology of Perception*, London: Routledge.

Mezirow, J. (1991), *Transformative Dimensions of Adult Learning*, San Francisco: Jossey-Bass.

——— (2000), 'Learning to think like an adult', in J. Mezirow and Associates (eds), *Learning as Transformation: Critical Perspectives on a Theory in Progress*, San Francisco: Jossey-Bass, pp. 3–33.

Niblock, S. (2007), 'From "Knowing How" to "Being Able": Negotiating the meanings of reflective practice and reflexive research in journalism studies', *Journalism Practice*, 1: 1, pp. 20–32.

Niedderer, K. and Roworth-Stokes, S. (2007), 'The role and use of creative practice in research and its contribution to knowledge', *IASDR International Conference 2007*, Hong Kong Polytechnic University, Hong Kong, 12–15 November.

Palmer, R. E. (1969), *Hermeneutics; Interpretation Theory in Schleiermacher, Dilthey, Heidegger, and Gadamer*, Evanston, IL: Northwestern University Press.

Piccini, A. (2004), 'An historiographic perspective on practice as research studies', *Theatre and Performance*, 23: 3, December, pp. 191–207.

Reason, P. and Rowan, J. (1981), *Human Inquiry*, Chichester, UK: Wiley.

Ryle, G. (1949), *The Concept of Mind*, London: Hutchinson.

Schön, D. (1983), *The Reflective Practitioner*, New York: Basic Books.

——— (1987), *Educating the Reflective Practitioner*, San Francisco: Jossey-Bass.

Schutz, A. (1976), *Collected Papers, Vol. II*, The Hague, The Netherlands: Martinus Nijhoff, pp. 91–105.

Sheridan Burns, L. (2003), *Understanding Journalism*, London: SAGE.

Stanley, J. and Williamson, T. (2001), 'Knowing how', *Journal of Philosophy*, 98: 8, pp. 411–444.

Steier, F. ([1991] 1992), 'Reflexivity and methodology: An ecological constructionism', in F. Steier (ed.), *Research and Reflexivity*, London: SAGE, pp. 163–85.

Stenhouse, L. (1985). 'Research as a basis for teaching' in Ruddick, J. and Hopkins, D. (eds.) *Research As A Basis For Teaching: Readings from the work of Lawrence Stenhouse*. London: Heinemann, pp. 124–126.

Stewart, R. (1996), 'Constructing neo-narratives: A qualitative research process for the visual arts', *Australian Art Education*, 19: 3, pp. 37–47.

Stewart, R. A. (2001), 'Practice vs praxis: Constructing models for practitioner-based research', *TEXT*, 5: 2, http://www.textjournal.com.au/oct01/stewart.htm. Accessed 9 March 2015.

Tierney, W. and Sallee, M. (2008), 'Praxis', *The SAGE Encyclopedia of Qualitative Research Methods*, Thousand Oaks, CA: SAGE Publications, pp. 675–80.

Tuchman, G. (1978), *Making the News*, New York: Free Press.

Wertz, F. (2005), 'Phenomenological research methods for counseling psychology', *Journal of Counseling Psychology*, 52: 2, pp. 167–177.

Wood, M., Ferlie, E. and Fitzgerland, L. (1998), 'Achieving clinical behaviour change: A case of becoming indeterminate', *Social Science and Medicine*, 47: 11, pp. 1729–1738.

Zelizer, B. (2004), *Taking Journalism Seriously: News and the Academy*, Newbury Park: SAGE.

Chapter 9

Minority Media as Intercultural Dialogue: Towards a Communicative Praxis

Fackson Banda

Introduction

My task in this chapter is to attempt an analysis of minority media in terms of its potential for intercultural dialogue in our societies, drawing primarily on the UNESCO World Report on Investing in Cultural Diversity and Intercultural Dialogue (UNESCO 2009). My aim is ultimately to show that the communicative aspect of such intercultural dialogue is the accentuation of democratic citizenship in multicultural societies. Conceptually, I use the term 'minority media' expansively, to refer more to a way of practicing journalism in intercultural settings than to any institutional structure of media. I thus see minority media as a typology of media that has a minority orientation in its editorial policies and makes good on that orientation. What this means is that I treat all media types – mainstream and alternative – as possibilities for minority-sensitive journalism or reporting. I recognize the fact that minority media can, and do, exist as such. But my approach is not so much about creating 'niche' media for minorities as advocating a resensitization and re-orientation of existing media forms to integrate minority cultures within their editorial practices and routines.

Focusing on all media types does not render insignificant all those media structures owned and operated by minority groups. On the contrary, by highlighting minority-sensitivity as an ideal feature of all free, independent and pluralistic media, the broad aim becomes one of universalizing minority discourse so that it can become an important part of the wider media ecosystem. Viewed that way, the political objectives of minority media and minority-sensitive media become closely intertwined.

To this end, I structure my chapter as follows: first, I justify the need for minority-sensitive media as a key element in the struggle for intercultural dialogue against the backdrop of the tendency towards cultural homogenization typical of mainstream media. Second, and by way of conclusion, I proceed to sketch what I consider to be the key normative communicative roles for minority media.

The case for minority media: Towards a journalism of cultural belonging

Why is the issue of minority-sensitive media so important in a multicultural setting? I would like to make three key arguments, namely: (1) the increasing recognition of minorities in international human rights discourse, (2) their continuing poor media representations and (3) the democratic potential of minority discourse in multicultural settings. I discuss each of these points in turn.

Minorities in international human rights discourse

The 1966 International Covenant on Civil and Political Rights and the 1992 Declaration on the Rights of Persons Belonging to National or Ethnic, Religious and Linguistic Minorities (also referred to as the United Nations Minorities Declaration) set out an international legal framework for recognizing and protecting the rights of persons belonging to minorities (United Nations 2010: 1). In the UN system, there is a recognition that the work by Francesco Capotorti, Special Rapporteur of the United Nations Sub-Commission on Prevention of Discrimination and Protection of Minorities (1979), reignited the spark of minority discourse, drawing special attention to minority rights (Aikio-Puoskari and Skutnabb-Kangas 2004: 60).

For its part, the United Nations Minorities Declaration refers to national or ethnic, cultural, religious and linguistic identity as constitutive of minorities. The existence of a minority is a question of fact, and any definition must include both objective factors (such as the existence of a shared ethnicity, language or religion) and subjective factors (including that individuals must identify themselves as members of a minority) (in United Nations 2010: 2). This approach generally agrees with that preferred by Aikio-Puoskari and Skutnabb-Kangas, who define a 'minority' as:

> a group which is smaller in number than the rest of the population of a State, whose members have ethnic, religious or linguistic features different from those of the rest of the population, and are guided, if only implicitly, by the will to safeguard their culture, traditions, religion or language [...] To belong to a minority shall be a matter of individual choice.
>
> (Aikio-Puoskari and Skutnabb-Kangas 2004: 66)

Writing within the US national context, Larry Gross extends this definition to include 'ethnically and racially defined people as well as to women (in terms of their relative powerlessness despite their numerical superiority)'. He points out that these descriptive categories are 'defined by their deviation from a norm that is white, male, heterosexual and (in most Western societies) Christian, and these deviations are reflected in the mirrors that the media hold up before our eyes'. Minorities, he goes on, share a common media fate of relative invisibility and demeaning stereotypes. He is quick to point out that there are differences as well as similarities in the ways in which various minorities are treated by the mass media. It is because of these differences in the conditions they face in our society that the effects of their media images are different for members of the various minority groups (Gross 1998: 89).

In general, then, both national and international definitions of the term would appear to lend themselves to objective and subjective criteria, whereby the deaf, for example, can legitimately be classified as a minority (Aikio-Puoskari and Skutnabb-Kangas 2004), and so can a multiplicity of linguistic communities, as is the case with the Baatombu in Nigeria (see, e.g., Kperogi 2006) and the Baswara in Botswana. Indeed, such a definition can be extended to include lesbian women and gay men (Gross 1998: 89).

In this regard, international human rights law seeks to achieve four key objectives, namely to: (1) secure the survival and existence of minorities, (2) promote and protect their identity, (3) ensure equality and non-discrimination of minority groups, and (4) enhance effective and meaningful participation of minorities in public affairs (United Nations 2010: 7–13).

This scope of protection of minority rights – and thus its global recognition – is reflected across a whole regimen of international treaties and agreements, such as:

- The 2001 Durban Declaration, which affirms that 'the ethnic, cultural, linguistic and religious identity of minorities, where they exist, must be protected and that persons belonging to such minorities should be treated equally and enjoy their human rights and fundamental freedoms without discrimination of any kind'.

- The 2001 UNESCO Declaration on Cultural Diversity, which encourages the production, safeguarding and dissemination of diversified contents in the media and global information networks, including promoting the role of public radio and television services in the development of audio-visual productions of good quality.

- The International Covenant on Economic, Social and Cultural Rights, which enjoins upon States Parties to guarantee that the rights enunciated therein will be exercised without discrimination of any kind as to race, colour, sex, language, religion, political or other opinion, national or social origin, property, birth or other status.

- General comment No. 14 (2000) of the Committee on Economic, Social and Cultural Rights on the right to the highest attainable standard of health, which states that health facilities, goods and services must be within safe physical reach for all sections of the population, especially vulnerable or marginalized groups, including ethnic minorities.

- The 2003 UNESCO Convention for the Safeguarding of the Intangible Cultural Heritage, which provides safeguards and promotes the practices, representations, expressions, knowledge, skills – as well as the associated instruments, objects, artefacts and cultural spaces – that communities, groups and, in some cases, individuals recognize as part of their cultural heritage.

- The 2005 UNESCO Convention on the Protection and Promotion of the Diversity of Cultural Expressions, which emphasizes the importance of the recognition of equal dignity and respect for all cultures, including that of persons belonging to minorities, and of the freedom to create, produce, disseminate, distribute and have access to traditional cultural expressions (United Nations 2010: 14–18).

It is evident, then, that there is no need for additional norm setting. What is important is to raise greater awareness about these instruments among media development actors, including media owners, editors, journalists, journalism educators and media policy-makers. We need to concentrate on better interpretation and more effective implementation of existing norms, particularly those relating to the promotion and protection of the human rights of minority groups.

Media under-representations of minorities

This takes me to the second aspect of the case for minority media: media under-representations of minorities. Without belabouring the point, there is ample evidence to prove that minorities receive the least exposure and most negative portrayals in mainstream media. Of course, we must recognize how the international and the national media landscapes have dramatically altered. As the UNESCO World Report on Investing in Cultural Diversity and Intercultural Dialogue (UNESCO 2009: 18–19) observes, recent years have seen the transnationalization of global multimedia corporations, many of them dominated by the OECD countries. The report goes on to note similar trends regarding the origin of content production in the radio, television and film sectors. In the case of cinema, the general trend is that of national productions struggling to compete with the blockbuster first produced by large movie conglomerates.

The vast majority of developing countries are still not in a position to harness their creative capacities for development in this sector, although intra-African trade in films produced by Nigeria's Nollywood shows the extent to which the African film industry is beginning to have resonance across the continent, contributing to what the UNESCO report refers to as 'counter-flows' in global information. Such 'counter-flows' are illustrated by the rapid increase in developing countries' exports of cultural and media equipment between 1996 and 2005 as a result of strategies to increase global competitiveness and an expanding demand for communication equipment. This trend facilitated the emergence of local markets for media content, though those markets remain fairly localized due to technological limitations and distribution difficulties (UNESCO 2009: 18–19).

Furthermore, the report concludes, the development in media exports from newly industrialized societies, the rise of new regional media hubs, the global significance of the Latin American audio-visual sector (telenovelas) and the rise of pan-regional/international news networks are visible signs of a 'globalization from below', which is creating new opportunities for alternative voices (minority, indigenous, diasporic communities or special interest groups) to be heard (UNESCO 2009: 18–19).

In general, however, the extent of minority penetration in international and national media outlets is still severely limited. Where it occurs, it does not reflect effective and meaningful participation by minorities, leading to what the UNESCO report refers to as a 'false diversity', masking the fact that a significant majority of people are still interested in communicating only with those who share the same cultural references (UNESCO 2009: 18–19).

Moreover, the limited range of representations in the larger national media and communication networks tends to promote the creation of stereotypes through what is often called the process of 'othering', whereby the media fix, reduce or simplify according to the dictates of standardized programmes and formats. Such media representations may serve to reinforce the power of vested interests and exacerbate social exclusion by excluding critical or marginalized voices, which usually belong to the category of 'others' (Van den Bulck and Van Poecke 1996: 159; Branston and Stafford 2003).

This process of mediated 'othering' can perhaps be better illustrated by Camilla Nordberg's study of how two of the largest Finnish and Swedish newspapers represent the Roma, a minority ethnic group. She concludes as follows:

> The narrow agenda on Romani issues covered in the Finnish press reproduces the familiar image of the Roma as outsiders, as entertainers, criminals and victims […]. This construction is underpinned by the lack of Romani representatives debating discrimination in the press. There is also a surprising shortage of feature stories recognizing the Roma not only as representatives of a collective ethnic identity, but as individual citizens with multiple identities triggered in different settings.
>
> (2006: 100)

On a more optimistic note, Nordberg argues that the shift towards more specific critical statements and the emphasis on empowerment from within could perhaps create an opportunity for increasing dialogue between a larger group of Roma and the state apparatuses about how to implement and transform those social and cultural rights that already exist in the form of legislation (2006: 100).

In Australia, a more nuanced media depiction of minority groups is offered by a content analysis that aims to examine the role representation and role evaluation of Chinese actors in English-language newspaper articles. A key finding was that:

> Chinese actors were predominantly portrayed as leaders, victims, ordinary citizens and criminals. While ordinary citizens were evaluated as neutral, and criminals as negative, both leaders and victims were evaluated in between.
>
> (Liu and Chen 2005: 144)

The study authors see the above ethnic characterization as a tempering of traditional negative stereotypes about Asian immigrants – a situation they attribute to 'multiculturalism and recognition of the increasing contribution of Asian immigrants to the Australian economy, education and culture' (Liu and Chen 2005: 144).

Minority discourse as democratic intercultural dialogue

This leads me to the third element in justifying the case for minority-sensitive media, namely that minority discourse can act as democratic intercultural dialogue. From what I have set out so far, it is clear that minority discourse calls attention to the discursive practices associated with the reality of mediated marginalization of minority groups and their attempts at self-empowerment through an alternative cultural narrative. A key feature of that minority project is to identify and expand a particular neutral setting or space for democratic dialogue with and within minority groups. In this regard, the UNESCO world report is instructive. It argues that:

> Intercultural dialogue is largely dependent on intercultural competencies, defined as the complex of abilities needed to interact appropriately with those who are different from oneself. These abilities are essentially communicative in nature, but they also involve reconfiguring our perspectives and understandings of the world; for it is not so much cultures as people – individuals and groups, with their complexities and multiple allegiances – who are engaged in the process of dialogue.
>
> (UNESCO 2009: 9)

As a communicative ability, dialogue has its problems, of course. As Cees Hamelink (2004: 29) helpfully reminds us, dialogue requires the capacity to listen and to be silent. But, he goes on, learning the language of listening is very hard in societies that are increasingly influenced by visual cultures, filled with 'talk shows' and no 'listen shows'. As such, Hamelink concludes, the essence of dialogue could and should be taught in the early stages of people's lives in school, at home, and through the media.

> As a feature of democratic (minority) discourse, (intercultural) dialogue should be seen not as involving a loss of self but as dependent upon knowing oneself and being able to shift between different frames of reference. *It requires the empowerment of all participants through capacity building and projects that permit interaction without a loss of personal or collective identity.*
>
> (UNESCO 2009: 10, emphasis added)

Within this interpretive framework, we can perhaps better appreciate why the UNESCO Constitution calls upon its Member States to promote 'the free exchange of ideas and knowledge' as well as to develop and increase 'the means of communication between their peoples and to employ these means for the purposes of mutual understanding and a truer and more perfect knowledge of each other's lives' (UNESCO 2004: 7–8).

In this regard, dialogue and intercultural learning have important effects on cultural identities produced through communication processes. More specifically, as Baraldi points out, 'research on *sojourners* in other cultures, *returnees* to their own cultures and above all *transients* between different cultures show how multicultural identities are shown in communication' (Baraldi 2006: 62).

Branston and Stafford reinforce this observation when they remind us that the media – as important vehicles of public communication – give us ways of imagining particular situations, identities and groups. These imaginings exist materially, as industries that employ people and can also have material effects on how people experience the world, and how they in turn get understood, or legislated for, or perhaps beaten up in the street by others (2003: 90).

For example, as Stuart Hall and others demonstrated, British media reporting of the so-called *mugging* phenomenon – often uncritically associated with ethnic minorities in urban cities – partly accounted for the resultant 'moral panic', which itself led to what were seen as disproportionate protective and defensive actions on the part of the judicial and police establishments (Hall et al. 1978: 20–52). Arguably, such defensive actions – rooted in the moral panic – became stumbling blocks to what should have been a robust democratic intercultural debate about questions of racial and ethnic identity vis-à-vis media representations and social regulation.

To summarize, the question of minority-sensitive media is one that, whilst commanding international recognition and harbouring the promise of democratic intercultural dialogue, echoes the continuing under-representation of minorities in media coverage. The above tripartite conceptualization offers the possibility for practical use in situations that are actually or potentially minority-insensitive. Against this background, then, let me move on to consider the question of the communicative praxis – or possible normative communication functions – inherent in the proposed theoretical framework.

Minority media as communicative praxis

Arguably, minority discourse can be appropriated as communicative praxis to stimulate informed dialogue about cultural coexistence. To this end, UNESCO is targeting minority-sensitive reforms in media and pedagogical practices. For example, through capacity-building, we can encourage news media to develop and apply minority-sensitive editorial guidelines, reflecting the campaigns currently being implemented by organizations like the Minority Rights Group International, a non-governmental organization (NGO) working to secure the rights of ethnic, religious and linguistic minorities and indigenous peoples worldwide and to promote cooperation and understanding between communities (Taneja 2009). We can also engage journalism educators to introduce intercultural competencies into their curricula. Indeed, these two approaches are the subject matter of UNESCO's project called 'Reporting on the other'. Through this project, UNESCO will be working with news media and journalism education institutions across the globe to integrate within their professional practices elements of cultural diversity.

The theoretical motif for such an intervention derives from the UNESCO world report, which offers a tripartite analytical framework for appropriating minority discourse as intercultural (dialogic) communication (UNESCO 2009: 9–10). The framework encapsulates the 'ways in which cultures relate to one another, awareness of cultural commonalities and shared goals, and identification of the challenges to be met in reconciling cultural differences' (UNESCO 2009: 9). As part of what some scholars refer to as the 'circuit of culture', news media and journalism education are interpenetrated in the cultural moments of production, identity, representation, consumption and regulation (Du Gay et al. 1997). As such, the communicative aspect of minority discourse entails treating news media and journalism education as part of that communicative-cultural nexus that can be enlisted in cultivating the kinds of democratic values and practices that can enhance cultural diversity. In this regard, three key normative communicative roles can be identified for minority media actors, namely: (1) facilitating cultural interactions, (2) unmasking cultural stereotypes and intolerance and (3) forging a common narrative.

Facilitating cultural interactions

To take the first element, facilitating cultural interactions, I see journalism and journalism education as critical to this process of cultural interactivity. Minority-sensitive editorial policy guidelines and journalism curricula could incorporate the fact that the 'intermingling' of dominant and minority cultures throughout history has found expression in a variety of cultural forms and practices, from cultural borrowings and exchanges to cultural impositions through war, conquest and colonialism. Critically important is the fact that 'even in the extreme circumstance of slavery, exchanges take place whereby certain discreet processes of reverse enculturation come to be assimilated by the dominating culture – a form of cultural "counter flow"' (UNESCO 2009: 9). As the UNESCO report further observes, recognition of the universality of human rights, along with respect for cultural diversity, has made it possible today to think in terms of genuine exchanges on the basis of equality between all the world's cultures (UNESCO 2009: 9).

Minority-sensitive editorial guidelines can help break down the barriers that often discourage and/or distort intercultural conversations. By interacting more with minorities, the often dominant-cultural inhibitions that define the operations of mainstream news media institutions could weaken, facilitating the emergence of a responsive and interactive professional culture that can accommodate minority representations.

As an example, the South African Broadcasting Corporation (SABC)'s editorial policy guidelines, which draw from a well-known past of racial disharmony, are underpinned by references to cultural diversity and human dignity – two features of minority-sensitive media. In terms of cultural diversity, the SABC undertakes to reflect 'South Africa's diverse languages, cultures, provinces and people in its programmes'. As for human dignity, it undertakes to respect 'the inherent dignity of all South Africans, reflects them in all their diversity, and does not use language or images that convey stereotypical or prejudiced notions of South Africa's races, cultures and sexes' (SABC 2004).

Furthermore, journalism education, for its part, can set in motion a long-term process of educational *conscientization* that could lead to critically-minded graduates, able to interrogate the stereotypical assumptions of dominant cultures in the newsroom. An illustration of this is the integration of dialogic intercultural journalism into existing journalism curricula as a way of expanding the repertoire of evolving journalistic literacies (Cabedoche 2013: 55).

Unmasking cultural stereotypes and intolerance

A necessary consequence of cultural interactivity could probably be the unmasking of cultural stereotypes and intolerance – which is my second point. Minority discourse attempts to unmask cultural stereotypes, which serve to 'demarcate one group from the alien "other"'. But more importantly, minority discourse, as democratic intercultural dialogue, seeks to negate the risk that dialogue may stop short at difference, which may engender intolerance.

As the UNESCO world report observes,

> most intercultural tensions are often bound up with conflicts of memory, competing interpretations of past events, and conflicts of values [...]. Where it has not been excluded by the will to power and domination, dialogue remains the key to unlocking these deep-rooted antagonisms and to pre-empting their often violent political expressions.
>
> (2009: 9)

Here, the news media, using their investigative capacities, are better placed to play a key role in unmasking any stereotypical hindrances to meaningful and effective dialogue. A particularly important role for journalists and journalism educators is to work towards reconciling 'the recognition of, protection of and respect for cultural particularities with the affirmation and promotion of universally shared values emerging from the interplay of these cultural specificities' (UNESCO 2009: 9–10).

In this regard, a capacity-building strategy to eliminate stereotypes could include media and information literacy – both for media personnel and the general citizenry. As the UNESCO world report advises us, such an initiative can help audiences to become more critical when consuming media and also help to combat unilateral perspectives. It is 'an important aspect of media access and a crucial dimension of non-formal education; it is imperative that it be promoted among civil society and media professionals as part of the effort to further mutual understanding and facilitate intercultural dialogue' (UNESCO 2009: 9–10).

For instance, the British Broadcasting Corporation's (BBC) editorial policy guidelines on the use of language amplify the need for a journalistic cadre that is *literate* about the role that media could potentially play in inadvertently fomenting intercultural strife. The guidelines stress the fact that:

> Different words cause different degrees of offence in different communities as well as in different parts of the world. A person's age, sex, education, employment, faith, nationality and where they live, may all have an impact on whether or not they might be offended [...]

Strong language is most likely to cause offence when it is used gratuitously and without editorial purpose, and when it includes:

- Sexual swearwords
- Terms of racist or ethnic abuse
- Terms of sexual and sexist abuse or abuse referring to sexuality
- Pejorative terms relating to illness or disabilities
- Casual or derogatory use of holy names or religious words, especially in combination with other strong language.

(BBC 2013)

Forging a common narrative of cultural pluralism

This leads me to the final point: forging a common narrative of cultural pluralism. The UNESCO world report observes that divergent memories have been the source of many conflicts throughout history. It goes on to argue that, although intercultural dialogue cannot hope to settle on its own all the conflicts in the political, economic and social spheres, a key element in its success is the building of a shared memory base through the acknowledgement of faults and open debate on competing memories. The framing of a common historical narrative, the report claims, can be crucial in conflict prevention and post-conflict strategies, in assuaging 'a past that is still present'. Here, an illustration cited by the report relates to South Africa's Truth and Reconciliation Commission and the national reconciliation process in Rwanda as recent examples of the political application of such a healing strategy. The showcasing of 'places of memory' – such as the Robben Island Prison in South Africa – is key to this process (UNESCO 2009: 9–10).

Arguably, news media and journalism education institutions constitute legitimate 'places of memory'. As cultural institutions, they can help a society to learn about and remember itself, shaping the understanding of values, customs and tradition to build a sense of community. By forging a common cultural-pluralistic narrative – one that builds bridges between the 'we' and the 'other' without obliterating or frowning upon difference – they can contribute towards affirming minority presence and agency in society. They can provide an inclusive and democratic platform for every group in society to gain visibility and be heard. By the same token, the media can engender suspicion, fear, discrimination and violence by strengthening stereotypes, fostering inter-group tension and excluding certain groups from public discourse, as was evident in the case of Rwanda's Radio Television Libre des Mille Collines – a private media outlet that spewed hate messages against an ethnic minority and moderate members of the Hutu majority.

Conclusion

In this chapter, I addressed the need for minority media, setting them out as a key plank of intercultural dialogue. First, I set out the case for minority-sensitive media, justifying them in terms of the increasing recognition of minorities in international human rights discourse, their continuing poor representations in the media, and the democratic potential of minority discourse as intercultural dialogue. Second, I proceeded to appropriate minority discourse as communicative praxis, sketching three key normative communicative roles for minority media actors. These are facilitating cultural interactions, unmasking cultural stereotypes and intolerance, and forging a common cultural-pluralistic narrative.

Ultimately, to speak of minority media as intercultural dialogue is to affirm the important idea that all free, independent and pluralistic media have the potential to cultivate democratic citizenship in intercultural settings. To paraphrase Peter Dahlgren (2000: 321–322), who refers to the 'empirical dimensions' of civic culture, minority-sensitive media can help us all in:

1. Providing an inclusive, pluralistic public sphere for imparting relevant (intercultural) knowledge and competencies to citizens.
2. Inculcating loyalty to (intercultural) democratic values and procedures and thus cultivating civic virtue (participation, solidarity, tolerance, courage, etc.).
3. Personifying the practices, routines, traditions associated with democratic (intercultural) citizenship.
4. Fostering the construction of the kinds of plural identities associated with democratic citizenship.

References

Aikio-Puoskari, U. and Skutnabb-Kangas, T. (2004), 'Exclusion or inclusion: Linguistic human rights for linguistic minorities', in P. Lee (ed.), *Many Voices, One Vision: The Right to Communicate in Practice*, Penang, Malaysia: World Association for Christian Communication, pp. 59–88.

Baraldi, C. (2006), 'New forms of intercultural communication in a globalized world', *The International Communication Gazette*, 68: 1, pp. 53–69.

BBC (2013), 'Editorial guidelines: Section 5: Harm and offence language', http://www.bbc. co.uk/ editorialguidelines/page/guidelines-harm-language/. Accessed 27 March 2013.

Branston, G. and Stafford, R. (2003), *The Media Student's Book*, 3rd ed, London and New York: Routledge.

Cabedoche, B. (2013), 'Intercultural journalism', in F. Banda (ed.), *Model Curricula for Journalism Education: A Compendium of New Syllabi*, Paris: UNESCO, pp. 55–64.

Dahlgren, P. (2000), 'Media, citizenship and civic culture', in J. Curran and M. Gurevitch (eds), *Mass Media and Society*, 3rd ed, London: Arnold, pp. 310–328.

Du Gay, P., Hall, S., Janes, L., Mackay, H. and Negus, K. (1997), *Doing Cultural Studies: The Story of the Sony Walkman*, London: SAGE.

Gross, L. (1998), 'Minorities, majorities and the media', in T. Liebes and J. Curran (eds), *Media, Ritual and Identity*, London and New York: Routledge, pp. 87–102.

Hall, S., Critcher, C., Jefferson, T., Clarke, J. and Roberts, B. (1978), *Policing the Crisis: Mugging, the State, and Law and Order*, New York: Holmes & Meier.

Hamelink, C. (2004), 'Grounding the human right to communicate', in P. Lee (ed.), *Many Voices, One Vision: The Right to Communicate in Practice*, Penang, Malaysia: World Association for Christian Communication, pp. 21–31.

Kperogi, F. (2006), 'Kparo: A study of the emergence and death of a minority language newspaper in Nigeria', in A. Salawu (ed.), *Indigenous Language Media in Africa*, Lagos, Nigeria: Centre for Black and African Arts and Civilisation (CBAAC), pp. 60–68.

Liu, S and Chen, G. M. (2005), 'Newspaper coverage of Chinese and group perceptions of Chinese immigrants', *Australian Journalism Review*, 27: 2, pp. 135–149.

Minority Rights Group International (2012), *Minority Voices Newsroom*, http://www.minorityvoices.org/pages/en/about.html. Accessed 5 March 2012.

Nordberg, C. (2006), 'Beyond representation: Newspapers and citizenship participation in the case of a minority ethnic group', *Nordicom Review*, 27: 2, pp. 87–104.

SABC (2004), 'SABC editorial policies', http://tinyurl.com/hbfgn4l. Accessed 27 March 2013.

Taneja, P. (ed.) (2009), *State of the World's Minorities and Indigenous Peoples 2009: Events of 2008*, London: Minority Rights Group International (MRG).

UNESCO (2004), *Constitution of the United Nations Educational, Scientific and Cultural Organization*, Paris: UNESCO, pp. 7–21.

——— (2009), *UNESCO World Report: Investing in Cultural Diversity and Intercultural Dialogue*, Paris: UNESCO.

United Nations (2010), *Minority Rights: International Standards and Guidance for Implementation*, New York: United Nations.

Van den Bulck, H. and Van Poecke, L. (1996), 'National language, identity formation, and broadcasting: The Flemish and German-Swiss communities', in S. Braman and S. Mohammadi (eds), *Globalization, Communication and Transnational Civil Society*, Cresskill, NJ: Hampton, pp. 157–77.

Chapter 10

Inside Out/Outside In: (Auto-)Ethnographic Work on the Position of the Newspaper Sub-editor

Astrid Vandendaele

Introduction

In today's globalized and increasingly digitalized world, newspaper circulation continues to fall. Many newspapers have either gone under or moved completely online. However, more than half of the readers (56 per cent) still prefer to read newspaper content in print only (Pew Research Centre 2015). Since those willing to part with cash for a newspaper understandably demand a 'good' one, a paper's quality has become more important than ever. Yet, the increase in errors causes trust in news media to remain poor, and consequently, sales to dwindle even further. Newspaper accuracy research in the United States (Charnley 1936; Meyer 1988, 2004, 2005; Maier 2005, 2007), Ireland (Fox et al., 2009), the German-speaking world (Baerns 1999; Breiden 2002), Italy and Switzerland (Porlezza, Maier and Russ-Mohl 2012; and more recently Bleyenberg forthcoming) shows that 'the press' frequently errs. Generally, vigilant readers find errors – ranging from sloppy spelling to misquotations and inaccurate headlines – in at least every other news article. Granted: journalism is a fast-paced field and therefore vulnerable to errors. In a time when newspapers sales keep recording losses, however, safeguarding quality becomes increasingly important. More and more, readers wonder: Who should make sure the much sought-after quality in newspapers is upheld?

As newspaper revenue declines, so does the industry's employment. In order to establish which newsroom jobs cannot be lost in the current economically-challenged news media landscape, determining what captures readers' attention holds great value. Eye-tracking studies found that readers do not really 'read' but rather 'scan' newspapers. Therefore, they have defined newspaper design as the task 'to give readers material that is worthy of their scan, that makes them stop scanning and start reading' (Garcia and Stark 1991: 67). Researchers in this field identified certain 'entry points', i.e. points where readers stop skimming through a page and start reading.[1] The most common entry points are (i) headlines, (ii) photos and photo captions, (iii) quotes and (iv) bulleted fact boxes (Holmqvist and Wartenberg 2005). When it comes to newspapers, what is seen is sold. Consequently, whoever is responsible for drawing the reader in is of great value for the newspaper business. After all: Those who create the aforementioned 'eye catchers' eventually attract readers. One can rightfully wonder: Who is responsible for an article's 'furniture', as sub-editor Charlotte Baxter wrote on *The Guardian* website (Baxter 2012). Who makes dry material vibrant? Who basically 'sells' the newspaper?[2]

Sub-editors and their craft

In general, readers are hesitant about whom to hold responsible. Mostly, they point to the journalist (Porlezza et al. 2012). He/she – or the publication as a whole – will have to bear the brunt of the readers' frustration in case of error, and will be applauded in case of an appealing story. But is it that straightforward?

Clearly, newswriting is seldom a solo performance (Bell 1991). Rather, a myriad of people and practices play their part. Journalistic practice embodies 'a broad range of activities' (Zelizer and Allan 2010: 62–63), including research, sourcing, narrative writing, reporting, judging, analysing, editing, cutting, typesetting etc. Just as revision is a crucial part of the writing process (Allal, Chanquoy and Largy 2004), so too is sub-editing and, thus, the sub-editors. Still, many are unsure what their role is – 'except perhaps to mess up copy or write boring/wrong/sensational headlines' (Baxter 2012). Sub-editors pride themselves on being 'the first reader'. Indeed, they are responsible for cutting copy to fit, checking journalists' copy for accuracy and correcting spelling mistakes as well as any other grammatical errors. Sub-editors or 'subs' also check copy for potential libel and contempt. Moreover, they contribute greatly to how an article is presented to the reader, which includes designing pages, selecting images and laying out stories. Clearly, sub-editors play a crucial part when it comes to both accuracy and appeal of a news story.

In an age when profit pushes newspaper management ever further to cut costs, it is common knowledge that newsroom employment has dwindled in all departments. Newspaper sub-editors have frequently drawn the short straw: signs point to a true 'endangerment' of the sub-editing profession. David Ayrton (research and information assistant organizer, National Union of Journalists) stated in *The Guardian* (Hattenstone 2009): 'There is little doubt the sub-editor has been a target for cost-cutting'. Although little research has been done on the number of sub-editors who have left journalism over the past few years, it is clear an increasing number of newspapers' editorial boards take the view that sub-editing is a functional task that no longer needs to be part of a paper's core activity.

Russial (1998) already emphasized the importance of the 'copy desks', in a time when several newspapers have, entirely or in part, dismantled them. Nearly a third of sub-editors working for US daily newspapers in 2007 were no longer employed in those positions in 2013, according to an American Society of News Editors' survey of 985 publications. Newspaper publishers around the world have been centralizing and also outsourcing their sub-editing operations to cut costs. So-called 'sub-hubs' are popping up, bringing together sometimes more than 100 sub-editors and layout designers to provide editing, layout and design for several publications at once. Possible consequences are a loss of connection with the publication. Not only style, but also local and regional specificity can be lost, in favour of a globalized take on events. Moreover, software options for journalists, such as Grammarly, PerfectIt, Tansa, the AP's StyleGuard and Lingofy, i.e. automated sub-editing subscription services, are being introduced. Increasingly, analysts are wondering if news organizations will perceive these newer automated editing tools as adequate replacements for human editors – and act accordingly.

Research focus

The aim of this chapter is twofold:

1. First of all, it zooms in on the 'forgotten stepchildren of the newsroom' (Wizda 1997: 38), the newspaper sub-editors, by summarizing research I conducted so far. As a first step towards shining a light on the sub-editors as overlooked cogs in the news production process, I consider their position within the larger organizational model of the newsroom.
2. Second, this chapter zooms out, and analyses the advantages, challenges and possible pitfalls media researchers are faced with when conducting research from within the newsroom (Outside => In). I also look at my own perspective, and discuss the potential benefits – if any – having a practitioner background as an academic can entail (Inside => Out).

The chapter is organized as follows: first, I provide a succinct overview of (the lack of) previous research on the sub-editor. Second, I briefly shed light on the first step I have taken in the study of the sub-editor and the sub-editing stage. Next, I focus on my own research perspective, wearing both the sub-editor's (Insider) and the academic's (Outsider) hats. Then, based on my own experiences, I discuss a few guidelines targeted at budding media researchers who choose a praxis-oriented perspective on their subjects/colleagues. This chapter concludes with some final remarks, and a number of avenues for further research.

Previous research: The sub-editor, a 'shady' character

As mentioned in the introduction, sub-editors are mostly forgotten by the readership. Since no byline is present to recognize their work, they tend to be overshadowed by journalists, the 'visible' experts, whose work is most noticeably on display in the newspaper as they are the credited authors. Similarly, academia has long omitted the sub-editor, as he has remained understudied in various disciplines related to the study of newsmaking and newswriting. In what follows, I provide a concise overview.

Since linguistic interest in the news has long been limited to analysis of the 'news product', the news production processes prior to its final materialization – be it on paper, online, on television or radio – have been ignored. However, as media linguists have come to learn from journalism scholars, it is exactly those processes that shed light on why the news is what it is, and how situated language activities in the newsrooms and contextual resources, social settings and the newsmakers themselves are related.[3]

Research into news production processes has shown how the production of news texts is complex and involves several skilled professionals besides the journalist. Just as the news foregrounds some stories and obscures others, the scope of journalism studies has been less than fully comprehensive. For one thing, when looking at the scholarship on news production processes, it is clear that journalists and editors are predominantly cast as the main 'actors', while other journalism professionals are ignored. Although their tasks have been listed in several journalism textbooks, when we look at classic newsroom ethnographies (White 1950; Breed 1955; Tunstall 1971; Epstein 1973; Schlesinger 1978; Tuchman 1978; Gans 1979; Fishman 1980), more often than not the spotlight has been on the journalist. Wahl-Jorgensen and Hanitzsch (2009) write:

> The neglect of journalistic practices marginalized within the newsroom is particularly alarming. Research tends to overlook particular categories of news workers. It predominantly charts the professional cultures of privileged full-time news reporters over casualized, multi-skilled, and free-lance journalists, to mention just a few neglected categories.
>
> (Wahl-Jorgensen and Hanitzsch 2009: 12)

Although news production studies dating back to the 1970s have captured the newsroom goings-on in considerable detail, little in-depth analysis has been done about the sub-editing stage. Moreover, research on sub-editing has been highly nationalized. There is a decent body of work on US newspaper sub-editors. Examples are Solomon (1995); Cook and Banks (1993); Cook, Banks and Turner (1993); Keith (2000, 2005a 2005b); Zahler (2007).

From a linguistics angle, the sub-editor has been somewhat ignored: Critical discourse analysts looking at newspaper headlines, for instance (Fairclough 1989), hardly ever recognize the sub-editor as their author. When headline authorship is attributed, this usually happens in passing, and in rather tentative terms: 'the newspaper', 'the journalist' or simply 'editorial changes' (Develotte and Rechniewski 2001), as well as 'writer' (Mahmood, Javed and Mahmood 2011) or 'headline writer' (Greco 2009; Vandenberghe 2014), to name but a few examples.

When it comes to writing studies, extensive research has been done on editing and revision (see e.g. Hayes et al. 1987; Hacker et al. 1994; Allal et al. 2004; Bisaillon 2007). However, little space has been devoted to professional editing. It is therefore not really surprising that revision/editing is often defined in terms of a 'subprocess' of writing (Alamargot and Chanquoy 2001; Fitzgerald 1987; Rijlaarsdam Couzijn and van den Bergh 2004; Laflamme 2007). Only on a few occasions the work of the sub-editor is recognized (Dahl 2015 and Ross 2013).

Consumption of newswriting – i.e. focus on those on the other end of the writing process spectrum, the readers – has been dealt with rather elaborately in research. Eye-tracking research has provided us with exhaustive insights into the reader's interaction with a variety of media stimuli and his priorities with respect to text. Moreover, this type of research helps to describe the distribution of the reader's attention, be it in print or in a digital publication (Garcia and Stark 1991; Hansen 1994; Stenfors et al. 2003; Outing and Ruel 2004; Holmqvist and Wartenberg 2005; Holsanova et al. 2006). With the exception of Wartenberg and Holmqvist (2004), this reception-oriented approach again overlooks the sub-editing stage.

By focusing on the sub-editors and their practices, this chapter aims to contribute to the (limited) work done in the past.

The story so far

This chapter features within a larger linguistic-ethnographic study of the (textual) interventions by newspaper sub-editors[4] and ties in with a shift in media discourse studies focusing on news production practices and their relation to text, talk and social meaning (Cotter 2010; Van Hout 2010; Jacobs and Tobback 2013).

Methodology: Into the newsroom

Our study of sub-editing practices draws heavily on ethnographic research methodologies: participant observation on the one hand, and interviews conducted at the news desks of a large Belgian broadsheet and a large Dutch national daily on the other. The Belgian Dutch-language newspaper has its headquarters near Brussels, and reaches about 251,000[5] readers a day. The Dutch paper has its headquarters in Amsterdam, and currently has a circulation (print) of 264,174.[6] They are both known as progressive quality papers targeting a wide, well-educated audience.

The two newspapers have become closely linked following the acquisition of the Dutch newspaper in 2009 by a Belgian publishing house. The arrival of the Belgian publisher was initially met with mixed feelings in the Netherlands. According to Sanders (2012), because it resulted in a considerable number of Dutch layoffs, mostly among journalists, and a growing 'interference' by shareholders in the newsroom, which 'could prove to be problematic for journalistic independence' (98).

My data include field notes, audio-recordings of storyboard meetings, recordings and transcriptions of semi-structured interviews with sub-editors, journalists and other key players in the newsroom, and (computer screen shots of) articles at various stages of production.

Collecting empirical evidence and additional materials from the newsroom, being able to observe newsroom interactions, participating in the day-to-day journalistic practices and being part of the newswriting process helped me to gain insights I could never have attained otherwise. When looking at media (discourse) clearly, an ethnographic approach brings along the added advantage of being able to find out where the community's priorities lie, rather than the linguists'.

Owing to a continuous back and forth between existing literature on the one hand, and the time spent in the field on the other, I was able to frame the sub-editing stage of newswriting within existing newsroom frameworks, and to analyse the level of interference in the sub-editing stage of newswriting. In what follows, I briefly go over some of our initial results.

The lowlands newsroom model

It is noteworthy that the focus on the relation of the newsroom space and journalistic work has been limited, especially when it comes to sub-editing. Whereas the traditional centralized newsroom setting may appear somewhat anachronistic in this age of digital and networked media (Rodgers 2014), sub-editing is still very much rooted in the newsroom. Researchers in media discourse have long been aware of the existence of different newsroom models: there are fundamental differences between newspapers' organizational structures, although the final product might not allude to that. Therefore, as an initial move in my aim to open the door to future journalism studies research of sub-editors, we considered their position within the larger organizational model of the newsroom (Vandendaele and Jacobs 2013). We observed how, at both the Belgian and the Dutch newspapers, the newsroom model differs from those previously described, which impacted on the sub-editing practices.

Esser (1998) discussed two ways a newsroom can be organized: the German model on the one hand, and the Anglo-Saxon model on the other. Whereas British and American newsrooms favour centralized newsrooms with a high division of labour, German newspapers tend to decentralize their work by maintaining many branch offices, completing various sections of the newspapers. Moreover, employees in German newsrooms tend to have more responsibilities than their Anglo-Saxon counterparts. In Germany, a 'Redakteur' will be involved in the entire production process: he will collect and select information – even pictures – he will write the actual piece and captions, will proofread the article, will be occupied with page layout and will coordinate all these activities. In British and American newsrooms, however, employees will be specialized, and asked to zoom in on one aspect.

In the Belgian newsroom, we noticed a strict division of labour termed 'In/Out'. In the early 1990s, the Belgian owner of the paper introduced 'In/Out' at the largest Belgian tabloid newspaper. The system has been jokingly referred to as 'The Gospel' (Oremus 2009: 16) in the newsrooms of several other papers belonging to the publishing house, where the model had been implemented. 'In/Out' is essentially a way in which to organize the newsroom. The most important divide within any newsroom is that between the 'news gatherers' (i.e. the general reporters and specialists) and the 'news processors' (i.e. the sub-editors and the layout sub-editors). According to a sub-editing chief, 'In/Out' actually divides the newsroom into 'two completely different worlds'; in the Belgian newsroom, there is a physical divide between the journalists ('In'), as they are placed on the far left of the newsroom, and the sub-editors/layout sub-editors ('Out') who are seated on the far right of the newsroom. The room is cut in half by the central news desk at which the chiefs of all the newspaper's sections and the editor(s)-in-chief are seated. In the morning, articles are started on the 'In' side and are then passed on to the 'Out' side, via the central news desk. One sub-editing chief compared them to 'diamonds in the rough', being fed through and processed by the sub-editing funnel. Once the boundary to 'Out' is crossed, stories are hardly ever sent back to the 'In' side, despite sub-editors' claims in the interviews. Although they stated repeatedly how confronting a journalist with a (finished) story that did not comply with standards is a must, during our fieldwork, this rarely happened.

'In/Out' can be placed roughly in the middle of the continuum described by Esser. However, the newsroom model we observed is closer in nature to the Anglo-Saxon system, than the German one. We therefore proposed 'Lowlands newsroom model' as a label, differentiating it from the Anglo-Saxon and German models. The Belgian newsroom was centralized and open-plan, as the Anglo-Saxon newsrooms tend to be. The sub-editors we observed did perform a distinct and rather specialized job, but were more involved in the 'newspaper making' process than their Anglo-Saxon colleagues. Although they are not as 'multifunctional' as the German 'Redakteur', they are charged with more responsibilities than their Anglo-Saxon counterparts.

When discussing the 'In/Out' system during the interviews, one sub-editing chief who had recently joined the Belgian newspaper after having worked at the Dutch daily in our study for 28 years, made looking more closely into the model of the 'sister newsroom' seem crucial when he said that even though both newspapers use 'In/Out', there are 'huge differences' between the functioning of both newsrooms. We discovered that, although the Dutch newspaper had adopted the (Belgian) 'In/Out' system relatively recently, they were somehow able to implement it more successfully, as it was claimed the daily battle with the deadline was won more frequently. In order to compare, we decided to continue research in the Dutch newsroom. There, we uncovered a number of 'huge differences' between the newsrooms, concerning organizational structure, workload and sub-editor profile.

Newsroom layout

At both newspapers the editorial floor was roughly divided into two parts – not only organizationally, but also physically. The 'In/Out' system was thus reflected on both those levels. At the Belgian paper, the newsroom was basically divided into two halves, with 'In' and 'Out' each at opposite sides of the rectangular newsroom. In the middle, the central news desk, headed by the editors-in-chief and the chiefs in charge of every news section, separated it. As articles were passed on from the journalists to the sub-editors and layout sub-editors they literally and figuratively went through the editorial filter, represented by the news desk. At the Dutch newspaper however, the sub-editors' and layout sub-editors' desks ('Out') were centrally located in the newsroom, next to the central news desk. The desks belonging to all other sections were spread around the edges of the rectangular room. Each section consisted of a number of desks set up in rows, all directed towards the centre of the room, where the central news desk and the 'Out' side were situated. The sub-editors, 'almost as invisible in the newsroom [...] as they are to readers' (Keith 2000: 43), were thus made hard to overlook. Because of the sub-editors' physical proximity to the journalists, communication was clearly facilitated. A sub-editing chief who worked at both the Dutch and the Belgian newspapers stated that although 'In and Out are worlds apart, close communication is key; there is still need for close cooperation between sub-editor and journalist'.

It is precisely communication that seemed to be somewhat hindered in the Belgian newsroom. One could claim that because of the harsh physical divide between the journalists ('In') and the sub-editors/layout sub-editors ('Out'), news workers from either side were not as likely to walk over and discuss certain issues. In the Dutch newsroom, the physical set-up actually encouraged this. Observations taught us how, because of newsroom layout, it was in fact accomplished far more easily. They also revealed how, because of the physical closeness in the Dutch newsroom, employees from both sides actually seemed to be better acquainted.

The sub-editors' central location in the newsroom also underscored how sub-editors and reporters have a fundamentally different 'mission statement'. The importance of the sub-editor's task as 'paper maker' was highlighted in the Dutch newsroom by being placed at the heart of the busy newsroom.

Workload

In the Dutch newsroom, we observed how each sub-editor was paired up with a layout sub-editor, usually for the entire day. Both were, as a team, responsible for a spread, i.e. two facing pages, often with related matter extending across the fold. Contrary to most mid-sized and large US papers, where the unit assignment is the story, in the Belgian newsroom each sub-editor was assigned up to eight pages, often teaming up with several layout sub-editors. When we compared this to the Dutch newspaper, which is printed in a tabloid format, 'smaller, so fewer letters, less text', sub-editors were assigned a maximum of four pages. Moreover, in the Dutch newsroom, an additional proofreader is part of the 'Out' team. Whereas the sub-editor focuses on the editing job on his computer screen, the proofreader will only check printouts for spelling mistakes and layout inconsistencies. In the Belgian newsroom, proofreading their own pages on paper was also included in the sub-editor's job description.

Sub-editor profile

Our time spent in the Dutch newsroom actually revealed that the profile of a sub-editor is somewhat different to what we had previously experienced in the Belgian one. At the Dutch newspaper, it is exceptional for sub-editors not to write (or have written) themselves. The editors-in-chief are aware of the lack of appreciation for the job – this and gruelling schedules are mentioned first as reasons – but interviews revealed there is a system in place where, every couple of years, sub-editors can go back to full-time reporting, should they choose to do so. The previous job experience explains the noticeable seniority of the Dutch sub-editors, in contrast to the junior staffers in the Belgian newsroom's 'Out' side; a much larger proportion has recently graduated and they generally indicated how they do not see themselves employed as sub-editors for very long. A Belgian sub-editor stated that 'a good sub-editor' should have the 'authority to tell a journalist what needs to be altered, or what just isn't good enough', and how he should 'be in a position to be able to rectify' an article. Our fieldwork showed, however, how the sub-editors' youth and relative lack of experience make exercising authority over senior colleagues at the 'In' side challenging.

The sub-editors in the Netherlands were often more senior. Most of them could look back on a full career, and had already proven to be valuable members of the reporting staff. The newsroom juniors most often took on the reporter role. From our observations, it seems that, in the Belgian newsroom, this is the other way around.

Although voicing opinions and engaging in dialogue with the 'In' side seems to happen more easily in the Dutch newsroom, our informants on both sides insist there is still a long way to go. Sub-editing chiefs from both Flemish and Dutch sides commented: 'The authority of the sub-editors should be made bigger; this is the only way to make a decent newspaper' and 'The power should gravitate to the Out-side'.

In sum, by taking this first step we have shown how the model in place in the newsroom, including its spatial layout, largely determines the sub-editor's modus operandi. The model we encountered in the Belgian and Dutch newsrooms was termed the 'Lowlands newsroom model', as it proved to be different from the ones in Germany and the United Kingdom described by Esser.

When looking at the Lowlands newsroom model we observed that the Dutch version demonstrates better sub-editing practice in terms of timing, communication and visibility because of newsroom layout, division of workload and a varied sub-editor profile.

Research perspective: Inside out/outside in

It is clear that in this case the boundaries of practice and academia have been blurred from the start. On the one hand, being a researcher with a journalistic background proved to be most beneficial for this study. On the other, being part of both worlds turned out to be problematic at times – A *double identity* within this strand of research is not always the gift media scholars believe it to be.

Advantages and challenges

Being a media practitioner and researcher at once provided me with *first-hand experience of a lack of knowledge of the sub-editor's* job contents beyond the newsroom. Moreover, the current turning point in the world of journalism, and the possible extinction of sub-editors, made me fully understand *the urgency of research into sub-editing*: how will the danger of extinction of the profession, and the upcoming centralized and automated editing impact on sub-editors?

Because of my professional link with a Belgian newspaper, I was quickly allowed to enter the newsroom as a participant observer. The all-important issue of *access* for this type of media research, and the necessary level of *trust*, was a given, since I was regarded a 'fellow practitioner'. Having 'insider knowledge' is clearly beneficial. Giddens (1982), for one, stated that valid descriptions of social activities presume that researchers themselves possess those skills necessary to participate in the activities described: 'It involves "mutual knowledge," shared by observer and participants whose action constitutes and reconstitutes the social world' (Giddens 1982: 15). Being a sub-editor, and thus possessing the necessary skills and sharing (professional) knowledge, allowed me to quickly participate to a high degree in newsroom activities, to 'make the invisible visible' (Cottle 2007: 5).

Being granted access for academic purposes should not be treated lightly in these economically challenging times for news media. As mentioned, the newspaper publishing industry is currently under threat since competition from other forms of media is increasingly limiting its market. The newspaper we used for our fieldwork is currently facing similar problems, forcing its (ever-changing) editorial board into taking radical decisions, in order to constantly stay one step ahead of the game, and to keep the paper looking 'fresh' and appealing to an ever-dwindling readership. As I switched from an employee to an observer role, *confusion* arose about my role. I was repeatedly faced with *limitations to a once quasi-unlimited degree of access* and with *varying degrees of trust*. For instance, at the start of our study, I was allowed to attend and record numerous editorial meetings and conduct interviews with a great variety of news workers, ranging from layout-editors to the former editor-in-chief. Unfortunately, growing job insecurity, increasing threat of mass lay-offs and the newspaper's continuous attempts to reach the diminishing readership put strains on the tentative and carefully-built relationship. We saw how the added external economic pressure on the newsroom significantly impacts not only the newsroom dynamics, but also the 'insider' attitude towards 'outsiders', and the threat they potentially pose. Gaining and continuing a relationship of trust and constantly negotiating my position and access therefore made for a treacherous journey, influencing (and inhibiting) data collection, but simultaneously providing a valuable insight into a present-day newsroom.

Up, down and sideways

The dual position of being an Insider (practitioner) looking Out, to the world of academia versus that of an Outsider (researcher), looking In, into the newsroom, brings with it a great deal of tension. However, the three-way approach anthropologist suggested by Laura Nader (2008) can be of great value to researchers going into the field of media, either being full-time academics or as those with a 'double identity'. Nader claimed that researchers should study 'up, down and sideways simultaneously'. In what follows, I shall briefly illustrate how this helped shape our research. Continuing to wear both the practitioner's and the academic's hats myself, my goal is to provide budding media researchers who choose a praxis-oriented perspective on their subjects/colleagues with a few helpful guidelines.

It has been argued that journalism researchers have focused on 'studying up' or have been engaged in 'elite research' (Conti and O'Neil 2007), by 'paying a disproportionate amount of attention to elite individuals, news organizations and texts' (Wahl-Jorgensen and Hanitzsch 2009: 12). This is illustrated by myriad studies of news organizations, which have mainly focused on journalism produced in large (national) television and newspaper newsrooms in elite nations. Based on the choice of newsrooms, it could be argued that I too have been susceptible to this tendency. The newsrooms selected as preferred research loci belong to two, large national broadsheets. However, as it 'is in the big, highly-tuned newspapers that the craft of subbing is developed to the highest degree' (Sellers 1986), this seemed a valid choice.

At the same time, in focusing on the sub-editor, 'labouring anonymously' (Keith 2000: 43) at 'the peripheries of the newsroom' (Wahl-Jorgensen and Hanitzsch 2009: 12), I am in a way 'studying down', and attempting to acknowledge an overlooked part of the news production chain.

Finally, 'studying sideways' is an integral part of my research stance: I procured 'insider knowledge' as both a researcher and a sub-editor. This way, I simultaneously observe colleagues as a researcher, and should be fully aware of the (possible) intrusiveness of an onlooker as a professional. In fact, all investigations into journalism can be seen as 'studying sideways' as we, researchers, are looking into a craft not that different from our own. This stance could be a way of slowly bridging the gap between the separate worlds of media studies and the media.

Concluding remarks

Media practitioners have been known to claim they get little in return for the access they grant to academics to interpret their world. Moreover, they feel that the research that has been done is rarely of any practical use. By focusing on the disappearing craft of newspaper sub-editing as a researcher with a practitioner background, I aim to counter this view, and help build a bridge between academic media and journalism on the one hand, and media and journalism practitioners on the other.

In my research, I shed initial light on the previously understudied sub-editor. Due to the nature of their job, sub-editors tend to be not fully recognized for their knowledge, skills and know-how. This is especially true in a time when it is argued that production outsourcing is the way ahead, meaning entrusting sub-editing to 'subbing factories' staffed by people who are usually unfamiliar with a newspaper's style or identity. First, I looked at the larger newsroom structures in which sub-editors operate (Vandendaele and Jacobs 2013) by describing his place in the 'Lowlands newsroom model' at work in a Belgian and a Dutch daily newspaper. I demonstrate how, although the same newsroom model is in place in both newsrooms, the spatial setting, division of workload and the sub-editor's profile impact on the sub-editor's ability to intervene in the news production process. Exploring this newsroom model is necessary, not only to considering the study of general newsroom flow, but also as a valid contribution to the debate surrounding the future of the newspaper 'subber'.

In order to approach my subject, I took on the role of participant observer, bringing to that role my professional experience as a sub-editor. This additional knowledge helped to bring about insights about the urgency of this study, as well as news worker interaction, job satisfaction and the sub-editor's position within the dynamic constellation of the newsroom. Difficulties did arise related to my 'double identity' in the newsroom, yet by simultaneously studying 'up, down and sideways', I was able to continue and gain results that I would not have attained otherwise.

Further academic research into sub-editing from this perspective is needed. Another step was therefore an investigation of the micro-discursive practices sub-editors use to revise news articles before publication (Vandendaele, Van Praet and De Cuypere 2015). Sub-editors contribute a considerable amount to how an article is presented to the reader, thus influencing the way readers are drawn into the story. Their role as 'marketeers' of a newspaper is worthy of more in-depth scholarly scrutiny in order to move towards a more complete definition of the sub-editor as a – in the language of Gieber (1964) – genuine 'newspaperman'. After all, as their ranks keep diminishing and more is outsourced to 'subhubs', closer scientific analysis of sub-editors' interventions in the news production process is not only of great value for the future of journalistic writing, but for journalism as a whole.

References

Alamargot, D. and Chanquoy, L. (2001), 'General introduction: A definition of writing and a presentation of the main models', in D. Alamargot and L. Chanquoy (eds), *Through the Models of Writing*, College Studies in Writing, Boston, Dordrecht, New York and London: Kluwer, pp. 1–29.

Allal, L., Chanquoy, L. and Largy, P. (eds) (2004), *Revision: Cognitive and Instructional Processes*, The Netherlands: Kluwer.

Baerns, B. (1999), 'Kommunikationsrisiken und Risikokommunikation: Das Nationale Risiko- verfahren (Stufenplanverfahren) zur "Pille der dritten Generation"' ('The risks of communication and risk communication: The national risk method [step plan] for the "Pill of the Third Generation"'), in L. Rolke and V. Wolff (eds), *Wie die Medien die Wirklichkeit steuern und selber gesteuert werden*, Wiesbaden, Germany: Opladen, pp. 93–125.

Baxter, C. (2012), 'What do subeditors do?', *The Guardian*, 26 July, https://www.theguardian.com/commentisfree/2012/jul/26/subeditor-role-changed. Accessed 7 November 2016.

Bell, A. (1991), *The Language of News Media*, Oxford: Blackwell.

Bisaillon, J. (2007), 'Professional editing strategies used by six editors', *Written Communication*, 24: 4, pp. 295–322.

Bleyenberg, L. (forthcoming), *Onderzoeksrapport foutenratio bij 'De Standaard'*, Ghent, Belgium: Ghent University.

Blommaert, J. and Dong, J. (2010), *Ethnographic Fieldwork: A Beginner's Guide*, Bristol, UK: Multilingual Matters.

Breed, W. (1955), 'Social control in the newsroom: A functional analysis', *Social Forces*, 33: 4, pp. 326–35.

Breiden, A. (2002), 'Die Rolle der Nachrichtenagenturen im Zusammenspiel von Öffentlichkeitsarbeit und Journalismus (The role of news agencies in the interaction of public relations and journalism)', Master's thesis, Freie Universität Berlin.

Charnley, M. V. (1936), 'Preliminary notes on a study of newspaper accuracy', *Journalism Quarterly*, 13, pp. 394–401.

Conti, J. A. and O'Neil, M. (2007), 'Studying power: Qualitative methods and the global elite', *Qualitative Research*, 7, pp. 63–82.

Cook, B. and Banks, S. R. (1993), 'Predictors of job burnout in reporters and copy editors', *Journalism Quarterly*, 70: 1, pp. 108–18.

Cook, B., Banks, S. R. and Turner, R. J. (1993), 'The effects of work environment on burnout in the newsroom', *Newspaper Research Journal*, 14: 3–4, pp. 123–36.

Cotter, C. (2010), *News Talk: Investigating the Language of Journalism*, Cambridge: Cambridge University Press.

Cottle, S. (2007), 'Ethnography and news production: New(s) developments in the field', *Sociology Compass*, 1: 1, pp. 1–16.

Creese, A. (2008), 'Linguistic ethnography', in K. A. King and N. H. Hornberger (eds), *Encyclopedia of Language and Education, Vol. 10: Research Methods in Language and Education*, 2nd ed, London: Springer Science + Business Media LLC, pp. 229–41.

Dahl, T. (2015), 'Contested science in the media: Linguistic traces of news writers' framing activity', *Written Communication*, 32: 1, pp. 39–65.

Develotte, C. and Rechniewski, E. (2001), 'Discourse analysis of newspaper headlines: A methodological framework for research into national representations', *Web Journal of French Media Studies*, 4: 1.

Epstein, E. (1973), *News from Nowhere: Television and the News*, New York: Random House.

Esser, F. (1998), 'Editorial structures and work principles in British and German newsrooms', *European Journal of Communication*, 13: 3, pp. 375–405.

Esser, F. (1999), 'Tabloidization of news: A comparative analysis of Anglo-American and German press journalism', *European Journal of Communication*, 14: 3, pp. 291–324.

Fairclough, N. (1989), *Language and Power*, London: Longman.

Fishman, M. (1980), *Manufacturing the News*, Austin: Texas University Press.

Fitzgerald, J. (1987), 'Research in revision in writing', *Review of Educational Research*, 57: 4, pp. 481–506.

Fox, C., Knowlton, S., Maguire, Á. and Trench, B. (2009), *Accuracy in Irish Newspapers*, Report for the Press Council of Ireland and the Office of the Press Ombudsman, Dublin: Centre for Society Information and Media, Dublin City University.

Gans, H. J. (1979), *Deciding What's News: A Study of CBS Evening News, NBC Nightly News, Newsweek, and Time*, New York: Pantheon.

Garcia, M. and Stark, P. (1991), *Eyes on the News*, St. Petersburg: The Poynter Institute.

Giddens, A. (1982), *Profiles and Critiques in Social Theory*, London: Macmillan.

Gieber, W. (1964), 'News is what newspapermen make it', in L. A. Dexter and D. M. White (eds), *People, Society, and Mass Communication*, New York: Free Press, pp. 173–82.

Greco, S. (2009), 'Metaphorical headlines in business, finance and economic magazines', *Linguistica e Filologia*, 28, pp. 193–211.

Hacker, D. J., Plumb, C., Butterfield, E. C., Quathamer, D. and Heineken, E. (1994), 'Text revision: Detection and correction of errors', *Journal of Educational Psychology*, 86, pp. 65–78.

Hansen, J. P. (1994), *Analyse af læsernes informationsprioritering*, Kognitiv Systemgruppen, Forskningscenter Risø, Roskilde, Unpublished report.

Hattenstone, S. (2009), 'Goodbye to all this?', *The Guardian*, 23 February, https://www.theguardian.com/media/2009/feb/23/subeditors-cost-cutting-newspapers. Accessed 11 April 2017.

Hayes, J. R., Flower, L. S., Schriver, K. A., Stratman, J. F. and Carey, L. (1987), 'Cognitive processes in revision', in S. Rosenberg (ed.), *Advances in Applied Psycholinguistics*, 2, pp. 176–240.

Holmqvist, K. and Wartenberg, C. (2005), 'The role of local design factors for newspaper reading behaviour – An eye-tracking perspective', *Lund University Cognitive Studies*, 12, pp. 1–21.

Holsanova, J., Rahm, H. and Holmqvist, K. (2006), 'Entry points and reading paths on the newspaper spread: Comparing a semiotic analysis with eye-tracking measurements', *Visual Communication*, 5: 1, pp. 65–93.

Jacobs, G. and Tobback, E. (2013), 'Is language a news value in Belgium? A case study of the use of Dutch-language quotes in the French-language TV news', *Journalism Studies*, 14: 3, pp. 407–22.

Keith, S. (2000), 'The existential copy-editor', *Journal of Mass Media Ethics*, 15: 1, pp. 43–57.

Keith, S. (2005a), 'Copy editor job satisfaction lowest at small newspapers', *Newspaper Research Journal*, 26: 2–3, pp. 6–26.

Keith, S. (2005b), 'Newspaper copy editors' perceptions of their ideal and real ethics roles', *Journalism and Mass Communication Quarterly*, 82: 4, pp. 930–51.

Laflamme, C. (2007), 'L'autorévision et la révision professionnelle: Un regard sur les contexts de production de l'activité révisionnelle', in J. Bisaillon (ed.), *La révision professionnelle: Processus, stratégies et pratiques*, Québec City, Canada: Éditions Nota Bene.

Mahmood, M. A., Javed, S. and Mahmood, R. (2011), 'A critical discourse analysis of the news headlines of budget of Pakistan FY 2011–2012', *Interdisciplinary Journal of Contemporary Research in Business*, 3: 5, pp. 120–129.

Maier, S. R. (2005), 'Accuracy matters: A cross-market assessment of newspaper error and credibility', *Journalism & Mass Communication Quarterly*, 82: 3, pp. 533–51.

Maier, S. R. (2007), 'Setting the record straight: When the press errs, do corrections follow?', *Journalism Practice*, 1: 1, pp. 33–43.

Meyer, P. (1988), 'Defining and measuring credibility of newspapers: Developing an index', *Journalism Quarterly*, 65: 3, pp. 567–574.

Meyer, P. (2004), *The Vanishing Newspaper: Saving Journalism in the Information Age*, Columbia: University of Missouri Press.

Meyer, P. and Kim, K-H. (2005), 'Survey yields five factors of newspaper quality', *Newspaper Research Journal*, 26: 1, pp. 6–15.

Nader, L. (2008), 'Strategies of subordination – In reverse', Key note address at Fifth Annual Public Anthropology Conference: Supporting Social Movements, College of Arts and Sciences, American University, Washington, DC, 31 October–1 November.

NT&T (2011), 'Towards a linguistics of news production', *Journal of Pragmatics*, 43, pp. 1843–1852.

Oremus, F. (2009), 'We zijn geen wonderjongens' ('We are no wonder boys'), *De Journalist*, 114, p. 16.

Outing, S. and Ruel, L. (2004), 'Eyetrack III: Online news consumer behavior in the age of multimedia', http://www.poynterextra.org/eyetrack2004/history.html. Accessed 13 March 2015.

Pew Research Centre (2015), 'State of the news media', http://www.journalism.org/2015/04/29/newspapers-fact-sheet. Accessed 22 May 2016.

Porlezza, C., Maier, S. R. and Russ-Mohl, S. (2012), 'News accuracy in Switzerland and Italy', *Journalism Practice*, 6: 4, pp. 530–46.

Rampton, B., Tusting, K., Maybin, J., Barwell, R., Creese, A. and Lytra, V. (2004), 'UK linguistic ethnography: A discussion paper', *UK Linguistic Ethnography Forum*, http://www.lingethnog. org. Accessed 5 February 2015.

Rijlaarsdam, G., Couzijn, M. and van den Bergh, H. (2004), 'The study of revision as a writing process and as a learning-to-write-process', in L. Allal, L. Chanquoy and P. Largy (eds), *Revision: Cognitive and Instructional Processes*, Boston/Dordrecht, Netherlands/New York/ London: Kluwer, pp. 189–207.

Rodgers, S. (2014), 'The architectures of media power: Editing, the newsroom and urban public space', *Space and Culture*, 17: 1, pp. 69–84.

Ross, D. (2013), 'Common topics and commonplaces of environmental rhetoric', *Written Communication*, 30: 1, pp. 91–131.

Russial, J. (1998), 'Goodbye copy desks, hello trouble?', *Newspaper Research Journal*, 19: 2, pp. 2–17.

Sanders, M. (2012), 'Wie bezit het nieuws? De doortocht van De Persgroep in Nederland' ('Who owns the news?'), *Apache*, 27 January, http://www.apache.be. Accessed 7 November 2016.

Schlesinger, P. (1978), *Putting Reality Together: BBC News*, London: Methuen.

Sellers, Leslie. 1972. *The Simple Subs Book*. Oxford: Pergamon Press.

Solomon, W. S. (1995), 'The site of newsroom labor: The division of editorial practices', in H. Hardt and B. Brennen (eds), *Newsworkers: Toward a History of the Rank and File*, Minneapolis: University of Minnesota Press, pp. 110–34.

Stenfors, I., Morén, J. and Balkenius, C. (2003), 'Behavioural strategies in web interaction: A view from eye-movement research', in R. Radach, J. Hyona and H. Deubel (eds), *The Mind's Eye: Cognitive and Applied Aspects of Eye Movement Research*, Amsterdam: Elsevier, pp. 633–44.

Tuchman, G. (1978), *Making News: A Study in the Social Construction of Reality*, New York: Free Press.

Tunstall, J. (ed.) (1971), *Journalists at Work*, London: Constable.

Vandenberghe, J. (2014), *Economic Conquistadors Conquer New Worlds: Metaphor Scenarios in English-language Newspaper Headlines on Spanish Foreign Direct Investment*, London: Continuum.

Vandendaele, A. and Jacobs, G. (2013), 'The Lowlands Newsroom Model: Fieldwork notes on the position of the newspaper sub-editor', *Journalism Studies*, 15: 6, pp. 879–97.

Vandendaele, A., Van Praet E. and De Cuypere, L. (2015), 'Beyond trimming the fat: The sub-editing stage of newswriting', *Written Communication*, 32: 4, pp. 368–95.

Van Hout, T. (2010), 'Writing from sources: Ethnographic insights into business news production', Ph.D. dissertation, Ghent University.

Wahl-Jorgensen, K. and Hanitzsch, T. (2009), 'On why and how we should do journalism studies', in K. Wahl-Jorgensen and T. Hanitzsch (eds), *The Handbook of Journalism Studies*, New York and London: Routledge, pp. 3–16.

Wartenberg, C. and Holmqvist, K. (2004), 'Daily newspaper layout designers' predictions of readers' visual behaviour – A case study', *Lund University Cognitive Studies*, 126, pp. 1–11.

White, D. M. (1950), 'The gate keeper: A case study in the selection of news', *Journalism Quarterly*, 27, pp. 383–90.

Wizda, S. (1997), 'Copy desk blues', *American Journalism Review*, 19: 7, pp. 36–41.

Zahler, A. (2007), 'One-third of copy editors dissatisfied with their jobs', *Newspaper Research Journal*, 28: 3, pp. 20–36.

Zelizer, B. and Allan, S. (2010), *Keywords in News & Journalism Studies*, Maidenhead, UK: Open University Press.

Notes

1 Later studies pursuing user-friendly newspaper design and looking into entry points and reading paths were carried out by Stenfors, Morén and Balkenius (2003), Outing and Ruel (2004), Holmqvist and Wartenberg (2005) and Holsanova, Rahm and Holmqvist (2006) among others.

2 See Vandendaele, Van Praet en De Cuypere (2015) for an extensive look at the sub-editor as 'marketeer'.

3 See NT&T (2011) for a position paper on this strand of media linguistics.

4 See Rampton et al. 2004; Creese 2008 and Blommaert and Dong 2010 for more on linguistic ethnography.

5 Readership in 2014. Numbers provided by CIM (Centrum voor Informatie over de Media; www.cim.be).

6 Circulation in 2014. Numbers provided by NOM (Nationaal Onderzoek Multimedia; www.nommedia.nl).

Chapter 11

Photojournalism and the Role of Images as Part of Design and Branding

David Machin and Lydia Polzer

Introduction

Academic theories and empirical work on photojournalism tend to be highly critical of the idea that the photograph can provide visual evidence or bear witness. In this chapter we look at this issue from the perspective of the professional photojournalist and page editor and as regards to the way that images are actually used, commercially by news outlets. To some extent, we show, photojournalists are aware of many of the limitations identified by academic work, yet formulate them in different terms. For the professional photojournalist the limitations of the photograph appear to be well understood but incorporated into how, in the first place, a photograph can best resonate with the requirements of different genres of news outlets and to the need to allow specific readers, in an increasingly niche-driven market, to feel that they are being personally addressed.

In the second case, and most salient for what we want to do in this chapter, there has been a wider shift in design culture in news that can be traced back to the 1980s, but which has taken a sharper turn in the second decade of the twenty-first century. This shift has involved a transformation in the way that news is built upwards from its visual appearance where design elements, across print, digital and television, are systematically deployed to communicate ideas and values about the news as a whole and the specific outlet, and as regards its relationship with the viewer. This must also be placed alongside the shift to online culture that has fostered different ways of dealing with content on behalf of the reader. In this new context, the photograph itself becomes part of design and composition. In its newer role, the image, along with typeface, colour and page composition, plays a part in signalling the kinds of attitude taken by the particular title, the kind of looking at the world it provides. From interviews with leading newspaper and Web designers around the world, it is clear that the news photograph is one part of building a brand; a way to communicate about the ideas and values carried by the outlet. In an age of intense branding, a shift to niche markets with the Internet and a change brought about partly by social media (as regards to the way readers must be addressed and engaged) visual communication, including the photograph, has a new role to play.

In this chapter, we begin by looking briefly at the core ideas in academic critiques of photojournalism. These raise important points for the role we can attribute to the news photograph. The chapter then proceeds to look first at how two newspaper designers talk about the use of news photographs as part of design. We go into detail as to how both photographs and other design elements are used precisely and strategically. We then look at the work of three photojournalists, reflecting on how their work fits into this new design culture. This allows us, at the end of the chapter, to reflect on how the academic theories now sound, asking where the best kind of dialogue can take place.

Academic work on photojournalism

Photojournalists have provided many iconic images of our times, such as Nick Ut's image of the naked girl fleeing her napalmed village during the American war in Vietnam, or Jeff Widener's *Tank Man* in Tiananmen Square. These are thought of as both bearing witness to such events and capturing the essence of the specific wider context. In the first case, we find the innocent victim of a complex and ugly war – one of the few where photojournalists were given free access; the second is a symbol of the ordinary person willing to face an oppressive regime. Books that celebrate photojournalism point to its important role in documenting and giving wide public access to key moments in history, helping to lead to social change.

It is with this point of view that academic criticisms of photojournalism take issue, not against the kind of everyday practical news work that we look at later in this chapter. And in their criticisms it could be argued that academic theories and empirical work on photojournalism hold the individual photograph against a very high bar that would not be asked of individual news texts. The photograph carries what has been called a 'burden of truth' (Newton 2000). They are held up to a standard of bearing witness to reality to which, academic work shows, they fall short for a number of reasons. Unlike the single text, of course, the photograph appears to provide an unmediated view of a scene as it happened, as if we had been there. And for authors like Barthes (1977) this is the trick of the photograph, since it conceals how and why it has been made, yet seems to provide a window to the world.

Academic work has pointed to what can be grouped here as three problems with the news photograph. First, photographs do not simply show events as they happen. Rather, they are selected moments from the flow of reality. In other words, photographs are representations that are isolated from the events that come before and afterwards. Berger (1980) described them as something seized from ongoing experience. They are not, therefore, authentic representations of that process of events. Sontag (2004) puts it that photographs are 'reality interrupted', yet are used in news media precisely as they do appear to encapsulate a series of complex events. Put simply, the photograph may be an exceptional moment and generally not characteristic of the whole.

For Sontag (1973), one danger with this process is that news photojournalism has encouraged us to think about the world of events in terms of memorable moments rather than lengthy complex processes. And to some extent, the fragmented nature of these compelling images also encourages us to accept a news world of unconnected, largely de-contextualized events (Morley 1992). Sontag (1973) argued that with news images anything can be separated or framed as adjacent to anything else. The world becomes 'a series of unrelated, free-standing particles' (22). The image of the naked girl becomes disassociated from the wider political issues of which the events were a part. Or it becomes a symbol for the American war in Vietnam, and not for the everyday squalor, suffering and degradation that happen in war zones, from which the public are normally protected.

The second kind of criticism is that the processes that lie behind the taking of a photograph also pose a challenge to its eye-witness status. A photograph is not simply a neutrally recorded moment. Each photograph is a result of a number of decisions as regards things like angle, proximity, exposure, cropping, later editing and then the editorial decision to choose this particular image over another. As we look at an image on a news website, such things are all invisible due to the compelling nature of having the visual document in front of our eyes (Goldman and Beeker 1985).

Huxford (2004) argues that, since the conventions of photography go unnoticed by the viewer, they will tend not to see how their understanding of a moment is being shaped. An image that appears uneven can suggest frank and immediate reporting where there is none. Closer shots can create greater senses of intimacy or threat. She notes that it is easy to mistake proximity with association and an uneven, candid shot with frank and immediate reporting. An accused person comes across as evil simply because the picture of them frowning has been chosen over one with a neutral expression. Of course, another thing we don't tend to see as viewers is the way images are placed on a page, how they are juxtaposed with headlines, page borders and other images.

Third, and of central importance to the way professionals we interviewed work, is that photojournalists have to provide images that fit with established news frames. News frames are basic themes that have become established within news culture. They signal to a journalist that an event is newsworthy and how this event should be covered, who the key actors are and how they should be treated. It is thought within journalism that such frames are often necessary for the public to recognize an event as news, although to some extent they have become invisible to the practitioners themselves. These frames, therefore, are routinely used to structure how events are represented. For example, a complex war, involving more than two parties and also very specific interests from global powers in how subsequent oil deals will be organized, will tend to be presented visually as a 'people's uprising'. Images will focus on the 'human toll' of the conflict where we see children or women suffering. We will see images of 'militia' or 'rebels'. Yet, as a number of scholars point out, this may provide very little sense of the actual, complex, ambiguous and shifting nature of the conflict (Bouvier 2014).

While academic work points to these limitations, it does in some way appear idealized in the context of contemporary photojournalism, comprised mainly of freelance workers who must be sharply aware of markets and brands. On the one hand, these photojournalists are aware of news-frames, news-flows, the need to capture the 'essence' of a story, which are largely defined by pre-existing ideas. It is the need to fulfil these frames and structures that guides their work. But what they also show a great awareness of is that the photographs they take must fit with particular kinds of page design, and that this is part of creating a kind of visual form of address. Since news outlets now tend to build upwards from visual design, photographs, like-choices in layout, colour and typeface, they must also provide a clear sense of what kind of looking at the world the outlet provides. This can also communicate the social relations between the outlet and the reader, whether the title speaks authoritatively or more on a mutual footing with informed and savvy readers. Later in this chapter, we look at the work of three photojournalists and how they talk about the demands of news frames and news cycles, but also about brands and visual design. First, we look at the way the photograph has become integrated into design and how it is now used in contemporary newspapers.

The contemporary use of the photograph as design

In an interview with Michael Crozier, who has redesigned newspapers around the world, we were told how in the 1990s, in particular, newspaper design transformed as things like colour, font, composition and the use of photographs became thought of in much more systematic ways. It was not just that newspapers began to become colourful or more visual versions of their former selves, Crozier said, but that they needed to rethink how these resources could be harnessed to speak to readers. One of Crozier's award-winning and innovative redesigns in the 1990s involved the British broadsheet *The Independent*, seen in Figure 1. Crozier spoke of the way that, in this case, the editor gave over the entire cover to the graphics team. Rather than conceiving of the cover in terms of columns of text, they began to think about the way that images, colour and fonts could help to communicate about issues. Entirely new graphic elements and shapes were introduced, completely reframing the look of newspapers.

The point here is that these design choices should not just be thought of as being based on fashion or aesthetic changes. The *Independent* began to address the public as a specific kind of reader, while attitudes and ideas about news were infused into design.

Dagens Nyheter, in Figure 2, is one example, according to its designer Javier Errea, of the contemporary use of the news photograph that follows such principles of building from design. This particular example is a Swedish newspaper that has won awards for its design. The main photograph plays its role as 'bearing witness' to a specific event. It claims to provide the viewer with a sense of 'being there'. But according to Errea this image has to do a number of other things that he would suggest are priorities. Importantly, the style of the image has to also signal the ideas and attitudes carried by the title itself. This works alongside other page elements, such as the use of restricted number of fonts, spacing and boxing, that are deployed to the same end.

The main photograph on the front page in Figure 2 provides an over-the-shoulder viewpoint. For Errea, this communicates a more up-to-date, involved, view on the world, as opposed to a former type of static image where we simply look on to a scene. Such changes in how we look is on the one hand related to shifts in design culture. But it is also about a shift in the relationship readers have with news. Many news designers we interviewed

Figure 1: *The Independent,* 1992, with innovative design.

Figure 2: *Dagens Nyheter*, 2013, providing a more involved viewpoint.

told us that, whereas formerly news outlets, including news and television, needed to connote 'information', 'authority' and 'formality', such things will now simply alienate readers and viewers. Lee Bearton art director for *The Standard* in London told us that, in a complete redesign, they had to successfully communicate with a newer generation of young professional newsreaders, who were intolerant of what they saw as an older, pompous, self-important and patronizing style of news delivery. These readers, who had simply stopped reading the older version, needed to be engaged with, addressed as if they have an existing viewpoint and not, as in former times, as passive and uniformed learners.

Designers spoke of the way that, in part, the rise of the Internet and social media with their scan-and-go, interactive cultures has played a big part in such shifts. Other scholars suggest that this must be placed into the context of wider changes in power of centralized and dominant systems of knowledge (Dean 2010). Here there has been an erosion of the power of nineteenth-century institutions and of professional knowledge. Some scholars, such as Dean, would suggest that online culture and social media have also fostered a culture where everything is viewed as opinion. For designers like Bearton and Errea, these shifts simply must be incorporated, not simply into how news is presented, but what news is per se. News itself must shift to meet these new cultures.

For the designer in this case, the photograph becomes one part of how the news title signals these ideas, values and attitudes. This can be thought of as part of how the news outlet communicates about both what 'news' is and also about the newspaper brand that will then run across different platforms. Such photographs are not so much about 'bearing witness' in the case of *Dagens Nyheter*, as such, but are part of a communicative strategy that suggests a more creative and thoughtful way of looking at the world. This, then, is not so much about what photographs depict, but about the ideas and attitudes the style of the photograph can get across.

The other images on the *Dagens Nyheter* page also play an important role, but in a slightly different way. In the first place, all the photographs on the page have been chosen for the way they fit with the overall design and brand. The images themselves are all optimistic through their use of exaggerated brightness, even though the larger image shows soldiers and the smaller images depict persons with stern expressions. Images tend to show ongoing moments and avoid anything static.

The cropping of the smaller images at the top also work, Errea said, as part of the spacious layout. The persons depicted sit with room to move. The designer of many international newspapers, Ron Reason, told us that here space can metaphorically mean 'room to think', in a shift away from a more densely populated older-style informer, where it was important to connote a sense of content and 'all the news'. The larger image too is not cramped in its composition. The smaller images, Reason said, must be able to capture the idea of attitude of a story in a way that is much more symbolic than on former designs, and is much closer to magazines' and advertising's use of images.

Clearly all these issues have an ideological consequence, as regards what kinds of events and issues the news photograph represents and how it represents these. And, in a sense, bearing witness becomes deeply interrelated with issues of branding with the matter of market-lead image production, which sit alongside the older issues of the nature of the news cycle and the need to make issues consonant with the values of the viewer.

Aamulehti, Finland

Javier Errea had been involved with many rebrandings of newspapers around the world as outlets shift to keep pace with changes in visual culture and reader expectations. The Finnish *Aamulehti* was one particularly interesting project. Here, we look at a more recent rebrand, considering the use of images in each, but also going deeper into the way these 'rhyme' with other design features. This is an important step to show how the photograph itself shifts to become one design component.

For over 100 years, until the spring of 2014, *Aamulehti* (seen in Figure 3) had been what Errea called a standard format newspaper, with a broadsheet-type identity. This recent redesign was part of a complete overhaul of the title, including the editorial team and type of contents. The newspaper was to switch to a more tabloid style and have two types of content with both professional journalism, providing content with a strongly informative identity, and local public-driven content, including short stories, commentaries, complaints, etc. The aim was to create a newspaper that was clearly in dialogue with its readers. Also, the redesign had another aim that follows a more international pattern. *Aamulehti* was the leading title of a group of local and regional titles. The redesign was to facilitate easy sharing of pages and contents across the different papers.

Javier said that the old version, however, did carry many of the more contemporary uses of photography. We see the photograph of the politicians reveals a more intimate and stylized, action shot. Other smaller images bring brightness and optimism. The image of man on the bench resembles a stock-image – here the composition of the image is used to carry text – as does the image showing a city-scape for a story headed 'Good life'.

Nevertheless, for Errea, the older design was very masculine. He saw it as hard and distant. This was partly down to the choice of font, mainly Flama and Morgan Avec, but also to its ordered appearance. The older version used more borders and hierarchies of headings. It was a smart-looking design in the direction of the Metro-style look with image cut-outs, but appears text heavy and with short introductions to many stories appearing on the front page. There are many photographs and cut-outs but they sit in layered rows and columns. Again, this suggests order and regulation. For Errea, this still points to something too authoritative for the contemporary reader.

Javier said that the challenge for this redesign was to adopt a tabloid format but maintain a serious feel. In terms of content, one innovation has been to include public commentaries on the front page. In terms of visual design, the aim was to lose some of the hardness and to make it more accessible, more optimistic and, importantly, more feminine and delicate. So the first step was to get rid of lines and the rows and columns of image, which

Figure 3: *Aamulethi,* front pages.

dominate the older version. New typefaces were brought in – Metric for information and Prumo for softer material. Metric is a typeface constructed from geometric shapes and connotes order in a simple and direct way. It also offers combinations of sharp angles and soft curves, as can be seen in the headline. For Javier, it was a fresh and gentle typeface. We can also see on the cover that the headline is lower-case and not particularly bold but a simple geometric font. The letter 't' has complete symmetry, for example. The 'o' is close to being a simple circle. All these kinds of devices help to communicate ideas of simplicity, ease and accessibility.

In terms of page structure, the design makes use of a complex grid based on 30 columns. Errea said that this was perfect for controlling distances between elements and also for creating space, important to bring in the gentleness and serenity they were looking for. We can see from the redesign that the amount of white space created is striking. Along with the simple fonts this becomes almost meditative. While there has been a decrease in the use of borders for segregation, there has been an increase in the use of space for separation. The masthead is allowed to sit in luxurious amounts of space as is the headline. But the higher number of columns used, along with the teasers at the bottom of the design, maintains the sense that the title is still information rich.

Colour has also been changed in the redesign. On the old design, colours such as orange were used well for linking elements on the page and for communicating hierarchies. But the new design has moved away from this model. A cheerful green box predominates below the masthead containing the sports headline and a bright yellow highlight in the photograph. Green is used for sports throughout. There is a clear emphasis on bright, vibrant saturated colours, and colours are used as accents. Importantly, regulation and excessive rhyming is avoided.

Javier said that photography and picture editing are thought of as part of these shifts in fonts, creation of space and colour. Grids are used to create space, fonts to create roundedness and colour to create a sense of more optimistic emotions. The photograph is seen as another component that must play the same role.

We see this on the main photograph on the new design. We are given the perspective of the men standing on the steps with the men in uniform facing us. Such images engage the reader and create interest in the page. There is much depth in this image, which our interviews with photojournalists revealed, and this was one requirement of these more 'engaging', rather than informative, images. We can also see the brightness rhyming from the man's hat to the left of the image, with the brighter background and the lettering on the jacket. We look more at the exact features of how such images work in the following section. Here, we seek to emphasize the way they are used in the same fashion, with the same attention to detail as other design components.

How the images are placed on the page is also important. There is an avoidance of symmetric structures and rhythmic patterns. But at the same time, space, regular use of a limited font palette and these more stylized images mean that this never takes on the cluttered appearance of a tabloid title. Inside the newspaper, the primary image on each double page will also usually cut across the fold. Again, for the designer this communicates a clear attitude with regards to the brand identity. Errea said that it is also useful to change the configuration of photographs on consecutive pages. So on one page they may be positioned in blocks, away from text, and, on the next, interact with wrap-around text and overlap with text. This can also provide a sense of changing reading rhythms, which he said should be used for titles that need to communicate a more 'alternative' viewpoint, even though this is simply one more branded set of ideas and values.

On the new design there was also the introduction of a cut-out image in the masthead, now typically used by contemporary newspapers to suggest a more magazine-like 'snippets' and entertainment feel. Overall, the number of images, as with the amount of text, has been reduced. It may be the case that newspapers are becoming more visual but this is not so much about more images per se. These titles should not communicate information, but 'interest'. Of course, this means that how these topics are presented itself has changed. Political events can be positioned alongside lifestyle items, linked to them by colour coding and font rhyming. For the designers, it is not unlike social media and, now, online news sites where people might browse 'what others like', or what 'others are reading'. The importance of events can now no longer be defined by the authoritative voice.

On the new design there has also been a reduction in the portraits of people attached to thumbnails of stories. This is also important with regards to the way that the newspaper seeks to create a sense that it offers participation rather than information or, even, authoritative opinion. The image of the 'mummy man' preparing food in the bottom left corner has been presented in ample white space. Like the text and other content, this is presented in the context of 'room to breathe' or 'room to think'.

What we have indicated so far is the way that the news photograph must be thought about in terms of design and brand, and creating a form of social relations with the reader. In what follows, we look at examples of the work of three photojournalists who are clearly aware of this process alongside the needs to work with news frames and different genres of news outlet.

The national newspaper and the symbolic image

Photojournalist David Levene has worked as a leading contributor to British titles such *The Standard*, *The Independent* and *The Guardian*. David was very much aware of producing images that, he suggested, must be on the one hand beautiful, but are also able to connote a particular kind of viewing process, one which itself is stylish and educated. The designer of *The Standard* in London told us the importance of visual design, including images and composition, to communicate to readers that they are being addressed as a knower and as stylish, as opposed to the more patronized reader of older newspapers. This was, he said, even though these readers may be much less informed.

Figure 4 shows a photograph taken by David for *The Guardian* newspaper for a series called 'Eyewitness'. This was a double-page spread given over entirely to one or several news photographs. Such images, he said, while being of interest to the reader, were also important in giving the newspaper a particular branded look. These are about connoting ideas and attitudes as much as bearing witness.

For the Eyewitness spread, national and international photographs are used that document the world on a given day in a 'unique way'. But David said that this 'uniqueness' tended to have typical features: the brief was for the picture to be taken at eye level, to create an all-consuming shot, with everything in focus and in wide angle. There must be many details to catch the eye in the foreground, but also points of interest at various distances from the camera.

While on an assignment in Panama, David heard talk about the way recession and the drying up of investment had led to the mushrooming of 'ghost towers' – unfinished high-rise buildings. He had noticed the scene in Figure 4 from the road and saw it as an ideal Eyewitness subject. Describing the photograph, he said that interest is generated by the activity at the front of the image, like the line of the pipe that draws the eye to the background, and the contrast of the boats and mundane everyday life with the failed ambitious developments towering over them.

While such images are clearly stunning, they could be argued to represent, in classic *National Geographic* style, the meeting of different worlds (Lutz and Collins 1993). The

Figure 4: Ghost towers, 'Eyewitness', *The Guardian*.

past and tradition is juxtaposed with the future and technology. The contrast between the poverty of the slums and the floundering wealth of property speculation is made apparent. Importantly such images do not create a depressing view of the world, even when they look onto scenes of poverty. These images are designed to be of the order we saw above in the Finnish newspaper. They use bright and coordinated colours to provide a lively and adventurous take on humanity. They are designed to invite a response of curiosity rather than shock or outrage in the viewer. Above all they are designed to sit alongside a range of other design features that connote a set of brand values. There will be softer fonts that bring a sense of emotion and space that suggests 'room to think', and, as Errea suggests, these can be presented on a page in a way that suggests 'alternative'. These are the kind of images that he, as an award-winning deisgner, pointed to as being important, not so much for what they depict, but the kind of looking that they represent. In this case *The Guardian* reader is offered not the literal look at the scene, as we might find in a local newspaper, where a row of local people will stand in a row frowning in protest at the closure of a local library, but the connotations of a more creative, adventurous and involved viewpoint through the use of perspective.

Our interviews with newspaper editors spoke of the fact that the younger generation of news readers would simply not accept the flat, formal, authoritative representations of photographs of a former era. Errea himself, along with other world-leading designers, in fact, said specifically that titles are now often built from the visual identity first. So, rather than thinking in terms of written content, the starting point is column number and width, use of colour boxes and the kinds of photographs. From the point of view of the scholarly work on the news photograph, we might ask what happens then when these typical news frames, where poverty meets the high tech, become used as part of a brand. The world of events for readers becomes always angled for them visually to connote an attitude. This may be an attitude of intelligent reflection, or of something alternative. But this may be only at the level of connotation, clearly communicated across design features. In the next section, we explore how slightly different markets require different viewpoints to be created by the photograph and through design.

Photographs and news frames

One major criticism of the news photograph has been that it is mainly used to anchor typical news frames. This is done both to make stories graspable to readers and to allow journalists and news outlets to manage resources with regards to how events are dealt with. Again, this must be linked to communicating a kind of viewing and also to the requirements of composition and the ideas and attitudes it must communicate.

One field of reporting where academics have been particularly critical of photographs providing little other than news frames is war reporting. We look at some examples of this from two photojournalists in what follows, Michael Graae and Louis Quail who both produced images of the conflict in Libya in 2011, again showing how this too must be related to the requirements of design and brand.

There is a sense that, apart from the case of Vietnam, photojournalism for the most part shows a highly managed version of war. We do not see wounded people, the daily horrors and brutality suffered by civilians or the battle itself. We tend to find photographs that point to the high level of technology and specialist soldiers being used (Griffin 2004), or to the war being a vague humanitarian matter (Parry 2010), where the enemy are delegitimized by presenting them as disorganized, scruffy and undisciplined (Machin 2007). Carruthers (2011) argues that the news media tend to cover war in terms of a particular set of frames and a typical cycle, so there is the outbreak of war that is exciting and then manoeuvres. There is a villain to be defeated in the name of something noble (Graham, Keenan and Dowd 2004). Here, we look at the work of two war reporters who explain how their images relate to news frames and also communicate to particular kinds of viewers.

We look at the photographs taken by these two photographers during and after the conflict in Libya in 2011 that led to the end of the Gaddafi regime. In fact, the British news media have themselves expressed regret about the lack of quality and simple errors in their coverage of this particular conflict, including their visual representations of it. Put simply, the complexity of the interests involved in the conflict and their relationships to NATO powers interested in oil deals was grossly misrepresented and simplified as a people's uprising against a dictator (Bouvier 2014). Since this time, events have proven otherwise in Libya.

The two photojournalists both took photographs of the conflict that appeared in the British national press. The first produced images in Libya during the conflict, the second a year on. Michael Graae, a young photojournalist from New York, who had recently completed a BA in Photojournalism at the London College of Communication, decided to begin freelancing work in places like Libya during his studies.

Graae made some striking comments on which images tend to get chosen over those that do not, which help us to think a little more about why such images appear. He said that sometimes newspapers simply want photographs that sit well with their story. So *The Sun*, a tabloid newspaper, ran stories on what it was like living in Bengazi. They focused on Gaddafi's former compound that had been looted. They took the angle that Gaddafi was simply an insane dictator living like a king. Graae had a picture of the shattered compound so the *Sun* used this, along with an inset of Gaddafi. This was also used by *The Scotsman* as shown in Figure 5.

Graae said that he was aware that one important consideration as to which images would be used by a picture editor was layout. He said that he would find his images used according to how it sat next to or clashed with other images on the page, and that this would depend

Figure 5: Photograph by Michael Graae seen with inset in *The Scotsman* 25 February 2011.

on the kind of composition typically found in a title. For example, in a more upmarket title, a more detailed image may then need more empty images to sit on the same page. One that showed a particular scene would need accompanying with an image with people in. What is clear in the tabloid use of images here is that the whole set of events have been framed for the British reader in terms of WWII reference, where Gaddafi is very much like Hitler. With his palace destroyed and him on the run, we find a story where people shoot guns in the air in celebration. An image shows a man and two children crossing the road with a burned-out military vehicle in the background. These small groups of people were typical representative of 'the people' required by the news. One image of a local militia has been used as a cut-out.

Graae found that, on his first, trip there was more demand for 'destruction-type' images but that, as time went on, news attention shifted and interest turned to more 'humanitarian and recovery' images, even though after this point events in the country became more and more chaotic.

In the 'recovery' images, we would find people carrying out more mundane activities amidst scene elements that indicated that there had formerly been conflict. And later there would also be the chance for the 'one year on' images as in the photograph of the young girl in Figure 6 with the flag captioned as 'Celebrating Their Freedom' in *The Independent*. At the same time this image was taken, Libya was in fact in violent turmoil as different factions struggled for power. But news organizations were not covering this with any emphasis. These kinds of images could be used as both larger and smaller images on the page as they communicate a very simplified news frame where the smiling child, representing ordinary uncomplicated people here, waves a flag.

We see something slightly different in the photographs of Libya taken by Louis Quail which appeared in *G2*, the supplement of the British *Guardian* newspaper. Quail is a photographer with many years of experience working for many leading British publications such as *The Sunday Times* and *The Telegraph*. These images are intended for a very different kind of brand and different order of reader identity.

The photographs in Figures 7 and 8 were published in *The Guardian* on Monday 29 October 2012 titled 'Libya: life after Gaddafi – in pictures' with the strapline 'Photojournalist Louis Quail's reflective and surprisingly affirming images of post-revolution Libya tell the human stories behind the uprisings'.

These very striking, beautiful and moving photographs, we might suggest, are one way by which *Guardian* readers are taken to the events in Libya. Quail pointed out that these upmarket titles favour these kinds of personalized images when doing a focus on an event. Such images will be thought through carefully in terms of colour palette, composition and how they sit on the page.

One effect of such images, we could argue, is that they personalize events, often through how they resonate with American-European cultural values. The image of the older woman in the chair in her house with an automatic weapon is jarring for the Western eye. The novel, the quirky, that which places these events into the category of 'difference', is often what attracts a picture editor to particular photographs. The newlywed couple are seen in

Figure 6: Kids wave the new Libyan flag in Martyr's Square in Tripoli, Libya on the one-year anniversary of the revolution. Copyright: Michael Graae.

Figure 7: Mother who lost her son in the conflict.

Figure 8: Married couple.

a post-apocalyptic scene under a broken underpass, in front of a burned-out tank. In both of Quail's images the everyday is placed alongside the unusual and surprising. It is unusual to see children and women depicted with guns. In their study of *National Geographic Magazine*, Lutz and Collins (1993) pointed to the nature of striking and jarring images that also struck notes with Western values and expectations. Such images would be highly stylized.

Like the *Scotsman* above, these striking, yet slightly haunting images, are as much part of the newspaper brand and way of looking as they are merely bearing witness. The tabloid suggests a more aggressive and simplified way of looking where events and issues easily collapse together – the end of the road for Gaddafi can be easily likened to that of Hitler. The winners can be easily portrayed, although in this case they are only tiny figures and not prioritized for the reader where the 'fall of the dictator' is foregrounded. *The Guardian*, on the other hand, also skipping the complex politics and actual ongoing situation, favours a creative, almost poetic, jarring look on the world where ordinary people are shown not bitter, angry or unsettled but calm and measured; as thoughtful as the reader themselves.

All of these images convey a role of bearing witness to the destruction and carnage on an everyday level (Pantti and Wahl-Jorgensen 2011). In *The Scotsman* we see the wreckage and the local people. In *The Guardian* we see the ordinary people living in a real world rather than 'experts'. So they bring a sense of authenticity to the representation of reality. Yet none of these images, we might argue, helps the reader to understand the complex background and multi-facetted reality of the conflict described above, which in fact, at the time, was already growing in new ways and complexities. But additionally what we have shown in this chapter is that all such images must be seen as being designed for a particular kind of viewing. The act of engaging with the newspaper is infused with brand values through composition, font, etc. David Morley (1992) once asked about how the world 'out there' appeared to ordinary people, through the way the news presented a stream of largely de-contextualized, plucked-out-of-context larger sequences of interconnected issues never really followed through. The difference is that now news pays more attention to visually making this world of events convey a more localized way of looking. It may remain as fragmented and fundamentally incomprehensible, but it is presented as a thoughtful view on these events, or one loaded with closed pre-existing frames of reference; one that allows the reader/viewer to feel they are no longer patronized when engaging with it.

Conclusion

Photojournalism, as a profession, can promote itself as highly noble, as can journalism in general – the photojournalist is the eyes of the public. But, like journalism as a whole, a huge variety of work is done under this umbrella term. Academic theories appear to take this highest estimation, the idea of the photograph as bearer of witness to world events to show how this is not indeed the case. The criticisms made are indeed important ones. But then, seen from the position of the contemporary photojournalist, most often freelancing, and the shifts in how news is perceived – the demise of the acceptance of an authoritative and slightly self-important news out – and huge changes in design culture as well as the influence of social media, it does become clear that there is a disjunction between theory and practice.

Put simply, photojournalists don't necessarily work to document reality but rather to sell images. These photojournalists are professionals who must understand the different markets and different kinds of images that they require. They must also understand the changing nature of visual communication and the new kinds of images this requires. And this presently involves the broader shift in status of news itself – away from a more formal, authoritative knowledge provider – to a genre that must communicate on a more equal footing with the reader, address them as having opinions, as needing to be entertained, and acknowledge that we now live in a click-and-go media environment. This involves a process where news outlets are built first from visual design, which much often run across different platforms, maintaining a clear visual voice. There, the photojournalist seeking to sell their work needs to understand these processes. We interviewed award-winning photojournalist Tom Stoddard, known for his stark, gritty, black-and-white images of ordinary people in war zones and famines. Tom himself said that the kinds of images he is known for, what many would think of as classical photojournalism, are now unlikely to be produced for news itself, unless it was to be used to signify a particular branded look.

References

Barthes, R. (1977), *Image, Music, Text*, London: Fontana.

Bennett, L. (2005), *News – The Politics of Illusion*, London: Longman.

Berger, P. (1980), *Ways of Seeing*, London: Penguin.

Bouvier, G. (2014), 'British press photographs and the misrepresentation of the 2011 "uprising" in Libya: A content analysis', in D. Machin (ed.), *Visual Communication*, Berlin: De Gruyter, pp. 281–300.

Carruthers, L. (2011), *The Media at War*, 2nd ed, London: Palgrave Macmillan.

Dean, J. (2010), *Blog Theory*, London: Polity Press.

Goldman, R. and Beeker, G. L. (1985), 'Decoding newsphotos: An analysis of embedded ideological values', *Humanity & Society*, 9: August, pp. 351–63.

Graham, P., Keenan, T. and Dowd, A-M. (2004), 'A call to arms at the end of history: A discourse-historical analysis of George W. Bush's declaration of war on terror', *Discourse & Society*, 15, pp. 199–221.

Griffin, M. (2004), 'Picturing America's "War on Terrorism" in Afghanistan and Iraq: Photographic motifs as news frames', *Journalism*, 5: 4, pp. 381–402.

Huxford, J. (2004), 'Surveillance, witnessing and spectatorship: The news and the "War of Images"', *Proceedings of the Media Ecology Association*, 5, pp. 1–21.

Kress, G. and Van Leeuwen, T. (2001), *Multimodal Discourse*, London: Arnold.

Lutz, C. A. and Collins, J. L. (1993), *Reading National Geographic*, Chicago: University of Chicago Press.

Machin, D. (2007), 'Visual discourses of war: A multimodal analysis of the Iraq occupation', in A. Hodges and C. Nilep (eds), *Discourse, War and Terrorism*, Amsterdam: John Benjamins, pp. 123–142.

Moore, C. (2011), 'Britain shouldn't feel guilty about the part we played in ousting Colonel Muammar Gaddafi', *The Telegraph*, 26 August, http://tinyurl.com/3g23a8p. Accessed 7 November 2016.

Morley, D. (1992), *Television, Audiences, and Cultural Studies*, London: Routledge.

Newton, J. (2000), *The Burden of Visual Truth: The Role of Photojournalism in Mediating Reality*, London: Routledge.

Pantti, M. and Wahl-Jorgensen, K. (2011), 'Not an act of God: Anger and citizenship in press coverage of British man-made disasters', *Media, Culture & Society*, 33: 1, pp. 105–22.

Parry, K. J. (2010), 'A visual framing analysis of British press photography during the 2006 Israel-Lebanon conflict', *Media, War and Conflict*, 3: 1, pp. 67–85.

Sontag, S. (1973), *On Photography*, London: Allen Lane.

Sontag, S. (2004), *Regarding the Pain of Others*, London: Picador.

Turner, V. (1982), *From Ritual to Theatre*, New York: PAJ Publications.

Chapter 12

Notes on a Practice-based Media and Journalism Research from a Critical Cultural Perspective

Marcela Pizarro

The launch of Al Jazeera English in 2006 could be theorized itself as a rupture in the north/south, centre/periphery dynamics of power. At the time, the field of international news was for the most part dominated by channels emanating from the northern hemisphere; framed by western perspectives due to locations of its news centres; the ethnic and cultural identities of their journalists, the political centres being reported on. The arrival of Al Jazeera English, a 24-hour TV news channel funded by the Qatari state, was seen as a major opportunity for many journalists around the world to decentre the logic of news and information being disseminated from the western metropolitan centre and to disrupt the power dynamics implicit in global news. A number of strategies were employed to build a different kind of news product that would incorporate voices and narratives from locations around the world: less parachute journalism; more local reporters; and an array of journalists educated around the world who had cultural proximity to the places they were covering. The ethos of inclusion did not just involve featuring locals on the ground but an overall attempt to showcase discussions with intellectuals and commentators rarely seen on mainstream channels. In the early days, notions of 'global south' and the 'voice of the voiceless' came to represent a revindication of the *periphery* as a privileged space of news production that had come to disrupt hegemonic information structures from the North.

The healthy journalistic scepticism imbued in many who came to work at the channel added a critical angle to the culture of news production from the very outset – and it is fitting that a weekly slot was given to a programme that was to dedicate itself solely to media critique. Since its inception, *The Listening Post* has covered coverage, dissected the politics behind news narratives, and unveiled the modes of its production. My work on the show has aimed to bring theoretical material and aesthetic sensibilities to bear upon the reading of news media production. This could be understood as an interrogation of news material through interpretative languages that see news media as material to be analysed through the prism of culture.

Every week, the programme sets out to provide coverage of the main stories. In other words, our interest lies in the meta-narrative: stories, not of what there is to report on the ground, but how it is being reported; stories of the wars that are not just fought on the battlefields, but across the airwaves, the broadsheets and the Internet; stories that explore the economic relationships between media organizations and political power – stories often of complicity; stories of the fourth estate constantly under threat of censorship, or death; the story of the emerging fifth estate, marking a bold new frontier in the history of journalism and of its duty to hold power to account; stories of an epochal crisis – where hierarchies of knowledge and information have collapsed in the wake of the digital era – both because of the demise of traditional formats no longer financially viable – but also because of the cacophony of voices that have come to disrupt the authority of establishment journalism.

Over the years, I have covered different media stories from around the world. In the United States, the story of journalism in post 9/11 in which the relationship between the official discourse of the 'war on terror' has frequently been reflected by the establishment media. And when the fourth estate has failed to do its job, we have seen the rise of another form of truth telling, the rise of the fifth estate: Chelsea Manning, Julian Assange, Edward Snowden, all protagonists in a story of some of the biggest leaks in political history.

In the Middle East, the initial euphoria for citizen journalism during the Arab Spring has given way to a series of complicated scenarios. In Egypt, Al Jazeera was initially celebrated for, or accused of, fomenting protests that eventually brought down President Mubarak after decades in power. Since President Mohammed Morsi was overthrown by the Egyptian military in 2013, the media landscape under President Abdel Fattah el-Sisi has faced an intense crackdown in the name of national security.

In Syria, the initial pro-democracy protests of 2011 led to a bloody civil war. War reporters trying to cover this conflict have either been killed or told to stay away by their editors. News organizations have instead resorted to piecing together the grainy images uploaded to smart phones from those bearing witness on the ground, documents of history that are nevertheless visually and editorially shaky because, as the-oft repeated caveat states, 'the authenticity of these images cannot be independently verified'. The emergence of ISIL has been coupled with a slick and increasingly disturbing propaganda campaign. In 2014, the filmed beheadings of three foreign journalists – James Foley, Stephen Sotloff and Kenji Goto – were a clear signal that, for ISIS, the western media represent a mouthpiece for their governments and, therefore, a target per se. This story has left news editors around the world in a bind: how to cover a story without giving in to the ISIS propaganda machine the forum demands. As the war continues, more than 400,000 Syrians have died and the images of discarded life jackets littered along Greek coastlines have become visual metonyms for a humanitarian crisis history cannot contain.

Around Latin America, in Argentina, Bolivia, Venezuela and Ecuador, battles that pit left-wing governments against big media conglomerates have made headlines domestically and around the world in a story that either characterizes leaders (such as the former president of Venezuela, Hugo Chavez, Ecuador's president, Rafael Correa, and Argentina's former leader Cristina Fernandez de Kirchner) as pariahs of press freedom, or as reformers revising outdated laws that have spurned media monopolies. And in Cuba, after decades of antagonism, the current rapprochement in US–Cuban relations presents a new challenge for old state media on the island – as well as a new generation of budding journalists keen to add their voices to an emerging public sphere.

These are just some of the media stories unravelling around the world today.

My role as a media analyst has been to chronicle those narratives, to position them within the wider political contexts in which they reside and make meaning. This is a job that involves taking distance from the object of analysis, journalism, and subjecting it to a critical rereading.

As a cultural historian who initially worked in the field of literature, film and critical theory, a lot of my work on Al Jazeera English has concentrated on developing strategies through which to apply the work of a number of theorists, cultural critics and philosophers in the field of cultural studies and critical theory to the canvas of news.

Practicing theory

The attempts to bring theory to a global TV news channel have been a series of experimentations that are always being challenged by the tyranny of the visual. One of the first pieces took a look at the work of Marshall McLuhan.

> When you are saying the medium is the message, you're really saying the ground is the message, not the content.
>
> Everything happens at once, there's no continuity, no connection. There's no follow through, it's just now.
>
> When you don't have a physical body, you are a disconduct being. You have a different relationship to the world around you.
>
> There's a new kind of humour in America today, called the one-liner. You used to have jokes, stories, but no more, only one liners now.
>
> (1976)

In the 1960s, way before anybody ever updated their Facebook page, posted their whereabouts on Twitter, uploaded images on YouTube, or exposed government secrets on Wikileaks, one man made a series of pronouncements about the changing media landscape that resonate with the Internet world we live in today: Canadian, Marshall McLuhan, professor of literature turned high priest of media theory. His ideas had something of the prophetic – because in the tumult of today's digital revolution, a lot of what McLuhan said has even more relevance now than it did then. McLuhan had actually studied Renaissance Literature, but, strangely, created a second career for himself as a sort of media guru, explaining to people the effect of the mass media, which were relatively new in the 1960s, what effect they had on people's lives. Curiously enough, he became incredibly trendy. He even famously appeared in a Woody Allen film – *Annie Hall*.

> Cinema goer: 'Marshall McLuhan … in terms of it being a high intensity …'
>
> Woody Allen: I've got Marshall McLuhan right here.
>
> Marshall McLuhan: You know nothing of my work, you mean my whole fallacy is wrong.
>
> (1977)

When McLuhan famously pronounced that [t]he medium is the message', he was writing about the effects of the mass media on contemporary life and he was talking mostly about television. To this day, it is one of the most famous and yet controversial statements in media and communication studies. It refers to the significance of form over content:

> A medium is not something neutral, is does something to people, it takes hold of them, it rubs them up, it massages them, it bumps them around ... and the general roughing up of any society gets from a medium, especially a new medium is what is intended to be in that title.

> (1966)

McLuhan's privileging of form over content is a slippery one – it is hard to argue that what is being said is entirely irrelevant. But for anyone working in journalism, understanding the epochal shift in how news is provided and how that affects the way the narrative is formed is crucial. What the dictum does provide is a frame through which to think more about the effects of new forms of delivering information, their performative roles in making meaning and, importantly, having impact.

In the wave of uprisings that took hold around the Arab world back in 2011, the account of this phenomenon points to the fact that one of the extraordinary things about the so-called Arab Spring was that events were both understood and made through the new media. It was widely commented that forms of communication like Facebook and Twitter became the means whereby people could not just report the Arab Spring, but also foment it against the will of the authorities across the region. In that sense, to varying degrees, social media were able to create an alternative conversation outside of the official channels of communication – the traditional mass media – with monumental results.

The level of protagonism attributable to social media has of course been a source of debate, and, while McLuhan's quirky statements serve as suggestive pointers to think about the media, caution should be exercised at every corner. For example, during the Arab Spring, the fanfare about the revolutions being the products of Facebook and Twitter was a rather naïve reading that elided a much more complex story of grassroots political organization. The idealization of the social media during the period of the Arab Spring pointed in some instances to simplification and decontextualization that implicitly celebrated the western technology in the uprisings, while obfuscating the slow and difficult work of political movements on the ground.

In terms of journalism itself, however, the rise of 'citizen journalism' does represent a privileged space in which subaltern/marginal/ordinary voices with no access to establishment journalism have been able to generate their own stories. For the past decade, digital technology has opened up a space for voices on the ground to give testimony and to provide their own narratives. These stories would have been unheard of had it not been for the technology itself. We only have to think about stories such as Ferguson to see the gaping divide between the stories being produced by the mainstream and those by different players on the ground. During the riots in Ferguson last year, it was through social media that those on the streets could reflect back to the world the myth of the 'post'-racial America:

> Another effect of this electric environment is this total lack of secrecy. [...] No form of secrecy is possible at electric speed ... at electric speed everything becomes x-rayed ... With the end of secrecy goes the end of monopolies of knowledge. There can no longer be a monopoly of knowledge in learning, education or in power.
>
> (1970)

McLuhan's idea of information being much more ubiquitous has certainly come to pass – so too his insight into how hierarchies of knowledge would be pulled apart.

On 5 June 2013, Edward Snowden, a former US National Security Agency contractor, made headlines around the world when he revealed that intelligence agencies, through rules laid down in the US Patriot Act, were systematically tracking Americans' phone records and collecting their e-mails through a series of surveillance tools. Mainstream news coverage painted Snowden as either a hero or a pariah.

Official voices have rallied against figures like Snowden and instead favoured national security discourses that privilege secrecy over transparency in the interests of keeping the public safe. But for many others, marginal to mainstream media narratives, the likes of Edward Snowden, Julian Assange and Chelsea Manning have come to symbolize the decline of the monopoly of knowledge in the wake of the electronic media age. For many, the age of the social media has given the *polis* access to information free of government or corporate media control that provides a space to build up public opinion in terms of collective intelligence – in other words, a democratization of knowledge and information.

Marginal knowledges: Cultural studies and post-structural critique

Some of the most important ideas come from cultural studies: a pioneering field of study that started during the 1960s, gathered around Birmingham University's Centre for Contemporary Cultural Studies, and gained popularity in the following decades, seeking to encompass a variety of different shifts in the practice of of history and sociology in which meaning was sought out in different forms of popular culture.

One of the most important influences in this endeavour has been post-structuralist theory, which has provided a key set of tools with which to analyse news discourse by focusing on theories of language and the production of meaning. Swiss linguist, Ferdinand de Saussure, famously argued that meaning is always already constructed (Saussure 1978). Truth is not a given; it is not 'out there' but rather created in language as a re-presentation. Crucially, if meaning was not a private experience to be then translated into language, there was no essential human nature; an individual did not own meaning, he or she did not produce it; crucially, he or she was a product of it.

This demystification of language and truth shook up the empirical view of language reflecting the outside world. In the field of journalism, this is one simple yet crucial concept because it disturbs journalism's founding myth that its premise is to report the facts. Structuralism as a whole put scare quotes around the very idea of 'what really happened', question marks around the very notion that reality is unmediated – calling on the reader to see all representations as constructed texts made up of ideologically infused words and images. In the act of naming therefore is a function of power. That means that all language and representation is political and that it has to be x-rayed.

Over the years, the attention to semantics in news discourse has been one of the key elements in the critical discourse being elaborated on the show. In the post 9/11 media landscape, the news media terrain has become a complex representational minefield.

In the United States, every year on the last Monday of May, US news outlets dedicate their day's coverage to Memorial Day – commemorating soldiers killed in action. A few years back, Chris Hayes, a presenter on US network MSNBC, sparked controversy when he questioned the US media's habitual use of the word 'hero' when describing American soldiers fighting in Iraq and Afghanistan. 'I feel uncomfortable with the word 'hero' because it feels to me to be so rhetorically proximate to justifications of war', he said, and the firestorm began. Media figures rarely raise this kind of issue on the terminology being used in news coverage. But this one was important – the term 'hero' is loaded with implications not just about those in uniform but about the morality of the war they are fighting. It was a chance to ask whether those who die in war have perished in vain or, even worse, have been killed in a cause that was actually wrong, and to ask whose interests the rhetoric of military heroism serves. But his comments caused outrage among right-wing media outlets and Hayes was forced to publicly apologise. What Chris Hayes learnt is that, to many Americans, this is not a discussion even worth having. Instead of using this questioning of the term 'heroism' to open up a debate about what it means for the nation to be at war, the pushback suggested that the media thought this was not a conversation worth having. When the word 'hero' is used as a blanket term, it diminishes the distinction between soldiers who commit exceptional acts of valour and everyone else in uniform. In both Iraq and Afghanistan, the media have found themselves reporting on abuses committed by soldiers on prisoners of war – acts that are elided in the discourse of heroism used to propagate war on key dates like Memorial Day.

Another report was an attempt to zone in on style guides and the politics of their ever-changing meanings.

When we open a news organisation's stylebook, there are a range of dos and don'ts of terminology: what kind of language to use when dealing with contentious topics, and what terms to avoid. In 2013, the news agency the Associated Press called time on one phrase: illegal immigrant. The reason given was that the word 'illegal' should not be used to describe a person. 'Illegal', according to the AP, should only describe an action, such as living in a country illegally. The AP's style guide is among the most influential in the news business.

The agency provides wire services to thousands of news organizations – 1400 print outlets in the United States alone and 5000 broadcasters around the world. So when the AP makes a change, it matters: not just for the agency but for all who subscribe to its services and adopt its language. After illegal immigrant was dropped from the AP Stylebook, publications including *The New York Times* and the *Los Angeles Times* followed. Two days after changing the way it describes undocumented immigrants, the AP then announced it would be revising its use of the term 'Islamist'. The stylebook entry now reads: 'An advocate or supporter of a political movement that favours reordering government and society in accordance with laws prescribed by Islam. Do not use as a synonym for Islamic fighters, militants, extremists or radicals, who may or may not be Islamists'. Just after 9/11, news organizations were changing their use of language. Reuters issued an internal memo about the use of the word 'terrorist'. The news agency ruled that the word was only to be used if accompanied by quotation marks. After the 2005 bombings in London, the BBC issued new guidance for staff to opt for less-loaded terms than terrorist', like 'militant' or 'extremist'. Journalists reporting political events have to be careful, because the stories they report are already framed by the language used by those in positions of power. And in the world of 24-hour news increasingly driven by digital content, some say style guides may not be as influential as they once were, since social media and citizen journalism are undermining traditional news institutions using new terminology.

Deconstruction

Often on *Al Jazeera English* I catch the word being used rather liberally – a reference to the process of unpicking the edifice of news. Deconstruction, as put forward by Jacques Derrida, gives a far richer, more challenging critical device. Derrida followed Saussure in describing language as a series of substitutions but introduced the concept of difference to suggest that language and meaning have no point of origin. In structuralism, meaning is predicated on binary oppositions – and that one element is always dominant – male/female, black/white, north/south, rational/religious, culture/nature, etc. (1962). As Derrida argued, the problem with seeing things in terms of binary oppositions was the process of privileging one side of the binary over the other. Derrida noted that those binaries are inherently unstable because the implicit hierarchy can be inverted – and therefore the job of the critical thinker is to seek out binaries in texts and to identify the point of ambivalence and to show up the artificial nature of their construction.

These are complex and nuanced theories that I have tried to translate on to television programming. The language is simplified and ideas condensed. The results are sometimes simplistic, but they represent an attempt to engage the audience with these kinds of discussions that usually reside in the realms of the ivory tower. One piece opened:

Regular viewers will know that here at The Listening Post. We're all about the narrative. We report on dominant narratives, alternative narratives and governments controlling the narrative. Narrative is defined as 'a story or account of events, experiences, or the like, whether true or fictitious'. And when media outlets report the news – they often present versions of the world, by packaging events and characters into some kind of narrative. They call them stories. Many of those stories are based on a simple storytelling device – binaries: stories organized around oppositions – good guys, bad guys – freedom, tyranny – the civilised versus the barbaric – the list is long, the issues are varied – however, the common element in them is that they privilege one term over the other, they produce a hierarchy of value. Often the mainstream media merely reinforce binaries offered up by the dominant political discourse – George W. Bush's post 9/11 speech, that idea – that 'you're either with us or against us' – grew into one of the biggest binaries of them all: the Global War on Terror.

One of the key slippages picked up by this piece was the migrant/refugee binary, which in 2015 underwent a semantic shift when Al Jazeera called out news organizations for using the word 'migrant' as an umbrella term. The channel's online editor wrote: 'The umbrella term migrant is no longer fit for purpose when it comes to describing the horror unfolding in the Mediterranean. It has evolved from its dictionary definitions into a tool that dehumanises and distances, a blunt pejorative'. The channel opted to use the word 'refugee' when describing those making the treacherous journey across the Mediterranean. This is, however, not a deconstruction but a reiteration of it. In a rather insidious kind of way, an implicit binary opposition is being set up between refugees claiming asylum, the good refugees, and the economic migrants, who were possibly still coming here on economic grounds 'to claim benefits'. By revealing the process of privileging one element over the other, we become acutely aware of how careful we must be to identify the exclusionary logics of the media narratives on this story.

Representing the other

> [...] as much as the West itself, the Orient is an idea that has a history and a tradition of thought, imagery, and vocabulary that have given it reality and presence in and for the West. The two geographical entities thus support and to an extent reflect each other.
>
> (Said 1991: 5)

It was Said's writing that came to so eloquently capture something many journalists, writers, artists perceived to be problematic about representations of their own cultures in the media of the cosmopolitan north. In his book *Orientalism*, Said explored how Western literature, anthropology, photography and science had constructed the eastern 'other' – the societies and peoples who inhabit the Middle East, Asia and North Africa (Said 1991). Through these various disciplines and genres, Western stories of the East had built a system of representation that functioned as powerful tools of colonial control. Said argued that, ultimately, Orientalist texts provided a rationalization for European colonialism based on a self-serving history in which 'the West' constructed 'the East' as different and inferior, and therefore in need of Western intervention. Said's work of course resonates because this imposed ventriloquism is far from being a thing of past. In his book, *Covering Islam* (1997), Said showed how these colonial notions continued to impact US news coverage of the Middle East in the 1990s.

In the post 9/11 media landscape, the news media terrain has become an even more complex representational minefield. Much of the US media have continued to portray 'Islam' as monolithic and synonymous with terrorism and religious hysteria. For the past 15 years, many in Said's wake have charted how mainstream news outlets have added layer upon layer to the construction of the terrorist, irrational other, the pervasion of orientalist ideas about the 'Arab mind'.

Over the years, the stories that have fed these notions are aplenty and there is scarcely space here to touch upon the surface. In 2015, this story seemed to reach its apex when two gunmen stormed an editorial meeting at the Paris office of the Charlie Hebdo satirical magazine killing 12 people in response to the cartoons that they, as Muslims, deemed blasphemous. The fatal attack quickly turned into a debate about freedom of speech around the world. At first glance it seemed reasonable and justified to do so. The edgy and provocative magazine exists in a country like France only because writers and journalists are protected in their right to do their work with sharpened pens. The violent deaths of the 12 staff members in an armed attack would intuitively seem to be a direct affront to this right. Freedom of speech is a function of the liberal, democratic value of tolerance and Charlie Hebdo's wilful courting of controversy has always been deemed to fall within its scope. Nevertheless, it would be all too easy for the emerging narrative of 'terror' to create a smokescreen. The very word 'terror' is sparingly applied – never to violence other than that which the media and public consciousness connects with Muslims.

Furthermore, the premise of much of the mainstream media narrative quickly resorted to a meta-binary in order to tell this story. Wherever you looked, freedom of expression was part of one of the foundational pillars of Western contemporary thought: Voltaire (1763) made a major come back – fittingly, on Twitter – to remind the world that the West were the owners of the Enlightenment. The pen and the sword came back again and again as tropes idealizing the dichotomy between the West and the barbaric other.

The mainstream commentary on the event – the taboo built around contesting the notion that freedom of speech was anything but an absolute – seemed to reiterate what Edward Said had exposed when he wrote about the unholy alliance between the enlightenment and colonialism (Said 1978). Modernity, science and the privileging of technological knowledge, fact over belief, empiricism over myth – all these ideas were there, lingering beneath the reams of copy being written during the Hebdo affair. There for anyone to trace was the historical line of progress that posits itself ahead – and therefore sees every other cultural belief system as lagging behind. Freedom of expression, alongside notions of other rights – human rights, women's rights – has become a powerful cause célèbres in mainstream media discourses in the 9/11 era – and the closer we look, the more frequently one could argue that they have been used to window dress and morally justify the wars fought in their name. Edward Said gave us a lens – not without its cracks and contradictions – through which to read media narratives.

The popular

Cultural studies proposed an interdisciplinary mode of studying society through its cultural forms, beginning with a democratic critique of an elitist perspective to culture and recognizing the fundamental importance of 'popular culture'. 'Culture is ordinary', it was claimed – but it is in the everyday forms of culture that political dynamics can be traced and thought about. Cultural studies straddled sociology, literature, media studies and a range of subjects that had up until then been deemed unworthy of intellectual attention. Hugely influenced by continental philosophy and Marxist theory, one of the key aims was to unravel the processes used by official structures to disseminate ideology.

Crucial to my work in media is how cultural studies has benefited from – but pushed beyond – Marxist-orientated scholars from the Frankfurt School. The work of Horkheimer and Adorno (1997) provided an analysis of the 'culture industry', which was thought to be a method of control and exploitation of the masses. But in counterpoint to these bleaker, more pessimistic evaluations about the mass mediatization of culture, cultural studies not only sought to denounce but also to show how these notions of power, control, domination and exploitation gave way to pockets of potential resistance from the ground upwards. In his essay, 'Notes on deconstructing the "Popular"' (1981), Stuart Hall argued that the term 'popular' pointed to a process whereby 'the people' erupted, made their culture known to the ruling classes in unpredictable ways, and thereby complicated the transformative projects of capital and state bureaucracies. A lot of our work on the show is dedicated to looking at how to study popular culture as a space of critical meaning.

The police thriller

One example was a drama broadcast on Chilean television in 2011. Packaged for the TV viewing masses, this was a popular genre where the trauma of the past managed to rupture cultural taboos on the subject. During Augusto Pinochet's 18-year rule, thousands of Chileans were murdered or had gone missing. But due to tight censorship, it was a story the country's media failed to expose. Chile returned to democracy in 1990, but the media have been reluctant to touch on the thorny issues of the country's past, until recently. *Los Archivos de Cardinal* ('The Cardinal's Archives') tells the story of a team of lawyers working with the Catholic church to expose the torture and killings carried out by Pinochet's regime – and that still divides Chile. The series was based on real testimonies collected by the Catholic Church during the dictatorship and it took Chileans back to their troubled pasts. Although there have been many essays, books and plays written in this time, this was the first time the past had been presented in this way. Mauro Valdez, the head of the TVN, explained:

> We are telling the truth through fiction. I think it has been difficult to talk about these issues so I think that the series has given us the opportunity to face this experience. Fiction is a legitimate genre for this. The aim is not such much to convey information as it is to describe the experience on a human level.

The series was broadcast by the national TV channel that, at the time of the dictatorship, gave the least amount of information about what was going on in the country. For those running TVN today, the series didn't just address Chile's traumatic past, but the station's complicity in it. 'TVN is settling a debt. We are balancing out a historical vision', Mauro Valdez (2011) told us in an interview we had with him in Santiago de Chile in 2011. Unsurprisingly, the series provoked a fierce debate about the role of public broadcasting, with some right-wing politicians denouncing TVN for having aired the series. Interestingly for the discussion on journalism in Chile, the series also provoked some of the country's most prominent journalists doing research at the University of Diego Portales in Santiago to carry out their own investigation, using Cardinal Raul Silva's original archives to look into the real facts behind the cases dramatized on screen – a slippery dance between fact and fiction.

The narco novela

Colombia has been the long-time regional hub for famed telenovela. A few years back, the industry underwent a rebranding in which it moved away from the fairy-tale tone of earlier years and started making grittier dramas about narcotrafficking. Reading these cultural productions through an Adornian lens, one would have concluded that the soap opera simply performed its function to dupe the ignorant masses. However, in 2013, one narco novella sparked a new kind of controversy – because the story went to the heart of Colombia's painful political history. *Los 3 Caínes* ('The Three Caines') (2013) told the story of the Castaño brothers – the real-life founders of one of Colombia's most notorious paramilitary groups. Set up to fight left-wing guerrillas, they killed thousands and were knee-deep in drugs trafficking – often with the blessing of the country's political elite. The series sparked unprecedented controversy. Critics said the show made heroes out of murderers and silenced the voices of the victims and journalists who have tried to tell the real story. They denounced the series as a gross misrepresentation of history. Interestingly, the show prompted protests that managed to convince big companies to pull their advertising.

The reality show

A few years back, Norway's public TV channel, NRK, decided to broadcast live coverage of a seven-hour train ride. Seven hours of simple footage; a train rolling down the tracks. In 2011, it broadcast 134 hours non-stop of a cruise ship going up the Norwegian coast to the Arctic, winning the world record for the longest continuous TV programme. Norwegians, more than a million of them, according to the ratings, loved it. A new kind of reality TV show was born – and it goes against all the rules of TV engagement. No storyline. No script. No drama. No climax. It was called Slow TV. During the summer of 2013, Norwegians watched a cruise ship's journey up the coast, foggy days included. 'I think filming a boat is not a great philosophical achievement. But I think depth can be in many things and I think the gift or just sitting back and watching nature come at you and move past your window through your television [...] It has a relaxing effect', Per Arne Kalbakk, the deputy CEO of NRK told me at the time, with a straight face (2013).

A whole slew of different variations appeared soon afterwards: a 12-hour knitting show; another 12-hour show on firewood, featuring discussions about stacking and chopping, and a debate on whether the bark should face up or down; a marathon 30-hour interview; salmon swimming upstream.

'Norway's Slow TV' is one of the more light-hearted stories I have done, but there is a side to this story through which to think critically about news. Slow TV brings into sharp relief how the structural demands of the news media echo the dynamics of the capitalist market. In the age of the 24-hour news cycle, and indeed, the age of the Internet, the commercial value of the 'new' exceeds its journalistic one. News, like any other commodity on the market, must be new because the market needs to constantly update and replace commodities to ensure it continues to generate profit. Read allegorically, Slow TV reminds of the effects of the capitalist market on modern culture by providing a thought-provoking antithesis.

Roland Barthes

I resented seeing Nature and History confused at every turn, and I wanted to track down, in the decorative display of what-goes-without-saying, the ideological abuse which, in my view, is hidden there.

(Barthes 1972: 11)

To analyse the news media is to study signs – it is the work of a semiotician.

It is Roland Barthes' *Mythologies* that has often informed my way of looking at the media. Published in 1957, the book flits from food to horoscopes, to religion, to detergents, to toys, to photography, to advertising. But what runs through the multiple and seemingly discordant subjects is a continuous critique of what Barthes called 'myth' and what he saw as the repackaging of historically specific values of the ruling elite into natural, immutable, absolute truths. Take what Barthes wrote about a photograph in which a black soldier salutes the French flag. There, he dissected how the insidious myth of multi-ethnic Frenchness and empire is created. Herein lies the critical and political importance of Roland Barthes' writings. For, if when history is transformed into nature what it veils over are the political discourses that construct those signs, then we must surely always be attuned to the myth-making machine par excellence: news.

Barthes saw the work of the critic as a process of unmasking codes of the obvious cultural forms and teasing out the meanings that lie between the lines. Media for Barthes were anything from films, to photographs, fashion and advertising. His ability to defamiliarize the obvious in order to expose the potential political power behind these texts provides a key tool to pull the news media apart critically.

Take a subject as inoffensive as fonts for example. Imagine a world where all fonts were the same, where words wore a uniform, where letters spoke in monotone. The local newsstand would look a whole lot duller. For most people, fonts may seem inconsequential. Typography, the way letters are dressed and the way words are designed, may seem secondary to the meaning of the words they house. Through a Barthesian lens things look different, however. The way we consume news can be influenced by the way the information is presented, how it is edited, the choice of images to illustrate the accompanying text and the choice of typeface itself. Editors of a newspaper, a TV station or an online outlet know that the font they choose is key to the message they want to convey. In the process of storytelling, fonts are used to set the tone and project authority. Without reading one word, an outlet can convey gravitas simply by the fonts they use. And in a world where news can be agenda-laden and where information is often being framed in a particular way, something as subtle as the choice of a typeface plays a central role in that framing. Helvetica conveys more neutrality than Lucida. Arial more sobriety than Comic Sans. If you look at your regular newspapers, be it the *New York Times, Le Figaro, The Hindu*, and you presented those papers in an unfamiliar typeface, your understanding would be confused: like you're talking in a different accent.

Last year, when the *Sydney Morning Herald* used Comic Sans on a front page news story, an almighty furore ensued about a lowly font that had infiltrated the sacrosanct space of news. To use another term from Barthes (Barthes 1993), the incident represented a punctum (the moment in the photograph that 'pricks', 'bruises', 'wounds') in the myth of authority constructed around what the very font connotes. The moment this aesthetic conceit is demystified, so is its authority.

There was a postcolonial angle to this story too. Historically, it is Latin typeface that has dominated the market – both in Latin script and in the process of imposing the aesthetics of that script on to other languages.

In most cases, technological and production limitations overwhelm other factors. For example, a dearth of Thai text typefaces may shine a light on issues such as local literacy, the presence of an aspirational middle class and the cost or technical difficulty of developing new typefaces for a specific typesetting technology. The shapes of the letterforms themselves have more to do with the tension between traditionalism and modernity, and the marginal cost for each new typeface released.

But typefaces themselves can also sometimes embody an explicit political choice when their shapes are identified explicitly with modernity, Western-ness. Designers of non-Western fonts are therefore faced with a struggle not least because the homogenizing effects of a market dominated by Latin script means their own scripts are in danger of losing their authenticity. When I spoke to Neville Brody, legendary designer of fonts, he talked about how fonts in other languages are being standardized due to the hegemonic advance of the Western script. What is lost, he suggested, are the very histories those languages carry and therefore the cultures they represent. Fonts have memories, too – and the loss of that memory is a chapter of a cultural and political history of a form forced into disappearance by the banalizing effects of globalization.

Walter Benjamin

Importantly for a discussion on journalism, Walter Benjamin imagined the critic as a 'polytechnical engineer' (Benjamin 1983: 90). Capable of taking on new forms of media and incorporating them into a new, visual critical language, this radical writer or artist would use technical advances to renew his/her own critical approach. Benjamin sought to capture and safeguard images in which the incidental, the marginal and the neglected are disclosed and remembered. These are forgotten images, returned to the present, re-cited incongruously alongside other images, in order to feed the struggles of the present.

These theoretical points provided me with a useful canvas upon which to think about a radio station in Argentina called Radio La Colifata. Set up more than 20 years ago in Buenos Aires, it is the first radio station to broadcast from inside a mental hospital. La Colifata (slang for 'loon' or 'crazy person') has been broadcasting from Hospital Jose Borda every Saturday afternoon ever since, to give those suffering from mental illness a space to speak freely and to help confront the stigma around mental illness, breaking through the wall in AM, FM and now online. I have been to the radio broadcast on several occasions – probably one of the most interesting experiences I have had in journalism. In-patients produce and present the shows that range from politics to sports – and, over the years, millions of Argentinians have been tuning in to hear this cacophony of voices.

The radio was never intended as a serious journalistic enterprise per se. But the voices it includes, the things that are said, the way the stories are told are enough to make anyone in the mainstream world of journalism stop, listen and think about how their own voices are repressed, censored and sedated – and how truth lies beyond what has been institutionally prescribed. A regular listener told me:

The difference between La Colifata and other radio stations is that on a 'regular' radio station there are things that you can and can't say – because the medium has its filters. At La Colifata there aren't any – this is where the benefit lies – you can say what you think or what you feel and others will always listen and respect you.

Like Walter Benjamin's writings, La Colifata harbours what is unremarked, forgotten, cast adrift, pointing to a fascination with scraps of forgotten history. La Colifata echoes the Benjaminian call to retrieve out-of-date objects and to re-arrange them in new and surprising ways – to allegorically point to potentially new journalistic narratives.

As the founder of the radio, Alfredo Olivera told me in Buenos Aires in May 2015:

> It's not that people from La Colifata take a critical position on things – it's more that, in many cases, there is a tendency to interrogate what is obvious. What is seen as a mistake elsewhere is turned into a journalistic value here. There was a patient once who was going through a bad spell, and overthought the very steps she took – walking was not automatic for her. It was something that made her think about the experience of being 2 legged – and this was translated into a philosophical programme about human beings and their experience of walking. This person had no intention of posing philosophical questions but there was a critical effect. That is what La Colifata does.

The Colifata unleashes a polemical energy. Irreconcilable voices are forced to rub up against each other, setting off accidental meanings in a kind of performative act of inscribing a fragmented, uneven notion of historiographical reconstruction.

As Alfredo Olivera told me:

> La Colifata represents a broken space forgotten by others. Consumer society produces things and then it throws everything away. From that perspective we can think of mental asylums as huge reservoirs of society's psychological waste and so La Colifata is like great attempt to recycle those words and voices that have been discarded because they don't fit into the logic of the market.

I am not sure how *au fé* Olivera was with Walter Benjamin when he said this, but his elegant thoughts gave me an insight into how one can read La Colifata as a critical discourse based on the intrinsic relationship between what the mainstream forgets, the dynamics of the neo-liberal market and mass mediatization of culture. And for those of us who work in journalism, where mainstream news outlets are often too careful, too scared to tell it like it is, the uncut, uncensored voices of the patients at the radio station stand as a reminder of just how institutionalized we may have become.

Conclusion

The premise of this chapter emanated from a series of questions about how to bridge the gaps between the world of media scholarship and the world of journalism itself. My career path took a sharp turn from high theory into journalism because of my own questions surrounding the relevance of those writings: I felt I had an explosive collection of ideas but they resided in the confines of a world in which they circulated around like-minded thinkers, sometimes dressed up in impenetrable languages that aligned themselves high-mindedly with the excluded ('the other') while revelling in their own semantic exclusivity. So while this intellectual history was a crucial chapter of my own journey, I began to wonder whether it wasn't more pertinent to take them to a more public forum.

The notes written down here are chronicles of attempts, some more successful than others, to create a language of media critique that can incorporate ideas that defamiliarize and enrich. This endeavour is not easy: first because television is often a much harder medium to manage and write to. Ideas get condensed beyond recognition, subtlety falls by the wayside. Additionally, I have frequently found that anti-intellectualism is rife in the world of TV news. Journalists, impatient with complex and contradictory texts, have little time for it. Understandably, when one is trying to deliver news on the ground, keeping up with breaking stories, trying to simply get a bulletin out, the last thing on your mind is what Jacques Derrida might have meant by then eternal deferral of meaning in language. But while cultural theory has sometimes over-theorized its objects of study, I do not think that it is an act of intellectual vanity to push thought beyond conventional wisdoms regurgitated ad infinitum by the narratives of the media. If social consensus is built through the stories repeated through the mainstream, it is sometimes in the university libraries, in academia, where we can *unlearn* those myths.

References

Allen, W. (1977) *Annie Hall*, Beverly Hills, CA: United Artists.

Anon. (1966), 'This hour has seven days', CBC, http://www.cbc.ca/player/play/1403659265. Accessed 7 November 2016.

—— (2012), 'Chile's collective trauma', Al Jazeera English, 11 June, http://www.aljazeera.com/programmes/listeningpost/2012/06/2012611101114900626.html. Accessed 10 September 2016.

—— (2012), 'US Memorial Day: A semantic minefield', Al Jazeera English, 18 June, http://www.aljazeera.com/programmes/listeningpost/2012/06/201261894353963597.html. Accessed 15 August 2016.

—— (2013), 'Colombia's Narconovelas', Al Jazeera English, 16 November, http://www.aljazeera.com/programmes/listeningpost/2013/11/colombia-narco-novelas-20131116102548621427.html. Accessed 10 September 2016.

—— (2013), 'Norway's Slow TV', Al Jazeera English, 15 September, http://www.aljazeera.com/programmes/listeningpost/2013/09/20139141111740850.html. Accessed 10 September 2016.

—— (2013), 'Of mediums and messages', 31 August, Al Jazeera English, http://www.aljazeera.com/programmes/listeningpost/2013/04/20134683632515956.html. Accessed 30 August 2016.

—— (2013), 'Stylebooks: The politics of naming',. Al Jazeera English, 25 May, http://www.aljazeera.com/programmes/listeningpost/2013/05/201352512137941940.html. Accessed 2 September 2016.

———— (2015), 'Argentina's Loony Radio', Al Jazeera English, 19 April, http://www.aljazeera. com/programmes/listeningpost/2015/04/argentina-loony-radio-150419152903774.html. Accessed 10 September 2016.

———— (2016), 'Fonts in the news media', Al Jazeera English, 2 December, http://video.aljazeera. com/channels/eng/videos/listening-post---feature%3A-fonts-in-the-news-media/3919417 725001;jsessionid=5F0E7F7BA480C676BA3A833FC24C4003. Accessed 10 September 2016.

———— (2016), '"Us" and "them" in media discourse', Al Jazeera English, 25 October, http://www. aljazeera.com/programmes/listeningpost/2015/10/media-discourse-151025072759187.html. Accessed 5 September 2016.

Barthes, R. (1972), *Mythologies* (trans. A. Lavers), London: Paladin.

Barthes, R. (1993), *Camera Lucida: Reflections on Photography*, London: Vintage Classics.

Benjamin, W. (1983), *Understanding Brecht* (trans. A. Bostock), London: Verso.

Culler, J. (1976), *Saussure*, London: The Harvester Press.

Derrida, J. (1977), *Of Grammatology* (trans. G. Chakravorty Spivak), Baltimore, ML: Johns Hopkins University Press.

Eagleton, T. (1996), *Literary Theory*, Oxford: Blackwell.

Forgacs, D. and Hobsbawm, E. (eds) (2000), *The Antonio Gramsci Reader: Selected Writings 1916–1935*, New York: New York University Press.

Hall, S. (1981), 'Notes on deconstructing "The Popular"', in R. Samuel (ed.), *People's History and Socialist Theory*, London: Routledge.

Horkheimer, M. and Adorno, T. (1997), *The Dialectic of Enlightenment*, London: Verso.

McLuhan, M. (1970), 'Living in an acoustic world', http://marshallmcluhanspeaks.com/ lecture/1970-living-in-an-acoustic-world/. Accessed 19 June 2015.

National Broadcasting Corporation (1976), *Marshall McLuhan Speaks Special Collection: The Tomorrow Show*, http://marshallmcluhanspeaks.com/interview/1976-what-television-does-best/. Accessed 4 November 2013.

Radio La Colifata (2016), 'La la la la la Colifata', http://www.vivalacolifata.org. Accessed 10 September 2016.

Said, E. (1991), *Orientalism: Western Conceptions of the Orient*, London: Penguin.

Said, E. (1997), *Covering Islam: How the Media and the Experts Determine How We See the Rest of the World*, London: Vintage.

Saussure, F. de (1978), *Course in General Linguistics*, London: Bloomsbury

Voltaire (1763), *Traité sur la tolerance,* http://www.gutenberg.org/files/42131/42131-h/42131-h. htm. Accessed 10 November 2015.

Part III

Who Gets It Right?

Chapter 13

Journalists Do Live in a Parallel Universe: A Response to Practitioner Critiques of Journalism Academics

Jairo Lugo-Ocando

Journalism exposes a key paradox, one that many of us who worked in the field are aware of. On the one hand, there is the conviction that the newsroom is the centre of the universe and, on the other, the certainty that it is one of the most isolated places on earth. In fact, it is more of an oxymoron. While the newsroom is supposedly one of the most interconnected workplaces in this planet, embedded in the structure of power with good access to the rich and the powerful, it also appears to be very detached from reality and far away from the daily lives of most of the audiences it claims to represent. Indeed, the newsroom can be at times a lonely place in which individual world-views and group thinking are incapable of self-awareness and which remains impenetrable by critical self-reflection. The predominant organizational culture in which journalists operate and are trained is one that tends to reject straightforward external criticism that questions the structural role of the commercial media and the prevalent world-views among journalists (Eldridge 2014; Haas 2006).

Resistance to criticism

Historically speaking, the news media has resisted change and criticism (Brown 1974; Carey 1974; Haas 2007). This is why official efforts and civic attempts to change and improve the way journalists go about their work have mostly been ignored.

One can cite two good examples of how journalists are reluctant to change and improve their work: the first is the McBride Report (1980) produced by UNESCO, and the second is most recent, the Leveson Inquiry in the United Kingdom (2012). These efforts, which in their time enjoyed considerable support from governments, international organizations and important segments of the public, had almost no effect on the way news media organizations behave or journalists go about their work.

One should not forget, as Upton Sinclair (1919) suggested in one of the first serious critical studies of the press, that news media outlets operate within an atmosphere of power and that it would be naïve to think that most of those who own and control them would be willing to relinquish that power for the public good.

Learning from mistakes

If truth be told, to use a classic journalism cliché, journalists are the most reluctant people to listen and learn from their own mistakes (Fahmy and Johnson 2005). We always find legitimate reasons to justify what we did and, particularly, what we did wrong. We dismiss criticism under the assumption that unless you worked as a proper reporter, with a daily beat, facing the pressures of power and deadlines, you have no 'legitimate' right whatsoever to criticize what we do.

We dismiss reports and scholarly research based on a systematic and structured study of our work, because – we say – it is 'irrelevant' or presented in convoluted language and terminology that makes it 'inaccessible'. Some of us have gone on to claim that we do not have time for scholarly criticism that overlooks the pressures we face and undermines the democratic value of what we do.

Denial

All these arguments, of course, are discursive strategies of evasion coming from a profession that lives in a state of denial. A professional body that, mostly and with very few exceptions in the mainstream, went along, deeply embedded, with Bush and Blair to illegally invade Iraq in 2003, opening a Pandora's box of terrorism and political instability (Lewis 2006; Miller 2004; Tumber and Palmer 2004).

It was this same professional body that overall, and again with few honourable exceptions, was unable or unwilling to challenge bankers and financial markets in the run-up to the crisis of 2008 (Schiffrin 2011; Starkman 2014). It is the same professional body that has never understood the challenges faced by its own industry in light of globalization, digital technology and de-politicization of society (Chyi, Lewis and Zheng 2012), something that has inexorably led to audience fragmentation and a decline in ratings, sales and income across the sector.

So for us to preach to academic researchers that their work is worthless unless it is made accessible and relevant to us journalists, or unless it has an immediate and direct impact on our daily practice, is nothing less than arrogance and a dire statement on the degree of disconnection between the newsroom and the real world.

Widening gap

Overall, the gap between journalists and academia needs to be acknowledged for what it really is: a flawed anomaly that rarely happens in other fields of social science knowledge.

For instance, institutions such as the Political Studies Association in the United Kingdom have continuously served as forums where politicians, activists, civil servants and officials of all sorts share ideas and discussions with academic researchers about their work. This also happens with the British Sociological Association, the Royal Geographical Society and the Royal Statistical Society with regard to social services, NGOs, charities and government offices who not only read the work of academics but commission them to carry out research that allows self-reflection and improvement from each one of these organizations and institutions.

Instead, journalism as a professional body seems reluctant to engage in such forums despite numerous invitations to do so from organizations such as ICA, MECCSA, ECREA and many others. The common experience of many academics, again with honorable exceptions, is that they struggle to get news people to spend a couple of hours with them, not to say a whole day in a particular event. Reasons given are the following: the incompatibility of the long sessions with the prerogatives, dynamics and pressures within the newsroom to deliver on the deadline; the fact that the research being discussed has little relevance for journalism practice; and, of course, the fact that the academic work is unreadable. So, are we really saying that academics in politics, sociology, human geography and statistics somehow have been able to unlock a special and magical formula that allows practitioners of other discipline to engage? Are we really suggesting that media and journalism studies have not produced work that is somehow relevant to what we do?

Not for a minute do I think this is what my colleagues (Chapters 1, 3, 4, among others) seem to be suggesting in their chapters published in this book. I think that the authors are genuinely asking for a dialogue that is evidently absent. I agree with them in many of the points they are making.

However, where I depart and take my own position is in not reinforcing this false perception that most if not all academic research into journalism is somehow irrelevant or useless. Here are some citations from chapters the practitioners have contributed to this book:

'I cannot recall a single academic paper issuing from 'pure' media scholars that I found relevant or useful to the work I did or that resulted in me changing my practice in any way' (Chapter 3).

'It is not only practitioners who feel alienated by such writing. Media, journalism and communication students are rarely happy with the language of the academic texts they are forced to read as part of their curriculum' (Chapter 4).

'But we all have to remember – academics and practitioners – it is the taxpayers who pay for a lot of the research; therefore, the public have the right to know whether they will eventually get something in return for their money' (Chapter 5).

'The way scholars write is a direct offence to the craft skills of journalists. It goes against everything they believe and everything they teach their staff. They see their own job as achieving clarity and regard academics as delivering obfuscation – over-long papers, windy, jargon, cloudy meaning, invented language' (Chapter 1).

I do recognize that it is tempting to make these types of assertions. I myself, first as a reporter and subsequently as news editor, never found many academic paper relevant to my own practice. However, contrary to some of my colleagues, I have come to recognize in hindsight that it was more to do with my own prejudices and reluctance to accept criticism against my self-constructed pedestal as paladin of justice.

Long way to go

The fact that many mainstream journalists are still embracing uncritically liberal values such as 'objectivity' and 'balance' as universal paradigms of truth indicates the long path that we still need to transit. To be sure, and as John Steel (2014) says, since most calls for reforming journalism happen within the confines of neo-liberalism, it will be naïve to suggest that they would address the fundamental reasons as to why the profession has failed society so far.

To be sure, the same criticism practitioners make on the pages of this book against academic work for not having any impact on practice can be turned around to ask whether journalism has made us a better, more just and equal society. Similar arguments about public funding and people asking for their money's worth to academia can be also easily redirected to institutions such as the BBC and its very flawed coverage of many aspects of public life or lack of impact in changing policy.

Moreover, the 'lack of impact' argument, based on the assertion of 'useful' and 'accessible' research, is in itself very problematic. This because the idea of 'pure media research' as too abstract or too theoretical represents not only a naïve dismissal of the importance of critical thinking in our lives but also because it is a very unsophisticated way of trying to keep journalism de-politicized and de-contextualized from social practice.

The fact remains that the academic field of media studies has become indispensable to any full understanding of the organization of modern life, the play of power and the dynamics of change (Murdock and Golding 2015: 41).

Scholarly work on the history of commercial journalism, to cite a case, is by all means particularly relevant to journalism practice. The plethora of research in this area shows that modern journalism is a by-product of the Enlightenment project and that it played an important role in legitimizing the British Empire and slavery in Africa in the nineteenth century. Drawing on this historical knowledge could allow us to question the causes that mainstream journalism is currently supporting under similar flags and assumptions.

It is from this research that we can draw important lessons of how journalism fell for the false promises of bringing democracy to Vietnam in the 1970s and to Afghanistan and Iraq more recently. It is from it that I myself came to understand why I accepted so uncritically the structural adjustment programmes of the 1980s and 1990s in Latin America (Lugo-Ocando 2014: 9) and how I had failed in my own duty of defending those left behind.

Social responsibility

Yes, academics do need to understand that they too have a responsibility for the public engagement and it should never be about researching to score points in the academic career.

Yes, it is also true that academics working in this field have failed in many cases to articulate more vehemently their case, and that the academic study of journalism as a whole 'resembles in many ways a failed adoption' (Zelizer 1998).

However, journalists should not hang on to this as to excuse their lack of engagement with what is by far the only available and credible body of work concerning practice.

Journalists should also understand that academics have been working hard to improve journalism, not to undermine it. It is in the pages of journal articles and academic books that we can find the most vehement, articulated and substantiated defence for journalism and its undeniable role in society – even if at times it seems obscure and convoluted.

We need to read criticism in these pages not as an attack on journalism – even if it at times seems harsh and demolishing – but as a valid and healthy exercise of democratic engagement and committed debate with one of the most important social practices of our times. The work of Lewis, Williams and Franklin (2008), just to name one example, sheds light on the deterioration and decline of quality of journalism in the United Kingdom and why journalism needs more and not less support from society as a whole. It is in my eyes one of the best defences ever written for journalism as a public service.

Can academics help?

If these works remind us that the mainstream media systems and journalistic practices continue to be a megaphone for the rich and the powerful (Curran and Seaton 2009; Entman 2004; Franklin 1997), it is also these findings that highlight the need to improve newsrooms' practices and our relation to power.

It would be of course naïve to think that all these works have been dismissed by journalists over the years just because of the style in which they were written. The fact remains that seminal pieces of research such as those produced by Hall et al. on racism ([1978] 2013) or those by Schlesinger and Tumber (1994) on crime reporting remain largely ignored by many practitioners despite being very relevant and accessible.

Even very useful and accessible guides to improve the reporting of poverty, produced by a group of academics and commissioned by the Joseph Rowntree Foundation (2010), are set aside to continue with the systematic stigmatization of large segments of society as 'scroungers'. This despite the fact that these works were commissioned to be written in a very accessible way for the public and for non-specialist audience.

Indeed, we are right to point out that most of the research and knowledge about media and journalism does not seem to permeate into the newsroom. Not at least in the same way that academia seems to collaborate with other fields of knowledge and social practices such as politics, social policy and justice.

An honourable exception to this is perhaps the work carried out between the London School of Economics and the *Guardian* analysing the 2015 London riots (Lewis et al. 2011). This type of initiative reminds us, as sporadic as it might be, that despite assumptions and prejudices from both sides there are good things happening between journalism and academia and there is hope for engagement and dialogue.

Lack of collaboration

If we, practitioners and former practitioners, are more open to accommodate self-criticism and listen more carefully to what the academy has to say about us, then there is a wealth of knowledge to be learnt from both sides. It is that research that would have allowed some news editors and reporters to avoid, for example, their support for the invasion of Iraq in 2003 or at least to provide a more critical coverage of the war. It could have also helped them understand better the relationship between reporters and their sources (Manning 2001), which in some circumstances such as the sub-prime mortgage market crisis got too close and complacent (Manning 2013).

However, journalists have consistently dismissed whole chunks of research carried out by academics, notwithstanding its constancy and great deal of evidence. Despite all the lessons we could have learnt from the Glasgow Media Group's work on the systematic bias of organizations such as the BBC and CNN, in conflicts such as Palestine and Israel or in Northern Ireland (Philo 2014), active journalists are still too ready to go embedded with the status quo to the next battle.

It is this same professional body that remains largely uncritical of corporations and their power and influence over democratic institutions. This is partly because it has ignored extensive works on the damage that corporate public relations have done and continue to inflict onto journalistic ethics and credibility (Miller and Dinan 2007).

One might suggest that resistance to academic critique goes with journalism's broader tendency to resist critique as a whole, which is perhaps somehow understandable in light of the barrage of attacks that journalism suffers on a daily basis from many other sectors. In the case of journalism practice, resistance to academic critique is probably due to the perception that academics are 'evaluating' rather than interpreting the social reality of journalism.

This insularity is sometimes seen as a product of its feeling threatened economically (Conboy and Eldridge 2014) or in terms of its authority, and provokes a need to reassert its place at the centre of the universe.

If truth is to be told, once more, journalists do not engage with academia because they live in a different universe – one where self-criticism is not a part of the equation nor is it permitted to go too deep into critical self-reflection of practices.

Yes, we might agree that many academics tend to write too convoluted for our taste and produce a lot of work that we find hard to fit in our own world-view or urgent need to produce news within the tight schedule of a deadline.

Yes, that particular research piece on Harry Potter and childhood aspirations of self-image (Whitehurst 2012) or the other one about Buffy the Vampire Slayer (Blowers et al.

2003; Greenwood and Pietromonaco 2004; Owen 1999) and the role of media in anorexia among young people might seem to us at times irrelevant.

And some might even parade these types of work every time we want to discredit academia as a waste of tax-payers' money.

But we should know better than to repeat the *Daily Mail*'s anti-intellectual clichés (Blanchet 2013) and to use them as cheap shots against academia only because we have failed to engage with it.

I do agree with my colleague Kevin Marsh who points out to the fact that there is a growing number of academy/practitioner institutions/organizations who do manage to cross the divide. This signals somehow that the aim of bringing the universes closer is not an idle one.

Having said that, 'hackademics' (Errigo 2004; Harcup 2011) are only a small part of the solution. Overall and more broadly, we need to stop seeing journalism solely as a profession and understand it instead for what it is: a social practice (Reese 2010; Schudson 2001) deeply embedded across the whole of society.

Once we realize this, we will understand that there are far more important matters at stake in our debates about journalism. However, to do that there are questions that practitioners need to ask themselves.

Why have we failed to engage with proper academic research and debate as other fields of knowledge have done? Why have we remained isolated in our newsrooms when the rest of the social science and arts and humanities universe has collaborated so effectively with academia to improve understanding and practice?

Unless we answer these questions more honestly, without recurring to discursive decoys that distract and are overall unhelpful, journalism and academia will be condemned to live in parallel universes. One of them is expanding and growing all the time and linking with the rest of society; the other is shrinking while trying to encapsulate and isolate journalism practice in a space and time that never was.

References

Blanchet, B. (2013), 'Translating the intellectual in Britain: The Cenotaph yob and other representations of dissent', *Journal of European Studies*, 43: 1, pp. 60–74.

Blowers, L. C., Loxton, N. J., Grady-Flesser, M., Occhipinti, S. and Dawe, S. (2003), 'The relationship between sociocultural pressure to be thin and body dissatisfaction in preadolescent girls', *Eating Behaviors*, 4: 3, pp. 229–44.

Brown, L. (1974), *The Reluctant Reformation: On Criticizing the Press in America*, New York: David McKay Company Inc.

Carey, J. W. (1974), 'Journalism and criticism: The case of an undeveloped profession', *The Review of Politics*, 36: 2, pp. 227–49.

Chyi, H. I., Lewis, S. and Zheng, N. (2012), 'A matter of life and death? Examining how newspapers covered the newspaper "Crisis"', *Journalism Studies*, 13: 3, pp. 305–24.

Conboy, M. and Eldridge, S. (2014), 'Morbid symptoms: Between a dying and a re-birth (apologies to Gramsci)', *Journalism Studies*, 15: 5, pp. 566–75.

Curran, J. and Seaton, J. (2009), *Power without Responsibility: Press, Broadcasting and the Internet in Britain*, London: Routledge.

Eldridge, S. A. (2013), 'Perceiving professional threats: Journalism's discursive reaction to the rise of new media entities', *Journal of Applied Journalism & Media Studies*, 2: 2, pp. 281–99.

——— (2014), 'Boundary maintenance and interloper media reaction: Differentiating between journalism's discursive enforcement processes', *Journalism Studies*, 15: 1, pp. 1–16.

Entman, R. M. (2004), *Projections of Power: Framing News, Public Opinion, and US Foreign Policy*, Chicago: University of Chicago Press.

Errigo, J. A. B. F. (2004), 'Surviving in the hackademy', *British Journalism Review*, 15: 2, pp. 43–48.

Fahmy, S. and Johnson, T. J. (2005), 'How we performed: Embedded journalists' attitudes and perceptions towards covering the Iraq War', *Journalism & Mass Communication Quarterly*, 82: 2, pp. 301–17.

Franklin, B. (1997), *Newszak and News Media*, London: Arnold.

Greenslade, R. (2013), 'Sadly, too many journalists seeking academic credibility can't write', *The Guardian*', http://www.theguardian.com/media/greenslade/2013/aug/27/journalism-education-newspapers. Accessed 10 May 2015.

Greenwood, D. N. and Pietromonaco, P. R. (2004), 'The interplay among attachment orientation, idealized media images of women, and body dissatisfaction: A social psychological analysis', in L. J. Shrum (ed.), *The Psychology of Entertainment Media: Blurring the Lines between Entertainment and Propaganda*, Mahwah: Lawrence Erlbaum Associates, pp. 141–75.

Haas, T. (2006), 'Mainstream news media self-criticism: A proposal for future research', *Critical Studies in Media Communication*, 23: 4, pp. 350–355.

——— (2007), *The Pursuit of Public Journalism: Theory, Practice, and Criticism*, London: Routledge.

Hall, S., Critcher, C., Jefferson, T., Clarke, J. and Roberts, B. ([1978] 2013), *Policing the Crisis: Mugging, the State and Law and Order*, London: Palgrave Macmillan.

Harcup, T. (2011), 'Hackademics at the chalkface: To what extent have journalism teachers become journalism researchers?', *Journalism Practice*, 5: 1, pp. 34–50.

Joseph Rowntree Foundation (2010), 'Reporting poverty', http://www.jrf.org.uk/reporting-poverty?gclid=CIL47Z6Uv8UCFerKtAodRAYAnQ. Accessed 12 May 2015.

Leveson, B. H. (2012), 'The Leveson Inquiry into the culture, practices and ethics of the press', http://webarchive.nationalarchives.gov.uk/20140122145147/http:/www.levesoninquiry.org.uk/. Accessed 10 May 2015.

Lewis, J. (2006), *Shoot First and Ask Questions Later: Media Coverage of the 2003 Iraq War*, Oxford: Peter Lang.

Lewis, J., Williams, A. and Franklin, B. (2008), 'A compromised fourth estate? UK news journalism, public relations and news sources', *Journalism Studies*, 9: 1, pp. 1–20.

Lewis, P., Newburn, T., Taylor, M., Mcgillivray, C., Greenhill, A., Frayman, H. and Proctor, R. (2011), 'Reading the riots: Investigating England's summer of disorder', http://eprints.lse.ac.uk/46297/. Accessed 9 May 2015.

Lugo-Ocando, J. (2014), *Blaming the Victim: How Global Journalism Fails Those in Poverty*, London: Pluto Press.

MacBride, S. e. a. (1980), *Un Solo Mundo, Voces Multiples*, Mexico City: Fondo de Cultura Economica.

Manning, P. (2001), *News and News Sources: A Critical Introduction*, London: SAGE.

——— (2013), 'Financial journalism, news sources and the banking crisis', *Journalism*, 14: 2, pp. 173–89.

Miller, D. (2004), *Tell me Lies: Propaganda and Media Distortion in the attack on IRAQ*, London: Pluto Press.

Miller, D. and Dinan, W. (2007), *A Century of Spin: How Public Relations became the Cutting Edge of Corporate Power*, London: Pluto Press.

Murdock, G. and Golding, P. (2015), 'Media studies in question: The making of a contested formation', in M. Conboy and J. Steel (eds), *The Routledge Companion to British Media History*, London: Routledge, pp. 41–59.

Owen, A. S. (1999), 'Buffy the Vampire Slayer: Vampires, postmodernity, and postfeminism', *Journal of Popular Film & Television*, 27: 2, pp. 24–31.

Philo, G. (2014), *The Glasgow Media Group Reader, Vol. II: Industry, Economy, War and Politics*, London: Routledge.

Philo, G., Briant, E. and Donald, P. (2013), *Bad News for Refugees*, London: Pluto Press.

Reese, S. D. (1999), 'The progressive potential of journalism education recasting the academic versus professional debate', *The Harvard International Journal of Press/Politics*, 4: 4, pp. 70–94.

——— (2010), 'Journalism and globalization', *Sociology Compass*, 4: 6, pp. 344–53.

Schiffrin, A. (2011), *Bad News: How America's Business Press Missed the Story of the Century*, New York: The New Press.

Schlesinger, P. and Tumber, H. (1994), *Reporting Crime: The Media Politics of Criminal Justice*, Oxford: Oxford University Press.

Schudson, M. (2001), 'The objectivity norm in American journalism', *Journalism*, 2: 2, pp. 149–70.

Sinclair, U. (1919), *The Brass Check*, Pasadena, CA: Self.

Starkman, D. (2014), *The Watchdog that didn't Bark: The Financial Crises and the Disappearance of Investigative Journalism*, New York: Columbia University Press.

Steel, J. (2014), '"Liberal" reform and normativity in media analysis – Open democracy', https://www.opendemocracy.net/john-steel/%E2%80%98liberal%E2%80%99-reform-and-normativity-in-media-analysis. Accessed 7 May 2015.

Tumber, H. and Palmer, J. (2004), *Media at War: The Iraq Crisis*, London: SAGE

Whitehurst, K. (2012), 'Explorations of childhood in a modern age: A review of three books that engage with fairy-tale literature', *Jeunesse: Young People, Texts, Cultures*, 4: 1, pp. 190–200.

Zelizer, B. (1998), 'The failed adoption of journalism study', http://repository.upenn.edu/cgi/viewcontent.cgi?article=1325&context=asc_papers. Accessed 11 May 2015.

——— (2004), *Taking Journalism Seriously: News and the Academy*, London: SAGE.

Chapter 14

Linking Theory to Practice: Changing the Approach of Media and Journalism Research

Leon Barkho

Introduction

Daniel Perrin (2012: 2) introduces a new strand of research methodology in the sphere, which may be labelled 'praxis', 'practice' or 'applied'. Perrin (2012) focuses on 'research with an applied angle in which a clear link is made between the prevalent theories and paradigms media and communication scholars work with, and the real world where media and communication activities take place'. Perrin's transdisciplinary action research (TD) has a strong bearing on the notion of praxis because it is about not only understanding the real world, the 'life-world' out there, but also *improving* it. Perrin's (2012 and 2013) research has pioneered a reciprocal, collaborative, proactive and transdisciplinary approach, in which academics and practitioners are both involved. In TD, as Perrin (2012: 4) points out, 'academics from various disciplines collaborate with practitioners to investigate and sustainably solve a socially-relevant practical problem'.

Explaining social worlds is not enough if researchers fail to make these social worlds 'understandable [...] coherent and meaningful to various addressees', Perrin (2013: 219) says. Media and journalism have their own social worlds. Praxis-based research shares a common ground with Perrin's TD, in that researchers should not only try to explain these worlds for the purposes of their own investigation, but also for the purposes of helping practitioners, where appropriate, understand the disorder of their own social world and introduce some form of order and coherence to it. Perrin's TD is a relevant research framework with the capacity 'to bridge the gap between media and communication research and actors with a say in media production, i.e. broadcasters, newspapers, radio, Internet-based media outlets, etc.'

Barkho and Saleh (Chapter 7 in this book) lay down the conceptual and methodological underpinnings of praxis-based research in the field of media and journalism. They position 'praxis' within the main schools of thought and philosophical deliberations that have characterized research in mainstream social science. They trace the term and its development as it first emerged in the treaties of ancient Greek philosophers down to modern thinkers such as Emanuel Kant, Jürgen Habermas, Max Horkheimer, Karl Marx, Hans-Georg Gadamer, Robert Brandom, Richard J. Bernstein and John Dewey. The chapter recommends special streams for future praxis-based media research and puts forward ideas on how the gap between media theory and media practice can be bridged. Drawing on these deliberations, the authors find that there is an urgent need for 'research in which a clear link is made between the prevalent theories: the paradigms and theories media and communication scholars work with, and the real world where media and communication work takes place'. The people and organizations we academics research are not merely our subjects, objects or respondents: they are our partners – partners with whom we are required to cooperate on the basis of equality, reciprocity and reflexivity.

The article by Perrin (2012) and the chapter by Barkho and Saleh (in this book) do not represent a template for how theory and practice should follow one another. They are an attempt to hone the praxis-oriented niche. They call on media and journalism academics to free themselves from the 'cage' and confines of the academic method of research with regard to language as well as issues of epistemology, ontology and methodology. They urge academics to get engaged with those they are researching and provide not only analyses that interpret their real 'life-world', but also sustainable, empirically and theoretically grounded alternatives, solutions and suggested improvements.

The three key pillars of praxis strategy

Praxis as strategy is comprised of a number of pillars. The first pillar includes terms like praxis, applied, practice, performance, experience, action and interaction. The second pillar relates to practitioners. It is part of another bundle of terms, which includes subject, actor, person, agent, self, participant, individual and respondent. The third pillar of this dynamic is part of yet another bundle of terms, which includes analysts, researchers, scholars, thinkers, hackademics and scientists. It is important to have these three pillars represented as far as possible at all levels of praxis-based media and journalism research; to have them included in the niche praxis research tries to promote.

Praxis and theory

We do not yet have a theory for praxis but we can feel the need for formulating such a theory in media and journalism research. In his seminal paper, 'Theory in anthropology since the sixties', Ortner (1984: 144) says that praxis as an orientation is deeply rooted in social science and it is a theme that is widely discussed in anthropology and ethnography; but it still remains 'neither a theory nor a method in itself, but rather [...] a symbol, in the name of which a variety of theories and methods are developed'. Developing a praxis-oriented theory gets added significance when encountering questions for which we are still scrambling for answers: where are we going to situate ourselves as analysts or researchers in the two main paradigms or categories of ethnography: (1) practice, praxis, action, interaction, activity, performance, structure; (2) agent, actor, person, self, individual, subject, etc.? What do we do with the knowledge we get? Who is to benefit from it? Is it possible to make it available to the categories and actors involved in our research and other actors interested in it, and in what shape? Do we reiterate what those we research already know, or try to seek solutions and alternatives to improve their 'life-world'?

The issue of rendering research meaningful, practical and relevant to different addressees is widely discussed and accepted in ethnography literature (Perrin 2013). However, media and journalism research has hitherto paid insufficient attention to the practical needs of those we research since it has mostly relayed to them what they already know and mostly through a language, philosophy and methodology they find hard to understand. This is probably one of the main reasons media practitioners discard our investigations: we generally reiterate what they already know and rarely get engaged in a dialogue that seeks solutions and alternatives to improve their 'life-world' (Chapter 16).

There are different ways of approaching praxis. Whichever one we choose to supplement media and journalism research, it will entail a radical theoretical and methodological move because praxis treats actors in the dynamic of social science research on a level playing field. In praxis-oriented research, we need to turn our attention to symbols and discourses the researched employ to communicate their views of the world, and how and why these symbols obtain a degree of objectivity that makes it rather difficult for individuals, groups and institutions to replace them or give them different meanings, since applied research aims at improving the 'life-world' and not only explaining it (Geertz 1973).

Praxis calls for partnership, reciprocity and collaboration between all the pillars in the dynamic of media and journalism research. This perspective means that, if we really want to make sense of the world from the viewpoint of the researched, we should not only situate ourselves in their position but also help the researched situate themselves in different situations; to help them be aware of contradictions, anomalies and even injustices of their own status. Praxis-oriented research is not confined to making people aware of what they do or why they do it. It tries to explore the impact of what they do to themselves and those who are different from them (Foucault 1980).

In short, praxis-oriented research must draw on the hitherto overlooked Bakhtinian recommendation on how to design dialogism theories capable of explaining and improving our social world. Mikhail Bakhtin coins the expression 'carnivalesque egalitarianism', in which researcher and researched become equal partners, making it extremely difficult for outsiders or observers to discriminate between them because both are elevated to a state of 'temporary suspension of all hierarchic distinctions and barriers', as is the case with revellers in a carnival (Bakhtin 1984: 15).

The missing paradigm

The notion of praxis or applied does not overlook the powerful role social systems and mechanisms exert upon human beings and their institutions and their impact on shaping events. But it is a call, which Pierre Bourdieu ([1972] 1978) theorizes and operationalizes in his applied research, to redirect attention to the real 'life-world' needs of those we research, the how and why texts, structures, processes and practices obtain their meanings, the role of agents and actors in their construction, what their practice in reality does to society and what we (academics and practitioners) can do to improve their impact.

Michel Foucault, likewise, advocates praxis in his philosophy and his praxis-based concepts and interpretations have impacted on social science disciplines. He is probably one of the most quoted philosophers in media and journalism studies. However, his notion of praxis has yet to be applied and put into practice. Foucault, like Bourdieu, redirects researchers' attention to impact, emphasizing not only the interpretation of our senses and dispositions of the social world but the consequences of how we translate them into reality because we as human beings may not be aware of the fallout of our actions: 'People know what they do; they frequently know why they do what they do; but what they don't know is what what they do does' (Dreyfus and Rabinow 1982: 187). Media and journalism scholars trying to penetrate power asymmetries in social relations often start from the platform that people may not be aware of what they are doing and usually do not know why they do the things they do. The missing paradigm is to research the impact and the consequences of what people do – and not only believe or perceive – to their own way of life and to others, and see what we can do to ameliorate the impact of harmful actions on society.

Foucault and Bourdieu's praxis-oriented approach resonates in Berger and Luckmann (1967: 61), who summarize it in a terse three-sentence statement: 'Society is a human product. Society is an objective reality. Man is a social product'. Media and journalism studies, particularly in the United States, start from the standpoint that culture and discourse are part of objective reality in which actors and agency do not play a big role. Media and journalism academics and practitioners seem to agree. If we sift through their style manuals and internal guidelines, we will come up with the perception that, in their opinion, it is possible and feasible to tell things as they are (Barkho 2011). On the other hand, studies mainly in Europe have emphasized the role of human agency in shaping the social and cultural world – a rather subjective reality in which practitioners tell things as they see them and not as they are. I believe we have not investigated the first part of P. Berger and T. Luckmann's epigram, namely: 'Society is a human product'. Here comes the role of praxis with its notions of cooperation, reciprocity and solidarity, which should help us understand how and why discourse and culture patterns are built, produced and reproduced, as well as the intentions behind them, what they do when translated into action, where these patterns come from and how they might be changed.

Ethnographic praxis

Praxis recognizes the potential of ethnography in combining media and journalism analyses with the social and cultural dimensions of research. Sociolinguists have dealt with this social dimension at length, but it remains to be fully investigated in other areas where language and discourse are the major tools of communication, namely in the realm of media and journalism as practice. The people we research employ symbols and language to communicate their own social reality. These symbols develop specific social and discursive patterns and in the course of time, they become entrenched, tried-and-trusted practices that are not easy to replace or change, because language forces its patterns on us and, as a sign system, 'has the quality of objectivity' (Berger and Luckmann 1967: 53).

The linguistic text has been the focus of most media-based discourse analyses. Praxis with an ethnography approach that is intended to serve the practical needs of practitioners may lead to methodological tensions with researchers trying to balance linguistic analysis with the demands and complexities of cultural and social practices. But this does not answer whether praxis with an ethnographic angle is useful for research. D. Hymes (1977) answered the question in the early 1960s when he urged communication scholars to add a second descriptive science besides the descriptive frame that relied almost solely on text so that research will be more ethnographic rather than linguistic. The question is no longer, which of the two analytical frames of reference should come first. It is how to combine them: (1) to explain how and why organizations and their practitioners stick to their own social and discursive patterns; (2) to help practitioners see why and how things may go wrong; (3) provide alternatives and solutions to help them change the real 'life-world' for the better.

Praxis and learning

In praxis-oriented research, there is a genuine interest in the various kinds of problems practitioners and their institutions might face. But examination of problems and provision of possible solutions is a task that both academics and practitioners must shoulder together. Looking for problems and faults in praxis is reciprocal. Praxis researchers should be open to the possibility of those being researched turning into analysts and analysts turning into the researched. Reciprocity is a main pillar of praxis. Praxis research should never be one-way research because it sees learning and knowledge as both vertical and horizontal (Tusting and Maybin 2007).

In praxis, researchers gaining new knowledge and making sense of those researched is not merely for personal gain. While personal learning is important, researchers include the interests of those researched as part of their ultimate aim. Praxis research involves personal learning (vertical) and collective learning (horizontal). It does this through timely publishing, the use of a language and a format that addressees can understand, cooperation throughout the stages of research with practitioners and, finally, winning practitioners over by proving to them that the investigation and its outcome will be relevant and useful and, if applied, might change their routines and conditions for the better. Access to media and journalism organizations is something we all yearn for and it is of paramount importance to praxis-oriented research. However, a media organization and its executives or employees have the right to ask, as Matthew Eltringham of BBC College of Journalism says, whether they will eventually learn something in return for access (Chapter 2). Once access is granted, a researcher should remember that those being researched have the right to read the findings and ask whether there is anything there for them to use.

Conclusion

We still have no template for how to do a praxis-related research. However, I believe we have the theoretical and methodological platform to embark on such a research. We can lean on Bourdieu, Foucault, Berger and Luckman, among others, who share the view that society is a system and that culture and discourse constrain the system and its actions and, finally, human action and agency influence the system and its patterns. This view covers the pillars and constructs of praxis as outlined in this chapter and the three studies briefly reviewed in the introduction.

Praxis researchers can learn a lot from ethnography (Perrin 2013). But it has to go beyond the surface to collect and analyse everything that could prove significant in the eyes of all the pillars in the dynamic of media and journalism. It is important to note that the role of praxis does not end with meeting with those being researched and then withdrawing to analyse data. Getting back to the researcher role does not mean suspension of praxis. For the final product to be meaningful, relevant, practical and useful, it is important for all research participants to have a hand in it.

In praxis-oriented research, our aim is not only to make sense of the social field and its participants. It is engagement and immersion with the researched and their social field so that the construction of meaning, which is a joint and reciprocal effort, would lead to a deeper and fuller understanding that makes it possible to see things through different eyes and empower both researcher and researched with the ability to seek alternatives and solutions to improve conditions.

In praxis, researchers learning of new knowledge and making sense of the researched is not merely for personal gain. While personal learning is important, researchers include the interests of those researched as part of their ultimate aim. Praxis or applied research redirects attention to the real 'life-world' needs of those researched, the how and why texts, structures, processes and practices obtain their meanings, the role of agents and actors in their construction, what their practice in reality does to society and what we (academics and practitioners) can do to alleviate their impact on society.

References

Bakhtin, M. (1984), *Rabelais and His World*, Bloomington, IN: Indiana University Press.

Barkho, L. (2011), 'The role of internal guidelines in shaping news narratives: Ethnographic insights into the discursive rhetoric of Middle East reporting by the BBC and Al-Jazeera English', *Critical Discourse Studies*, 8: 4, pp. 297–309.

Berger, P. and Luckmann, T. (1967), *The Social Construction of Reality*, Garden City: Doubleday.

Bourdieu, P. ([1972] 1978), *Outline of a Theory of Practice* (trans. R. Nice), Cambridge: Cambridge University Press.

Dreyfus, L. and Rabinow, P. (1982), *Michel Foucault: Beyond Structuralism and Hermeneutics*, Chicago, IL: Chicago University Press.

Eltringham, M. (2013), 'Towards a new relevance: Why the new media landscape requires journalists and media scholars to forge a genuine partnership for the first time', *Journal of Applied Journalism & Media Studies*, 2: 3, pp. 387–396.

Foucault, M. (1980), *The History of Sexuality* (trans. R. Hurley), vol. 1, New York: Vintage.

Geertz, C. (1993), 'Religions as a cultural system', in C. Geertz (ed.), *Interpretation of Cultures: Selected Essays*, London: Fontana Press, pp. 87–125, http://isites.harvard.edu/fs/docs/icb. topic152604.files/Week_4/Geertz_Religon_as_a_ Cultural_System_.pdf. Accessed 21 May 2014.

Hymes, D. (1974), *Reinventing Anthropology*, New York: Vintage.

Nolan, K. (2010), 'Praxis', in A. J. Mills, G. Durepos and E. Wiebe (eds), *Encyclopedia of Case Study Research*, Thousand Oaks, CA: SAGE Publications, pp. 726–28.

Ortner, S. (1984), 'Theory in anthropology since the sixties', *Comparative Studies in Society and History*, 26: 1, pp. 126–166.

Perrin, D. (2012), 'Transdisciplinary action research: Bringing together communication and media researchers and practitioners', *Journal of Applied Journalism & Media Studies*, 1: 1, pp. 3–23.

——— (2013), *The Linguistics of Newswriting*, Amsterdam: John Benjamins.

Tusting, K. and Maybin, J. (2007), 'Linguistic ethnography and interdisciplinarity: Opening the discussion', *Journal of Sociolinguistics*, 11: 5, pp. 575–583.

Chapter 15

Media Academics versus Media Practitioners: Who Gets It Right?

Leon Barkho

Introduction

This chapter is derived from a conference organized in Sweden by Jönköping University's College of Education and Communication in 2013 on praxis-based media and journalism research, in which nearly a dozen practitioners took part. It starts with a short background and then considers the major concerns the practitioners voiced about much of the research media academics carry out. It then presents a synopsis of their responses to two major questions: (1) Why do media practitioners generally discard or not trust findings by media scholars? (2) Are media scholars under any obligation to relate their theories to practice? It ends with the lessons that academics can draw from the way practitioners view their world and assess their research.

Background

Praxis is based on a dual dynamic. Academic media and journalism research represents one pillar; media and journalism practitioners the other. It means that we employ our theoretical and methodological paradigms and approaches for the good of the society, which in our case mainly constitutes media and journalism academics and their students on the one hand and practitioners on the other. There is no template for how theory and practice should follow one another, but there should be a dialectical and dialogical cycle or bridge that allows the sides to 'operate concurrently with each other' (Nolan 2010: 726).

Praxis-oriented research encourages establishing a clear link between the prevalent theories: the paradigms and theories media and communication scholars' work with and the real world where media and communication work takes place. The people and organizations academics research should not merely be their 'subjects', 'objects' or 'respondents': they should be their partners, with whom they are required to cooperate on the basis of equality, reciprocity and reflexivity, tackling issues at the centre of research with an applied angle.

This chapter is an attempt to hone the volume's praxis-oriented niche. It frees itself from the 'cage' and confines of the academic method of research with regard to language as well as issues of epistemology, ontology and methodology. The chapter skips sections on literature review, theoretical framework, data collection and such, and draws on interviews with and the writings of renowned media scholars and representatives of some of the world's most influential media outlets. It starts with the analysis and throws in relevant literature and theory.

The idea is to try – as far as possible – to address some of the major concerns practitioners have about the nature of media and journalism research and the complexity of its language.

One world or two different worlds

The centre of my argument for praxis is that those of us who do media and journalism research from a critical perspective must find new ways to connect with the organizations and people we research. We must adopt approaches, methodologies and theoretical underpinnings that will help actors in the dual dynamic of communication to learn from each other. Today, the two pillars of this dynamic (academics and practitioners) stand apart in terms of dialogue, reciprocity and partnership. Media practitioners complain they get little in return for the access they grant to academics to interpret their social world, and that the 'scientific' rigour and 'sophisticated' analyses, methods and style employed to study them are rarely of any practical use.

Academia is a 'hidden' and an 'obscure' world in the eyes of media practitioners. Universities and their faculties are not wholly unlike media organizations and their practitioners: they each have their own cultures, compete with each other, suffer from rivalries and 'petty' academic jealousy over publishing, rewards, grants, promotion, salaries, prestige, position, etc. (Parsons and Frick 2008). Media scholars claim to know a lot in relation to how media practitioners and their organizations go about their work. Their scholarly work, they say, deconstructs the social world of media organizations and their practitioners with the intention of exposing biases and power relations. Practitioners, on the other hand, make no such claims. They say academia's philosophical, methodological and organizational cultures are some form of 'mystery' for them – a mystified world they know very little about. The analysis below highlights the major concerns practitioners raised in the conference. They are summarized under four headings: mystification, critique, language and inertia.

Mystification

One way to demystify academia, according to BBC's Matthew Eltringham, editor of the BBC College of Journalism website, would be for academics to approach those they study and research from the angle of partnership, equality and reciprocity. Eltringham argued that practitioners want research that responds to the question: 'what's in it for me?' He urged media practitioners and academics to trade their 'fortresses' in exchange for 'practical partnership': 'So what should be the foundation of a fruitful – and genuine – partnership between academics and journalists? From where I stand, it has to be relevant, practical and useful to both journalists and academics'.

It was good to see practitioners so eager to know more about what Eltringham called 'Fortress Academia'. Some questioned whether the objective of media scholars has ever been to work for the benefit of people and organizations they research, or just respond to the organizational and cultural requirements of their own institutions.

Critique, critique, critique

Asked for the reason media practitioners generally discard or do not trust findings by media academics, Vin Ray, the founder and former editor of the BBC College of Journalism, said: 'Scholars only criticize, they never provide alternatives or solutions. This is a big issue'. Referring to the way media scholars carry out their research, Ray said:

> Many practitioners see selective research: reaching unfair conclusions from unrepresentative samples, biased questions or short runs of data that distort the reality – curiously, the very accusation that scholars often level at journalists. A lack of objectivity – setting out to confirm their own hypothesis.

Probably one major reason for the state of affairs Ray refers to is lack of reciprocity and trust between academics and practitioners, even though they are essentially dealing with the same subject. But is there anything in the media and communication literature warning academics against the criticism Ray makes about their research and its findings? In fact, more than 30 years ago, Heron (1981: 34) wrote that the researched should be treated 'as autonomous beings' with 'a moral right to participate in decisions that claim to generate knowledge about them'. He even called on researchers to share power with researched 'in the generation of knowledge ... to provide conditions under which subjects can enhance their capacity of self-determination in acquiring knowledge about human conditions'. In 1985, Ingram (1985: 45) struck a similar chord. He wrote that the 'very *modus operandi* of human understanding is teleologically oriented towards the recognitions of the "thou" as one whose individuality merits... to be respected and understood'. Almost a decade later, Tanno and Jandt (1994: 38) advised academics to free themselves from the 'cage' and 'confines' of their own methods of research if that were to help the organizations and people they study transform their world for the better. Academics, they emphasized, ought to show a willingness 'to work outside the constraints of a science-based model'. At the turn of the century, Roy and Starosta (2001: 14) called on academics to grant and not deny participants in their research the right to be the owners of 'the process of coproducing/co-owning knowledge'.

Issues of language

Practitioners strongly criticized the language media scholars employ in writing their research. They argued that academic language or 'jargon' was mainly geared towards special or specific purposes that served mainly the needs and interests of academic community; media academics used a form of language that was extremely hard for them to understand. A writer must take his or her audience into account when writing and there was a strong belief that academics targeted other academics and seldom the people they researched. David Elstein, founder of UK's Channel Five, currently chairman of openDemocracy and the Broadcasting Policy group said academics should not present 'abstract concepts' if they wanted their research to be read by practitioners: 'We need to demystify the language, and it is hard for academics to change their language to make it more accessible to journalists'. For Vin Ray (Chapter 1):

> The way scholars write is a direct offence to the craft skills of journalists. It goes against everything they believe and everything they teach their staff. They see their own job as achieving clarity and regard academics as delivering obfuscation – over-long papers, windy, jargon, cloudy meaning, invented language. Explaining complex issues in a way that can be universally understood is far more difficult than writing for a niche audience.

The fact that the language academics use in their research is characterized with high complexity has not been lost on prominent social science thinkers shaping much of media and journalism research. The thinkers urge academics to use lucid and simple language, which is not too hard for the people they research to understand. Habermas (1984), one of the most important and oft-cited thinkers in media and journalism research, cites simplicity of language in terms of grammar and semantics as the number one priority for research. Scholars, he says, need to present organizations and people they research with something they can understand. Fay (1975: 98; see also Heron 1981; Polani 1967; Lather 1986) warns against 'complexity' in all areas of academic research in social science. He says that academics write, and probably speak, a language that reflects the 'complexity' of their theories, methodologies and interpretations, and avoid 'ordinary language' that 'must speak to the felt needs of the groups and societies we research'.

Inertia

Nazar Daw of Sky News raised some crucial questions he thought academics needed to consider in relation to their research. According to Daw, the digitized media is moving, changing and transforming rapidly, while academic media research, or at least most of it, 'takes ages' to be published. Even when it is published it may never be brought to the attention of the practitioners who took part in it. Daw added:

> What we need is answers, and we need them now. We cannot wait for systematic academic ways of tackling things … We need more answers to daily questions that are up-to-date … Academics should serve answers in a language that I can understand. Develop ideas of

our work and criticize our work, but we need it quickly. Journalists are a moving target; academics must be too ... We need someone to advise us since we are constantly on the go.

For Ray:

Speed and relevance are crucial if academic research is to be useful. Practitioners have little time for reflection and this is where academic research can really help. If the media are giving too much time to a particular knife crime or missing child, can academics reflect on what the data tells us and suggest ways in which we can put these stories in better context? Can some content analysis tell whether our coverage of China is too focused on human rights issues at the expense of economic growth? Can some linguistic analysis tell us whether we are unwittingly adopting the language of one side or another in a long-running debate? These would be very helpful kinds of analyses – but only if they can be done in a timeframe that makes them useful.

What do media practitioners think of praxis-oriented research and are media academics obliged to respond to their needs and demands?

In an effort to understand what praxis-oriented media and journalism research might mean to the pillars in the dual dynamic of communication, two panels were organized, with each meant to answer one of the questions below. Here are excerpts from the deliberations that took place:

Q1: Why do media practitioners generally discard or do not trust findings by media scholars?

Pal Aam of Volda University, Norway:

I vividly remember my own frustrations over academic books as a student. It was a futile attempt to link the content and the realism of working as a journalist. I couldn't understand how the books could help me to become a journalist, since the books mainly pointed out what was wrong with, and the shortcomings of journalistic work.

Maron Medzini of Hebrew University, Israel:

Journalists are suspicious of academics, and academics address journalists, who, as said, don't trust them. What language are they using in academia? Prose vs technical language. Reporters feel that academics respect them, but also that they are inferior.

Colleen Cotter of Queen Mary University, UK:

Researchers aren't rooted in their reality, so it's almost a matter of a translation problem. What is well grounded, evidence based is not equivalent with the journalist worldview. Journalists mock academic projects.

Michal Krzyzanowski of Örbero University, Sweden:

A delicate question, relevance issue. The key to find the relevance is very often that we do things in a slightly different way. Journalists construct and academia deconstructs (and) gives different directions. Professors do things for academics and students. Journalists do things for the people so the language creates distrust.

Eltringham:

It's easy to make cheap jibes about dumbing down and hide behind the walls of fortress academia, in the same way that I used to hide behind the walls of fortress journalism... Tell us something we don't know; tell us something that matters to us; and tell us something that will make a difference to what we do.
Q2: *Are media scholars under any obligation to relate their theories to practice?*

Åke Petterson of Swedish public radio:

Media researchers could still be far more active in presenting their research in a popular fashion. It's the taxpayers' money since we pay for much research, and then the public should get to know what their money is used for.

Medzini:

We don't have an obligation, but a desire. We'd like to feel that we have an impact, that we can improve and raise the standards. There we can make an important point.

Sarah Niblock of Brunel University, UK:

Synthesize theory and practice, synergy emerges. I teach ethics, (and) how many stakeholders are affected by our choices... Engage ordinary citizens and consumers of media to be informed. There is lack of public engagement. They are not informed about how media affects them. This needs to be debated by both theorists and practitioners.

Daw:

The main issue is that there is no system to make it possible for theorists and practitioners to work together. The question 'who serves who' could be a start for finding a system. Journalists can serve academics and provide material. Academics can serve journalists with conclusions ... We need to make academics to fit into the newsroom.

Lessons to be learned

One can draw a few lessons that may help build new bridges between academics and practitioners. They are at the heart of any research that pursues an applied angle geared towards helping the researched transform and improve their conditions.

'Supremacy' does not help

It is obvious from the citations and deliberations above that academics and practitioners do not feel that they are equal or are in a position to enter into good partnership. They are, in fact, often at odds. The reason is probably the epistemologies and methodologies we academics employ to critique and denaturalize or demystify the organizations and people we study. We say 'we are scholars and not journalists', i.e. we can be patronizing, presuming that others (those we research or our 'subjects') are required to admire us or follow us because we have some 'philosophical', 'scientific' and 'methodological' power that others lack. This reflects in the type of language we use, which practitioners find hard to understand. On close examination, as demonstrated above, we can see that our own academic institutions survive on hierarchies of power and hegemony that we detect in those we research. We also have our own 'powerful' individuals or groups and 'weaker or less powerful' individuals and groups in terms of publications, academic or administrative titles, grants, awards and the like.

Power versus influence

Media and journalism literature with a critical approach focuses on issues of meaning and power but does not distinguish the difference between power and influence. One may lack power but that does not mean one cannot exert any influence in changing perceptions and assumptions. In his 'The end of power: From boardrooms to battlefields and churches to states, why being in charge isn't what it used to be', Moises Naim (in Cocozza 2013) differentiates between power and influence. He says both can change the behaviour of others but 'influence seeks to change the perception of the situation, not the situation itself'. Media and journalism research with a praxis angle must not aim at overthrowing, changing or transforming the centres of power. Media scholars should try to positively influence the way power players perceive the situation.

Dynamic engagement

Though not cited during the conference, I believe some ideas of the pedagogy philosopher Paulo Freire (2007) were there in the deliberations and discussions, particularly by the practitioners. Freire has transformed the world of teaching through his ideas. These centre on dynamic engagement, where all actors of pedagogy (academics, teachers and students) are involved in a dynamic communication. Freire urges the actors with a stake in research to work for each other, learn from each other, and cooperate and coordinate their activities to free themselves from domination and oppression. The ultimate aim of any good research and good teaching, he says, should be helping the researched acquire practical skills, new dispositions and fresh attitudes that can help develop a better, different and healthier course of life. That is exactly what the practitioners wanted to see from media and journalism scholars researching them.

No 'sacred cows' or 'ivory' towers

Technological change is forcing media organizations through rapid and dramatic transformations. In contrast, there has been little change or transformation in approach and methodology on the part of media scholars and the way they go about their research. In other words, most academics still adore their 'sacred cows' and bask in the comfort of their 'ivory towers', although as early as 1966, Frey et al. (1996: 15) wanted to 'draw a different set of virtues for research, overturning some of the sacred cows of conventional wisdom'.

Dialogical relationship with the organizations and people we research has even entered a new territory of effective participation and cooperation. Stewart (1978) urged academics to descend from their 'ivory towers' and mingle with the people they study to start appreciating them as they are: equals who work together for a better world. The knowledge we gather when operationalizing our theories must be applied to 'the concrete situation', otherwise it will remain 'meaningless and even risks obscuring what the situation calls for' (Gadamer 1989: 313).

Alternatives and solutions

Media and journalism academics need to find ways to persuade individuals and organizations to consider and apply what they see as better alternatives to the 'bias' they detect in their output. To do this, they need to enter into effective and constructive dialogue and partnership with media practitioners. Dialogism, reciprocity, partnership and reflexivity – the four major constructs of praxis – do not deny researchers the right to intervene in the social world of those they research. However, for human intervention to be effective it must be reciprocal (Lather 1986). Communication and media thinkers and philosophers allow human intervention but set tough conditions on how it is to be carried out. First, research must come up with useful, practical and relevant alternatives. Second, the researched must have confidence and trust that the solutions and alternatives academics have arrived at through their research are meant to change their world for the better. Third, practitioners must be persuaded through partnership, dialogue, cooperation, communication and community work that there is no attempt on the part of media scholars to have them accept pre-determined and pre-imposed philosophies, methodologies and solutions.

Conclusion

This chapter has mainly focused on the concerns of media practitioners and their views of academics researching and investigating their social world. Practitioners have problems with media and journalism research, which they find of little practical use in their daily work. They have grave concerns about the type of language and style academics use in their research. They believe that academics could be quicker, more relevant, practical and useful to their work and their organizations once they are prepared to gear their investigations towards meeting their practical needs and start seeing them as partners on a level playing field. The status quo can be transformed by building bridges to promote partnership, engagement, reciprocity and reflexivity. Without this, academics will fail to persuade practitioners to adopt their findings, solutions and alternatives.

References

Cocozza, P. (2013), 'What Bill Clinton wants to teach Nick Clegg about the end of power', *The Guardian*, http://www.theguardian.com/politics/shortcuts/2013/dec/12/bill-clinton-nick-clegg-end-of-power. Accessed 19 December 2013.

Fay, B. (1975), *Social Theory and Political Practice*, London: Allen & Unwin.

Freire, P. (2007), *Pedagogy of the Oppressed*, New York: Continuum.

Frey, L. R., Pearce, W. B, Pollock, M. A., Artz, L. and Murphy, B. A. O. (1996), 'Looking for justice in all the wrong places: On a communication approach to social justice', *Communication Studies*, 47: 1–2, pp. 110–27.

Habermas, J. (1984), *The Theory of Communicative Action, Volume 1, Reason and the Rationalization of Society*, Boston, MA: Beacon Press.

Heron, J. (1981), 'Experimental research methods', in P. Reason and J. Rowan (eds), *Human Inquiry*, New York: Wiley, pp. 153–66.

Gadamer, H. G. (1989), *Truth and Method* (trans. J. Weinsheimer and D. G. Marshall), New York: Crossroad.

Ingram, D. (1985), 'Hermeneutics and truth', in R. Hollinger (ed.), *Hermeneutics and Praxis*, Notre Dame, IN: University of Notre Dame Press, pp. 32–53.

Lather, P. (1986), 'Research as praxis', *Harvard Educational Review*, 56: 3, pp. 257–77.

Nolan, K. (2010), 'Praxis', in A. J. Mills, G. Durepos and E. Wiebe (eds), *Encyclopedia of Case Study Research*, Thousand Oaks, CA: SAGE Publications, pp. 726–28.

Parsons, J. and Frick, W. (2008), 'Why professors hate their jobs: A critique of the pedagogy of academic disengagement', *Culture Society and Praxis*, 7: 2, pp. 30–46.

Polani, M. (1967), *The Tacit Dimension*, Garden City: Anchor Books and Doubleday.

Roy, A. and Starosta, W. J. (2001), 'Hans-Georg Gadamer, language and intercultural communication', *Journal for Language and Intercultural Communication*, 1: 1, pp. 6–20.

Stewart, J. (1978), 'Foundations of dialogic communication', *Quarterly Journal of Speech*, 64: 2, pp. 183–201.

Tanno, D. V. and Jandt, F. E. (1994), 'Redefining the "other" in multicultural research', *The Harvard Journal of Communication*, 5: 2, pp. 36–45.

Notes on Contributors

Åke Pettersson is currently working as a part-time media reporter and commentator mainly for Kulturnytt, a news programme covering cultural issues for Sveriges Radio, Sweden's independent public service radio broadcaster. For nearly three decades, he was the chief editor of the weekly media programme Vår grundade mening, which later came to be called Publicerat and was broadcast from Radio 1. He has worked for Ekot, Sveriges Radio's main news programme. He has also received several journalist awards among them Stora journalistpriset, Sweden's highest journalistic award.

Astrid Vandendaele is a research assistant at the department of Linguistics at Ghent University, Belgium. She teaches English at post-graduate level. At present, she is writing up a doctoral dissertation on the role of the newspaper sub-editor. Her research interests include media discourse, newswriting, news production processes, journalism, and business communication. As she has been working as a freelance newspaper sub-editor since 2008, her research is mostly newsroom-based, and has a strong focus on the practitioner perspective.

David Machin is a professor in the department of Media and Communication, Örebro University, Sweden. His interests lie in multimodality, critical discourse studies and visual design. His books include *The Language of War Monuments* (2013) and *Visual Journalism* (2015). His current research focuses on the multimodal communication of administration in institutions.

Fackson Banda is a programme specialist in journalism education and knowledge-driven media development at UNESCO's headquarters in Paris, France. Prior to that, he was executive director of the Panos Institute for Southern Africa, based in Lusaka, where his focus was on promoting communication for sustainable development. As an academic, he has taught and published in the following areas: the political economy of communication; African political thought and African media; community communication policy; development communication and journalism; and new media policy and the African digital public sphere. He is currently editor of the *Compendium of New Syllabi* – a UNESCO publication that seeks to introduce and refine evolving journalistic literacies as an integral part of core journalism curricula.

Ibrahim Saleh is a senior lecturer (associated professor) and convener of political communication at the University of Cape Town (UCT). Saleh is a Fulbright scholar and chair of the Journalism Research and Education section in the International Association for Media and Communication Research (IAMCR). He is the author of three monographs, including *Unveiling the Truth About Middle Eastern Media: Privatization in Egypt: Hope or Dope?* and *Prior To the Eruption of the Grapes of Wrath in the Middle East: The Necessity of Communicating Instead of Clashing*. He worked as a print and TV journalist for seven years, and currently edits the *Global Media Journal African Edition*.

Jairo Lugo-Ocando is an associate professor in the School of Media and Communication at the University of Leeds, UK. Before becoming an academic he worked as a reporter, correspondent and chief news editor for several news media organizations in Venezuela, Colombia, Mexico and the United States.

Kevin Marsh was the longest serving editor of a daily news programme in the BBC when he retired in March 2011. His editing career began in 1989 with the drive-time PM programme and in succeeding years he edited *The World at One*, *The World This Weekend* and *Broadcasting House*. He was editor of *Today* from 2002 to 2006 – Britain's leading news and political programme with a daily audience of up to seven million. He won numerous national and international broadcasting awards. From 2006 to 2011, he was executive editor of the BBC College of Journalism and, since leaving the BBC, has taught and lectured in Washington, Geneva, Ramallah, Hilversum, Istanbul, Kiev, Tbilisi and Jonkoping, as well as the British Defence Academy and many British universities. He is currently a practitioner in residence at Bournemouth University Media School in the UK and is director of OffspinMedia. He is the author of *Stumbling Over Truth*, an account of the media battle prior to the 2003 invasion of Iraq, as well as numerous articles for academic and non-academic publications.

Leon Barkho is associate professor of Media and Communication Science at Sweden's Jönköping University and Qatar University. He is the author of *News from the BBC, CNN and Al Jazeera: How the Three Broadcasters Cover the Middle East* and *From Theory to Practice: How to Assess and Apply Impartiality in News and Current Affairs*. His research has appeared in the *Journal of Pragmatics*, *Babel*, *American Communication Journal*, *Journalism Studies*, *Critical Discourse Studies* and the *Journal of International Business Studies*. He spent seven years with Reuters as a correspondent before moving to the Associated Press as a staff writer.

Lydia Polzer presently works as editor of a travel magazine. Before this she worked as a freelance magazine designer, journalist and photojournalist for ten years. She has also presented lectures on magazine design, layout and production for journalism at Brunel University and has lectured at City University in the past. She is a winner of the UNESCO and The Independent World Press Freedom Award (2007). The visual presentation of news and feature content is part of her day-to-day working life.

Marcela Pizarro Coloma was born in Valparaíso, Chile, but history intervened and she came to London in 1976. She studied her first degree in Spanish and French at the University of Nottingham and then went to University College London to do an MA in Hispanics. In 1998, she won a British Academy award for a full doctoral scholarship. She has worked in international news and programmes since 2000, first as a producer at Associated Press then for Al Jazeera English in Latin American, Washington DC, Doha and London.

Matthew Eltringham joined the College of Journalism in May 2011 as head of the website and events operation, after spending more than 18 years working in the heart of the BBC's network news operation. In the spring of 2005, he was the founding editor of the UGC Hub – a team of BBC journalists who pioneered the incorporation of user-generated content by mainstream media in their journalism. Throughout his career he has produced interviews with more than a dozen heads of state – including Presidents Putin and George W Bush. But one of the jobs that has had more influence on his life than most was his first break into journalism as a district reporter in the Exeter office of the *Western Morning News* – a regional morning daily covering the south west of England. He is currently editor of the BBC College of Journalism website.

Sarah Niblock is associate dean and professor of journalism at the University of Westminster School of Media, Arts and Design, London. She is author and co-author of several books on journalism, and a number of journal articles and chapters on reflexive and practice-facing research. She is on the editorial board of number of distinguished journalism journals and is an academic fellow of the Dart Center for Journalism and Trauma. She spent several years in the local, regional and national press before entering academic life and continues to freelance as a broadcaster, reporter and feature writer.

Vin Ray is a writer, coach, consultant and visiting professor of Journalism at the Bournemouth University Media School. He is the lead trainer on the BBC's Editorial Leadership Programme. He left the BBC in 2010 after a 23 year spell in which he had been Foreign Editor, Executive Editor, the first Director of the BBC College of Journalism and, for five years, a member of the BBC's Journalism Board. Ray is probably best known for his work around talent development and storytelling. For many years, he had the additional role of recruiting and coaching on-air talent for BBC News and hired many of the BBC's best-known reporters and presenters. He was described as 'a revered teacher' by Andrew Marr who, along with many others, he trained and coached through his transition to broadcasting. In 1999, as Executive Editor, he was asked to look at improving the storytelling skills of the BBC's reporters and correspondents. He has written two books: *The Reporter's Friend* and *The Television News Handbook*, as well as numerous chapters and articles. In 2004, he was awarded the Dart Center's Distinguished Media Leadership Award at a ceremony in New York. In 2005, following the Hutton affair, he was asked to set up the BBC College of Journalism, which he ran until he left the BBC in 2010.